On This Day in North Carolina

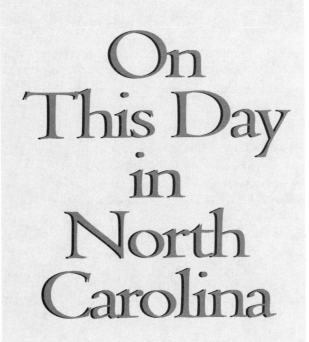

On This Day in North Carolina

LEW POWELL

JOHN F. BLAIR, PUBLISHER ▪ *Winston–Salem, North Carolina*

Cover photographs—

A. North Carolina suffragists (see page 142)
   Courtesy of North Carolina Division of Archives and History

B. Billhead for original Pepsi-Cola plant in New Bern (see page 104)
   Courtesy of North Carolina Division of Archives and History

C. Rocky Mount native Buck Leonard and Negro League team (see page 64)
   Courtesy of North Carolina Museum of History

D. Katharine Hepburn with North Carolina Governor and Mrs. Broughton (see page 2)
   Courtesy of The *News and Observer* of Raleigh

Library of Congress Cataloging-in-Publication Data

Powell, Lew.
    On this day in North Carolina / Lew Powell.
       p.   cm.
    Includes bibliographical references and index.
    ISBN 0-89587-139-4 (alk. paper)
    I. North Carolina—History—Chronology.   I. Title.
F254.P58   1996
975.6—dc20   95–41603

DESIGN BY DEBRA LONG HAMPTON
PRINTED BY R. R. DONNELLEY & SONS

To

Dannye

Contents

Acknowledgments

No manuscript is an island. I am pleased to have the opportunity to express my gratitude

To the editors of the *Charlotte Observer*, who sanctioned my interest in history and even granted me a six-week sabbatical in 1991 that accelerated what had been a snail's-paced pursuit

To my longtime friend Ed Williams, editor of the *Observer*'s editorial pages, who encouraged me to write a monthly history column that advantageously dovetailed with this book

To Jack Betts, Mary Boyer, Tom Bradbury, Jack Claiborne, David Goldfield, Tom Hanchett, Mary Norton Kratt, Dan Morrill, and M. S. Van Hecke, who have generously shared their historical research and insights over the years

To Sara Klemmer and her colleagues in the

Observer's library, who introduced this chronic technophobe to journalism's dazzling new electronic catacombs

To Mary Louise Phillips, Rosemary Lands, Pat Ryckman, and their colleagues at the Robinson-Spangler Carolina Room at the Public Library of Charlotte-Mecklenburg, who have been an indispensable resource since I first set foot in North Carolina two decades ago

To Alice Cotten, Harry McKown, and their colleagues at the North Carolina Collection at the University of North Carolina, who served uncomplainingly as detectives of last resort on my most intractable queries

To Steve Massengill at the North Carolina Division of Archives and History and Jerry Cotten at the North Carolina Collection, who reached into their respective files and pulled out striking images of bygone days

To the late Dr. Thomas Banks, who sent me information on Ava Gardner; Jim Harris, who turned up a rare episode of barbecue history; and Claire Ashcraft, who graciously tracked down clippings on her late husband Hugh G. Ashcraft, Jr.'s, famous "wing and a prayer" flight in World War II

To Peter C. Engelman, assistant editor of the Margaret Sanger Papers Project, sponsored by New York University and the Sophia Smith Collection, Smith College, who unearthed Mrs. Sanger's own account of her little-known appearance in Elizabeth City

To William King, Duke University archivist; Ted Mitchell, historic-sites interpreter at the Thomas Wolfe Memorial in Asheville; Wesley Paine, director of the Parthenon Museum in Nashville, Tennessee; Jim L. Sumner, researcher and writer at the North Carolina Division of Archives and History; Jan Blodgett, Davidson College archivist; Ronnie Pugh, head reference librarian at the Country Music Foundation in Nashville; Robin Farquhar, executive director of the Flat Rock Playhouse; Christie Cameron, clerk of the North Carolina Supreme Court; and Denise Weeks, clerk of the North Carolina House of Representatives, all of whom came through with information I was unable to find elsewhere

To librarians across the state—including those at the State Archives, Davis Library at the University of North Carolina, Pack Memorial Library in Asheville, Durham County Public Library, New Hanover County Public Library, Rowan County Public Library, and Forsyth County Public Library—all of whom responded helpfully to my long-distance requests

To Norman Welch, who indexed this book on a tight deadline and from across the Atlantic

To Hank Durkin, Mary Waterstradt, and Sarah Welch, who provided essential production assistance

To Sally Hill McMillan, valued neighbor and literary agent, for her encouragement, advice, and direction

To my allies at John F. Blair, Publisher—Carolyn Sakowski, who watched *On This Day in North Carolina* grow to twice its proposed size but never blinked, at least when I could see her; Steve Kirk, whose keen-eyed editing is responsible for untold accuracies (any inaccuracies are my own); and Margaret Couch, Debbie Hampton, Liza Langrall, Andrew Waters, Anne Schultz, Judy Breakstone, Lisa Wagoner, Sue Clark, and Heath Simpson, all of whom helped bring this book to reality with unflagging professionalism

And to my wife, Dannye, without whose love, support, and counsel I would be as lost as CROATOAN

Introduction

I recently happened onto a long-forgotten "Daily Reminder" book for 1981. (Apparently, as is my habit, I had waited for it to go on sale; it was penciled down from $6.75 to the unlikely price of $5.06.) In this red-bound volume, I had recorded half a dozen historical items that turned out to be the tentative beginnings of *On This Day in North Carolina*.

Although *On This Day* would come to include more than 1,000 such items, only two of those in the datebook survived—North Carolina's secession from the Union and the opening of the state's first McDonald's. Saul Steinberg's cartoon of the Charlotte post office published in *The New Yorker* and an NCAA record for free throws set in a Davidson College basketball game didn't make the cut; both were a shade too obscure, though in different ways.

It didn't take long for me to set aside the datebook in favor of a computer, but those early items remain typical of how I went about compiling *On This Day*—noticing, recording, rejecting, and, always, collecting, collecting, collecting. Although long periods went by in which I did nothing more than rip out newspaper and magazine stories and stuff them into the cardboard boxes that surround my desk, *On This Day* refused to die. I hope this is a sign of the idea's merit, not merely its hardiness.

I have been unable to turn up a comparable "book of dates" of any state's history. In content and tone, however, my model has been *The*

People's Almanac series (1975–81). Like David Wallechinsky and Irving Wallace, I am a collector, repackager, and unapologetic popularizer. Although I have included such historical staples as the birth of Virginia Dare, my bias is toward digging up and dusting off the almost-forgotten: John Lawson's early-18th-century encounter with barbecue, the train wreck that nearly killed Annie Oakley, the first electrocution at Central Prison, the coining of the term *air conditioning*, Yale first baseman George Bush's big day against North Carolina State.

No doubt, my idiosyncratic approach has resulted in omissions (as well as inclusions) that readers will consider curious. I hope they will forgive this shortcoming and judge *On This Day in North Carolina* to be a modest but worthwhile addition to the long, long shelf of North Caroliniana.

On This Day in North Carolina

Touring actress Katharine Hepburn
enjoys a smoke as she talks
with Governor and Mrs. J. Melville Broughton
at a party in the
Executive Mansion [January 30].

The *News and Observer* of Raleigh

January

Durham plays host to Rose Bowl
Lumbee Indians break up Klan rally
Nuclear warheads
imperil Goldsboro

JANUARY 1

1766

Moravian settlers found the town of Salem, which will become the hub of their self-contained community and eventually part of Winston-Salem. The name Salem means "peace."

The Moravians, tight-knit German Protestants, arrived in North Carolina from Pennsylvania in 1753.

1833

The state's first railroad opens in Raleigh. It is a temporary mile-long line built to haul granite from the quarry to the site of the new State Capitol. On Sundays, it takes passengers on outings.

1837

Edward Dudley of Wilmington, North Carolina's first elected governor, is sworn in. Previous governors were chosen by the legislature.

JANUARY I, 1864

Sergeant Bartlett Yancy Malone of the Sixth North Carolina Infantry records his New Year's Day as a Confederate prisoner of war at Point Lookout, Maryland: "The morning was plesant but towards evening the air changed and the nite was very coal. was so coal that five of our men froze to death befour morning. We all suffered a great deal with coal and hunger too of our men was [so] hungry today that they caught a Rat and cooked him and eat it."

1942

Out of fear the Japanese will bomb Pasadena, California, the Rose Bowl game is played in Durham. Oregon upsets previously undefeated Duke, 20–16.

1956

Jack Kerouac, Beat Generation icon-in-the-making, sits down at his sister's kitchen table in Rocky Mount and begins writing a novel.

Since Kerouac, 33, arrived last spring, he has been drinking moonshine, suffering nightmares about H-bombs, and waiting for a publisher to accept his oft-spurned *On the Road*.

With his hosts away on a trip, Kerouac begins filling a tiny pocket notebook with the story of his brother Gerard's death a year earlier. Fueled with Benzedrine, he writes furiously for 15 straight nights. After each session, he walks across a cotton field to a pine forest to meditate with his brother-in-law's hunting dogs. He sleeps in a sleeping bag on a cot on the back porch with the windows wide open.

When the manuscript is finished, he writes a friend that it is "a beaut, my best. . . . Enuf to make Shakespeare raise an eyebrow."

Reviewers are less enthralled. When *Visions of Gerard* is finally published in 1963, *Newsweek* calls it the work of "a tin-ear Canuck," while the *New York Times Book Review* dismisses it as "garrulous hipster yawping."

1962

Deputy Barney Fife (Don Knotts) first tells someone to "nip it" on *The Andy Griffith Show*.

JANUARY 2

1929

Meeting for the first time, Scribner's editor Maxwell Perkins and Thomas Wolfe discuss the manuscript of *Look Homeward, Angel*, Wolfe's first novel. His "wild hair and bright countenance" remind Perkins of the English poet Shelley.

JANUARY 3

1963

"If a novel of recent history should convey a

feeling of great events," the *Christian Science Monitor* says of Richard McKenna's *The Sand Pebbles*, "this one does."

McKenna, a 22-year navy veteran who afterward settled in Chapel Hill and earned a degree at the University of North Carolina, based his first novel on his experiences in the Far East. *The Sand Pebbles* proves a popular success and in 1966—two years after McKenna's death at age 51—is turned into a movie starring Steve McQueen.

JANUARY 4

1969

Siamese twins Daisy and Violet Hilton, once famed in vaudeville but most recently working in a supermarket, die in obscurity at their Charlotte apartment. Violet was ill with the flu.

The twins were born in Brighton, England, in 1908. Their mother, a poor, unmarried barmaid, sold them, and by the time they were three, they were being exhibited at circuses. Their brutal guardian increased their value by paying to have them learn to sing, dance, and play musical instruments. At her death, she willed Daisy and Violet to her daughter. Their slavery continued in vaudeville until the twins confided their story to a lawyer. In 1931, at age 23, they were freed.

For the next 20 years, the sisters profitably ran their own show. At the height of their success, they lived in a house in San Antonio, Texas, designed for them by Frank Lloyd Wright.

By 1962, however, their career had faded. That year, they came to Charlotte's Fox Drive-In to publicize the reissued 1932 documentary *Freaks*, in which they had appeared. The agent who delivered them to the drive-in never returned to pick them up. The sisters stayed in Charlotte and spent their last years weighing produce at a Park-N-Shop. "Most people did not realize they were tied together," said the store owner, who stationed the twins at two produce scales set at angles to serve two lines of customers.

JANUARY 5

1988

Basketball legend Pistol Pete Maravich, who played at Broughton High School in Raleigh when his father was coaching at North Carolina State, dies from cardiac arrest during a pickup game in Pasadena, California. He is 40 years old.

Less than a year earlier, Maravich had spoken in Charlotte about his recent conversion to Christianity: "My valley was the bar, it was alcohol, it was women. I had that external glow of happiness, but inside I was so empty. I wouldn't trade where I am right now for 1,000 NBA championship rings.

"If people just see a basketball player when they look at me, forget it, my life is nothing. The old Pete Maravich is dead and buried."

JANUARY 6

1870

A temporary state penitentiary, a compound of log cabins, opens in Raleigh.

After a half-century of failed efforts, the North Carolina General Assembly has put up the money and the city the land. The log buildings will be used while Central Prison, a massive Gothic fortress, is under construction.

1962

Richard Vinroot, a reserve forward for the University of North Carolina, hits a free throw in a game against Notre Dame at the Charlotte Coliseum.

It will be the only point Vinroot scores during his two-year, nine-game Tar Heel career. He proves more successful at politics, however, and is twice elected mayor of Charlotte in the early 1990s.

JANUARY 6, 1965

The University of North Carolina basketball team returns to Chapel Hill after a road loss to Wake Forest that brings its record down to 6–6. At Woollen Gym, the team bus encounters surly students chanting, "We want Smith, we want Smith," and a dummy of the fourth-year coach burning in effigy.

Dean Smith will survive the season and go on to become, as of this writing, the second-winningest coach in major college basketball history.

1864

The Confederate Navy Yard, housed in a converted ironworks in Charlotte, is destroyed by an explosion and fire of unknown cause.

The ordnance depot had been moved inland in 1861 when a similar facility at Norfolk, Virginia, was under threat from Union forces.

1989

The *News and Observer* of Raleigh breaks the news that Simon and Schuster will publish *Personal Fouls* by Peter Golenbock. The book's dust jacket alleges wrongdoing in the North Carolina State basketball program.

An investigation by the University of North Carolina system later clears coach Jim Valvano of breaking academic rules but finds his players violated NCAA regulations by selling game tickets and basketball shoes and accepting discounts on jewelry and food.

Fifteen months after the first story about *Personal Fouls*, Valvano is fired.

JANUARY 8

1815

Troops under Andrew Jackson win the Battle of New Orleans. Because of Jackson's canny fortifications, American losses are only seven dead, versus 700 for the British.

A peace treaty ending the War of 1812 was signed two weeks earlier in Belgium, but word has not yet reached New Orleans.

News of the great victory will inspire a Surry County innkeeper to write on Jackson's overdue bill, "Settled in full by the battle of New Orleans."

1903

In his biennial message to the North Carolina General Assembly, Governor Charles Brantley Aycock calls for legislation "in behalf of the children who are working in textile and furniture factories."

Manufacturers, who have beaten back previous restrictions on child labor, want no part of Aycock's proposals—"Yankee doings," in the words of W. L. London of Pittsboro. "You let us alone," says Moses Cone of Greensboro, "and the matter will come out all right."

But Aycock's vow to stump the state moves the manufacturers to compromise. The Child Labor Law of 1903 will prohibit industry from employing children under the age of 12 (except for young oyster shuckers, who are paid by the gallon or bushel). Children under 18 are barred from working more than 66 hours per week.

JANUARY 9

1887

At the University of North Carolina, the *Tar Heel* newspaper reports that "a lattice fence has been placed around the commons outhouses and adds greatly to the appearance of the place."

1939

At the Museum of Modern Art in New York, artist Josef Albers tells an audience about Black Mountain College's avant-garde educational philosophy, while Walter Gropius and Marcel Breuer—key figures in the modern architecture movement—display a model of their proposed new campus overlooking Lake Eden.

The approach of war in Europe will derail fund-raising efforts, however, and the college abandons the Gropius-Breuer concept in favor of something less ambitious.

1990

Dr. Henry Stenhouse, a Goldsboro ophthalmologist, announces his candidacy for Congress. At 100, Stenhouse is perhaps the oldest North Carolinian ever to run for office. "I'm a revolutionary," says Stenhouse, who opposes welfare, seat-belt laws, and AIDS research.

After a campaign that includes an appearance with Johnny Carson on *The Tonight Show*, Stenhouse finishes third in a three-man race for the Republican nomination, although he handily carries Goldsboro and Wayne County.

Dr. Stenhouse will live to be 105.

JANUARY 10

1905

After commuting a 15-year manslaughter conviction to six years, his last official act, Governor Charles Brantley Aycock proudly points out to the press his desk's bare top and empty compartments.

It is an appropriate exit for Aycock, who has set records by extending clemency in 458 cases and granting 369 full pardons. On one occasion, to his embarrassment, he even pardoned a man who had died in prison several months earlier.

1936

The state's first highway historical marker, designating the homesite of Declaration of Independence signer John Penn, is dedicated at the Stovall community in Granville County.

In coming years, the North Carolina Division of Archives and History will erect more than 1,200 markers across the state.

1942

Ava Gardner marries actor Mickey Rooney, the first of her three husbands, in Ballard, California.

1953

Two days after a demanding round of inaugural ceremonies—capped by his wee-hours harmonica solo—Governor William Umstead suffers a heart attack while closing his Durham law office.

Umstead remains frail and is hospitalized several times during the remainder of his 22 months in office. On November 7, 1954, he will become the state's only 20th-century governor to die in office.

JANUARY 10, 1979

Congressman Ike Andrews of Cary scoffs at the latest reports linking smoking and mortality. "I smoke regularly and happily," he says, "and I feel that I'm better off for it. . . . The more I smoke, the better I feel."

1982

Charlotte's Dwight Clark makes "the Catch," as it comes to be known in NFL lore, giving the San Francisco 49ers their first Super Bowl trip.

Clark's leaping, stretching grab of Joe Montana's last-minute end-zone pass beats Dallas, makes the cover of *Sports Illustrated*, and foreshadows the 49ers' dominance of the 1980s.

1994

Tales of the City, a miniseries based on the newspaper serial and novel by Raleigh-reared Armistead Maupin, debuts on PBS.

The three-part series—stations can choose from versions with or without nudity and profanity—satirizes San Francisco lifestyles in the 1970s.

Like fellow writers Reynolds Price and Anne Tyler, Maupin studied literature under Broughton High School's renowned Phyllis Peacock. After graduating from the University of North Carolina, he entered journalism as a reporter at WRAL-TV, where family friend Jesse Helms was an editorialist. A navy tour, including a year in Vietnam, was followed by an abortive try at the University of North Carolina Law School before Maupin, by now openly gay, made *Tales of the City* a daily institution in the *San Francisco Chronicle*.

1995

Hudson-Belk, founded in Raleigh in 1915, closes its Fayetteville Street location, leaving North Carolina without a major downtown department store.

Less than a week earlier, Briggs Hardware, a Fayetteville Street landmark since 1874, had moved to the suburbs.

JANUARY 11

1964

A report by United States surgeon general Luther Terry marshals evidence that smoking causes cancer and other diseases, effectively sending North Carolina's tobacco industry into a long, slow slide.

JANUARY 12

1865

Determined to at last break what Robert E. Lee considers the lifeline of the Confederacy, 58 Union warships in the Cape Fear River begin an unprecedented bombardment of Fort Fisher. At one point, an estimated 100 shells a minute are bursting above and inside the fort.

Three days later, 5,300 Union troops rush ashore, attack the fort from all directions, and overwhelm its 1,900 defenders in hand-to-hand combat.

Union casualties in the Civil War's largest sea-land battle exceed 1,300, Confederate casualties 500.

1909

Stonewall Jackson Manual Training and Industrial School, one of the first boys' reformatories in the nation, opens on a former 300-acre cotton farm near Concord.

Concord Standard editor J. P. Cook has advocated a reformatory since the early 1890s, when he saw a 13-year-old boy sentenced to three years at hard labor for a minor theft.

A key ally in his campaign: Anna Morrison Jackson, whose status as the widow of Confederate war hero Thomas "Stonewall" Jackson helped win over the many Civil War veterans in the 1907 legislature.

1915

In Congress, Representative E. Y. Webb of Shelby speaks against the proposed women's suffrage amendment: "Nature destined woman to be the home maker, the child rearer, while man is the money maker. I am unwilling, as a Southern man, to force upon her any burden which will distract this loving potentate from her sacred, God-imposed duties. I am unwilling to force her into the vortex of politics, where her sensitiveness and her modesty will often be offended."

1960

Bishop C. M. "Sweet Daddy" Grace, who began his colorful ministry in Charlotte, dies in Los Angeles at age 78.

Followers of the self-described "Boyfriend to the World" mourn him during a two-week cross-country funeral. In Charlotte, thousands view his body at the red, white, and blue House of Prayer for All People, as bands play around the clock. He is later buried in New Bedford, Massachusetts.

JANUARY 13

1981

The Washington Redskins name Joe Gibbs,

a Mocksville native, as their head coach. Gibbs will go on to coach three Super Bowl champions.

Although his family moved to California when he was 14, Gibbs had already picked up an appetite for stock-car racing—his sheriff father chased moonshiners and frequented dirt-track races. In 1992, Gibbs will form his own NASCAR Winston Cup team.

1982

The *Village Voice* profiles Gene Roberts of the *Philadelphia Inquirer* as "the Best Newspaper Editor in America."

Before retiring in 1990 as executive editor, Roberts, born in Pikeville and educated at Mars Hill Junior College and the University of North Carolina, will lead the *Inquirer* to 17 Pulitzer Prizes. His first newspaper job: farm editor of the *Goldsboro News-Argus*.

JANUARY 14

1937

Selected items from the schedule of fees adopted by the Wake County Medical Society:

Office calls: $1.50

Thorough physical exam: $5

Town calls within a radius of one mile: northern part of county, $3; eastern part of county, $2; southern and western parts of county, $2.50

Calls beyond one mile of corporate limit: $.50 per mile plus the amount of the town call

Roadside prescription or visit: $2

JANUARY 15, 1795

The University of North Carolina, the nation's first state university, opens in Chapel Hill.

Although the University of Georgia was chartered before the University of North Carolina, it doesn't open until 1801.

1925

The members of a nameless string band performing in the New York studios of Okeh Records tell promoter Ralph Peer he can call them whatever he likes—"We're just a bunch of hillbillies from North Carolina and Virginia anyway." Peer names them "the Hillbillies." The term *hillbilly* will later take hold as a label for commercial country music.

1959

Senator John F. Kennedy, characterized in the *Charlotte News* as "not improbably the next president of the United States," addresses the annual banquet of the Charlotte Chamber of Commerce.

Introduced by Senator Sam Ervin of North Carolina, Kennedy pushes his anti-racketeering bill and lambastes Teamsters boss Jimmy Hoffa.

Jacqueline Kennedy, 27, tells a reporter that she sees her role in her husband's campaign as "helping with baggage and seeing that he eats."

1987

RJR Nabisco, North Carolina's largest company, announces its intent to leave Winston-Salem—where it was founded 112 years earlier—for Atlanta.

The city loses 300 jobs, but the R. J. Reynolds Tobacco Company subsidiary remains, and RJR donates its 500,000-square-foot headquarters building to space-starved Wake Forest University.

Barbarians at the Gate: The Fall of RJR Nabisco, a best-selling account of the company's subsequent buyout by Kohlberg Kravis Roberts and Company, will attribute the decision to move to chief executive Ross Johnson, who describes Winston-Salem to an Atlanta interviewer as "bucolic."

JANUARY 16

1975

Black hecklers prevent David Duke, a little-known Ku Klux Klansman from Louisiana, from speaking at the University of North Carolina's Memorial Auditorium.

Chancellor Ferebee Taylor calls the incident "a transgression of one of the highest and noblest traditions of this institution."

Duke will go on to form the National Association for the Advancement of White People in 1980, be elected to the Louisiana legislature in 1989, and unsuccessfully challenge incumbent George Bush for the Republican presidential nomination in 1992.

1991

At Chapel Hill, a nationally televised basketball game between the University of North Carolina and North Carolina State is postponed when war breaks out in the Persian Gulf.

"This was a moment of recognition that our lives have changed," says University of North Carolina chancellor Paul Hardin. "It was not a moment to play basketball."

JANUARY 17

1874

Chang and Eng Bunker, the original "Siamese twins," die within two hours of each other at their home in Surry County.

Brought to the United States in 1829, the two became wealthy and world-famous touring for P. T. Barnum. In 1839, weary of life on the road, they settled near Wilkesboro and married local sisters. Their domestic system was to spend three days in one couple's house, three days in the other's. Chang fathered 12 children, Eng 10.

They are 63 years old when Chang succumbs to a blood clot in his brain; Eng, as best doctors can tell, dies of fright.

JANUARY 18

1958

Lumbee Indians, upset about two recent cross-burnings near their homes, break up a Ku Klux Klan rally in Robeson County. Klan leader James Cole planned to speak on "Why I Am for Segregation," but the program is cut short by gunfire, firecrackers, and tear-gas grenades thrown by sheriff's deputies. One Klansman is charged with public drunkenness.

1862

Private D. L. Day, Company B, 25th Massachusetts Volunteer Infantry, writes in his diary at Hatteras Inlet,

Witnessing boat collisions and wrecks is getting old and the boys are amusing themselves by writing letters, making up their diaries, playing cards, reading old magazines and newspapers which they have read half a dozen times before; and some of them are actually reading their Bibles.

Of all the lonely, God-forsaken looking places I ever saw, this Hatteras island takes the premium. It is simply a sandbar rising a little above the water. . . . I don't think there is a bird or any kind of animal, unless it is a dog, on the island, not even a grasshopper, as one would have to prospect the whole island to find a blade of grass, and in the event of his finding one would sing himself to death. . . . It is the key, or gate-way, to nearly all of eastern North Carolina and places us directly in the rear of Norfolk, Va.

JANUARY 20

1840

One year after the North Carolina General Assembly passed the Common School Law, the state's first public school opens in Rockingham County. The law requires schools to stay open at least two months per year.

1977

Joining the more traditional Guy Lombardo at Jimmy Carter's inaugural ball: Wilmington-born Charlie Daniels.

Two years later, the Charlie Daniels Band will hit number one on both the country and rock charts with the fiddle tour de force "The Devil Went Down to Georgia."

1993

Maya Angelou, professor of American studies at Wake Forest University, delivers her poem "A Rock, A River, A Tree" at the inauguration of Bill Clinton.

Angelou, 64, is the author of several volumes of poetry and five memoirs, including *I Know Why the Caged Bird Sings*.

She is the first poet to read at an inauguration since Robert Frost at John F. Kennedy's in 1961.

JANUARY 21

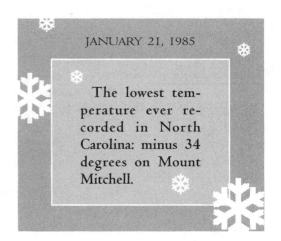

JANUARY 21, 1985

The lowest temperature ever recorded in North Carolina: minus 34 degrees on Mount Mitchell.

1816

Responding to a letter from Senator Nathaniel Macon, Thomas Jefferson offers his opinion "on the subject of the statue of George Washington, which the legislature of North Carolina has ordered to be procured, and set up in their Capitol."

Jefferson, retired at Monticello at age 73, proposes the state use an Italian sculptor, Antonio Canova, and Italian stone, Carrara marble. Washington, he adds, should be depicted in Roman costume: "I am sure the artist, and every person of taste in Europe would be for the Roman. . . . Our boots and regimentals have a very puny effect."

North Carolina follows Jefferson's advice, and the Canova statue is a source of state pride until it is crushed in the State Capitol fire of 1831.

In 1970, following heated debate in the North Carolina General Assembly over the appropriateness of Washington's "miniskirt," a privately financed copy of the statue is installed in the State Capitol.

1862

Private D. L. Day, Company B, 25th Massachusetts Volunteer Infantry, writes in his diary at Hatteras Inlet,

> A schooner came alongside today and left us rations of steamed pork, hardtack and condensed sea water. This was a very timely arrival as we have been very short of water for two or three days and pretty much everything else. Rattlesnake pork will taste pretty good again after a few days fast. Condensed sea water is rather a disagreeable beverage, but still is a little ahead of no water at all. I think, however, it might be made palatable by adding about nine parts whiskey to one of water.
>
> This water and pork is all manufactured here on the spot. They have a sort of rendering establishment where they make it, but I cannot believe that the pork would take a premium in any fair in the country unless it was for meanness.

1857

North Carolina native Miles Darden, the heaviest human being on record until the 20th century, dies in Henderson County, Tennessee. It takes 17 men to place his body in the coffin.

Darden was born on a farm near Rich Square in Northampton County but moved to Tennessee at about age 30. He was an innkeeper and farmer.

Darden, who stood seven feet, six inches, tall, apparently refused to be weighed after moving to Tennessee, but his neighbors, using rocks to duplicate the tension on his ox-wagon springs while he was aboard, estimated his weight at a little over 1,000 pounds. The *Guinness Book of World Records* will later list his weight at 1,020 pounds.

1931

R. J. Reynolds Tobacco Company begins wrapping Camel cigarettes in moisture-proof cellophane.

As soon as the new packages reach store

shelves, Reynolds plays up its edge on the competition by offering a $25,000 first prize for the best answer to the question, "What significant change has recently been made in the wrapping of the Camel package and what are its advantages to the smoker?"

In less than a month, the Winston-Salem post office is inundated with 952,229 contest letters.

1977

The largest audience in television history begins watching the eight-part ABC miniseries based on Alex Haley's best-selling *Roots*.

Growing up in Henning, Tennessee, Haley listened to his grandmother and her sisters tell stories about their ancestors who came to Alamance County as slaves.

Roots was born when Haley, a journalist and author, happened into the National Archives in Washington and asked to see the 1870 census. The discovery of his ancestors' names on the rolls of microfilm inspired him to visit Alamance County and eventually to trace his roots back to Kunta Kinte in Africa.

1978

Under pressure to confront one of the nation's most controversial civil rights cases, Governor Jim Hunt declares on statewide television that while the case against the Wilmington 10 may not have been perfect, the convictions were justified. Hunt does, however, cut their sentences dramatically. Some are immediately eligible for parole, although the most prominent—Ben Chavis—will remain in prison nearly two more years.

The case centered on the 1971 firebombing of Mike's Grocery during racial strife in Wilmington.

1986

Overall-clad Rufus Hussey, 66, a retired carpenter and chicken farmer from Randolph County, shows off his skills with a slingshot—a "beanshooter," he calls it—on *The Tonight Show*.

Johnny Carson asks his opinion of the show. "There's room for improvement," Hussey suggests.

JANUARY 24

1918

A spinal meningitis quarantine shuts down Charlotte's amusement places, churches, schools, and public gatherings.

The quarantine is lifted after two weeks, but 10 months later, the city is again quarantined, this time because of an epidemic of influenza.

1936

Allen Foster, rapist, becomes the first person to die in the gas chamber in North Carolina. The new procedure is so ineptly carried out that death takes 11 minutes. Even hardened witnesses at Central Prison are revolted, and civic clubs around the state petition Governor J. C. B. Ehringhaus to prohibit further executions until the method "has been perfected to the point of definite elimination of needless suffering."

1961

A B-52 bomber from Seymour Johnson Air Force Base crashes near Goldsboro. The air force denies the two nuclear warheads aboard could have detonated, but later revelations suggest the incident was the closest the nation has come to suffering an atomic-weapons disaster.

Defense Department reports made public in 1980 indicate that one of the 24-megaton bombs snagged in a tree and was only a final safety catch away from detonation. Eastern North Carolina would have experienced an explosion 1,800 times more powerful than the one that leveled Hiroshima.

Crews collect debris from the crash for more than four months, digging a hole 50 feet deep, but one piece of uranium will remain unaccounted for.

1965

Dynamite destroys the car of Julius Chambers, a black NAACP lawyer, while he speaks at a civil rights rally at a church in New Bern.

Ten months later, Chambers's house is among those in Charlotte hit by late-night explosions. In the early 1970s, during the Charlotte-Mecklenburg case that establishes busing as a tool for desegregating schools, arson strikes Chambers's law office once and his father's auto-repair shop in Mount Gilead twice.

In 1993, after nearly a decade in New York as director of the NAACP Legal Defense and Educational Fund, Chambers will return to his alma mater, North Carolina Central University, as chancellor.

1995

Fourteen years after being convicted of the rape and murder of a North Carolina Wesleyan College cheerleader, Kermit Smith is executed by lethal injection at Central Prison in Raleigh. Smith is the first white person in North Carolina, and the second in the nation, to be executed for killing a black person.

JANUARY 25

1994

Pat Crawford, the last surviving member of the famed "Gashouse Gang"—the 1934 world-champion St. Louis Cardinals—dies at a Morehead City nursing home at age 91.

Crawford was the top pinch hitter for the Gashouse Gang, named for its rambunctious style. Unlike such teammates as Pepper Martin, Leo Durocher, and Dizzy Dean, however, Crawford held two college degrees—from Davidson College and Ohio State—abstained from tobacco and alcohol, and preferred to turn in early.

The Gashouse Gang's next-to-last survivor, Burgess Whitehead, died two months earlier at his home in Windsor in Bertie County.

JANUARY 26

1826

Former governor Benjamin Smith, once among the state's wealthiest citizens, dies a pauper in his namesake town of Smithville—later Southport.

Smith is buried at night to prevent creditors from holding his body to force friends to pay his debts, a legal ploy of the time.

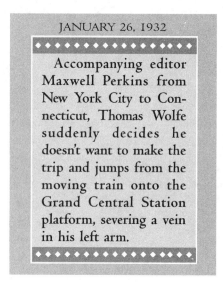

JANUARY 26, 1932

Accompanying editor Maxwell Perkins from New York City to Connecticut, Thomas Wolfe suddenly decides he doesn't want to make the trip and jumps from the moving train onto the Grand Central Station platform, severing a vein in his left arm.

JANUARY 27

1851

The North Carolina General Assembly creates Madison County, one of three counties in the state named for presidents. The others are Washington and Jackson; Cleveland, Lincoln, Polk, and Wilson Counties are not named for presidents.

JANUARY 28

1781

British forces occupy the port of Wilmington, which will become a key supply base for Lord Cornwallis's troops.

1916

Central Prison warden Big Tom Sale undertakes the electrocution of two men convicted of killing a Guilford County farmer.

Sale throws the current to the first murderer, whose body rises against the straps before the power fails. Sale calmly repairs a faulty rheostat, finishes the job of executing the first murderer, and then executes the second murderer without incident.

He walks to his office, signs the death certificates, leans over his desk—and drops dead.

1922

The University of North Carolina Press, the first university press in the South, begins operation. Its first book, *The Saprolegniaceae, with Notes on Other Water Molds* by William C. Coker, will appear a year later.

More typically, however, the University of North Carolina Press addresses such subjects as education, tenant farming, child labor, unions, chain gangs, and lynchings.

1959

Governor Luther Hodges of North Carolina wires Governor Ralph Herseth of South Dakota in response to a bill that would require tobacco to carry a skull-and-crossbones label and the statement, "Not recommended by state of South Dakota": "I know that you would not want the General Assembly of North Carolina to pass a law requiring that any farm products originating from South Dakota and offered for sale in North Carolina must carry labels warning that, according to the United States Department of Agriculture, South Dakota soil has the highest content in the nation of selenium, a well known poison."

Three days later, the South Dakota tobacco bill will be dead.

JANUARY 28, 1986

Seven astronauts, including Beaufort native Michael J. Smith and North Carolina A & T graduate Ronald McNair, are killed when the space shuttle *Challenger* explodes 73 seconds after liftoff.

JANUARY 29

1901

His reelection bid thwarted by the state's disfranchisement of blacks, Representative George H. White of Tarboro gives his farewell speech to Congress:

Now, Mr. Chairman . . . I want to submit a brief recipe for the solution of the so-called American Negro problem. He asks no special favors, but simply demands that he be given the same chance for existence, for earning a livelihood, for raising himself in the scales of manhood and womanhood that are accorded to kindred nationalities. Treat him as a man: Go into his home and learn of his so-

cial conditions; learn of his cares, his troubles and his hopes for the future; gain his confidence; open the doors of industry to him; let the word *Negro, colored* and *black* be stricken from all the organizations enumerated in the federation of labor.

Help him to overcome his weaknesses, punish the crime-committing class by the courts of the land, measure the standard of his race by its best material, cease to mold prejudicial and unjust public sentiment against him, and my word for it, he will learn to support, hold up the hands of, and join in with that political party, that institution, whether secular or religious, in every community where he lives, which is destined to do the greatest good for the greatest number. Obliterate race hatred, party prejudice, and help us to achieve nobler ends, greater results, and become more satisfactory citizens to our brother in white.

This, Mr. Chairman, is perhaps the Negro's temporary farewell to the American Congress, but let me say, phoenix-like, he will rise up some day and come again.

A white North Carolina legislator exults over George White's departure that now "we have a white man's government in every part of the old state. . . . For these mercies, thank God."

White will be the last black member of Congress for 25 years; it is 1992 before North Carolina elects another.

1902

Patrick Pearsall, secretary to Governor Charles Brantley Aycock, takes it on himself to appoint two maids of honor to a ball at the Charleston Exposition. The governor himself, sensitive to constituents who oppose dancing, has been unable to act.

1963

Jesse Helms, editorialist for Raleigh's WRAL-TV, reacts to Harvey Gantt's entrance into Clemson University:

> He has stoutly resisted the pose of a conquering hero for the forces of integration. He simply wants, he says, to be an architect—and Clemson is the only college in South Carolina that can teach him how to be one.
>
> He has rejected the fanfare and trappings of the NAACP. He has turned away from the liberal press and television networks which would glorify him. He has refused to make pompous speeches and statements.
>
> If ever a man put his best foot forward, Harvey Gantt has done so. His conduct will not cause South Carolinians to relish court orders relating to integration. But he has done a great deal, probably more than he himself realizes, to establish respectful communications across sensitive barriers in human relations.

Helms goes on to cast Gantt and James Meredith, who desegregated the University of Mississippi in 1962, as "a study in contrasts. . . . Meredith as a man handpicked as the showpiece of forced integration, Meredith as a man who never quite persuaded anybody that he was really interested in an education, Meredith as a man constantly and piously parading before the microphone and television cameras."

By 1990, when Gantt runs for Helms's United States Senate seat, Meredith has joined Helms's Washington staff.

1968

The all-time highest-rated episode of *The Andy Griffith Show* airs, during the last of the show's eight prime-time seasons.

In "Barney Hosts a Summit Meeting," former costar Don Knotts returns for a guest appearance as Barney Fife. Hoping to help his ex-deputy impress superiors at the Raleigh Police Department, Andy allows Barney to arrange an East-West summit at the Taylor household. The meeting fails miserably until an impromptu encounter in Aunt Bee's kitchen saves the day.

The episode wins Knotts a fifth Emmy for his portrayal of Fife.

JANUARY 30

1941

After appearing at Raleigh's State Theatre in the stage version of *The Philadelphia Story*, Katharine Hepburn attends an Executive Mansion cast party hosted by Governor and Mrs. J. Melville Broughton.

"Miss Hepburn wore a mink coat over tan gabardine slacks and jacket, with white blouse of crepe silk and brown suede shoes with crepe rubber soles," reports the *News and Observer*. "Her informal attire and equally informal manner put at ease all her admirers."

Hepburn, 33, tells reporters she hasn't seen enough of North Carolina to form an opinion, "but the beds in the hotel are nice."

1972

At Hatteras Inlet, James Hussey pulls in a world-record bluefish—31 pounds, 12 ounces.

The Outer Banks will also account for the world's largest red drum, or channel bass (94 pounds, two ounces, caught by David Deuel off Cape Hatteras in 1984) and largest Spanish mackerel (13 pounds, caught by Robert Cranton at Ocracoke Inlet in 1987).

JANUARY 31

1734

The first lots are sold in New Liverpool, which has sprung up, unplanned, at the junction of two branches of the Cape Fear River.

The town will later be renamed Newton, or New Town, then finally Wilmington.

1781

Two months after taking charge of the Continental Army in the South, General Nathanael Greene writes George Washington to lament the state of the North Carolina militia. He finds the men "poorly armed, poorly organized, untrained, and led by inexperienced officers. . . . It is impossible to carry on the war any length of time with the militia."

1890

James B. Duke of Durham organizes the American Tobacco Company.

His father, Washington Duke, had sparked the public's switch from chewing to smoking by turning his harvests into smoking tobacco and selling it from a wagon. Before its breakup in 1911, the American Tobacco Company will become the world's largest tobacco producer.

1927

Mayor H. A. Moffit of High Point orders that all future public dances must stop at midnight. According to a dispatch in the *Charlotte Observer*, the mayor's announcement follows "a series of four terpsichorean events staged in connection with the furniture exposition. The mayor made an exception . . . in order that the visiting furniture men might be entertained more elaborately."

Two years before Mayberry, Andy Griffith [February 15]
and wife Barbara return for a 1958 visit to
the University of North Carolina.

February

Lafayette visits muddy Murfreesboro
Jules Verne borrows Morganton's mountain
Pogo puts in a plug for N.C. candidate

FEBRUARY 1

1865

Zebulon Vance, governor of North Carolina, writes J. A. Seddon, Confederate secretary of war, about the condition of Union prisoners being held at Salisbury: "Accounts reach me of the most distressing character in regard to their suffering and destitution. I earnestly request you to have the matter inquired into, and if in our power to relieve them that it be done. If they are willfully left to suffer when we can avoid it, it would be not only a blot upon our humanity, but would lay us open to a severe retaliation. I know how straitened our means are, however, and will cast no blame upon any one without further information."

1886

As the legislature again rejects proposals for establishing a state agricultural and mechanical college, Walter Hines Page, a Cary native living in New York, sends a stinging letter to the *State Chronicle*, a Raleigh newspaper he once edited, comparing North Carolina's leadership to Egyptian mummies.

"The world must have some corner in it where men sleep and sleep and dream and dream, and North Carolina is as good a spot for that as any," Page writes.

> There is not a man whose residence is in the State who is recognized by the world as an authority on anything. Since time began no man nor woman who lived there has ever written a book that has taken a place in the permanent literature of the country. Not a man has ever lived and worked there who fills twenty-five pages in any history of the United States. Not a scientific discovery has been made and worked out and kept its home in North Carolina that ever became famous for the good it did the world. It is the laughing stock among the States.

The letter provokes a storm of protests—but a year later leads to the founding of what is now North Carolina State.

Page goes on to edit several national magazines, including the *Atlantic Monthly*, and to serve as United States ambassador to Great Britain during World War I.

1898

The state's first free library opens in Durham.

1960

Four black freshmen from North Carolina A & T ask to be served at the whites-only Woolworth lunch counter in downtown Greensboro, setting off a historic challenge to segregation across the South and bringing "sit-in" into the American lexicon.

Although sit-ins date back to the 1930s labor movement, the term has not yet gained wide usage. The 1960s will bring not only more sit-ins, but also kneel-ins, teach-ins, and love-ins.

1988

Two Tuscarora Indians armed with sawed-off shotguns take over *The Robesonian* newspaper in Lumberton. Eddie Hatcher and Timothy Jacobs, who say they are calling attention to corruption and discrimination in the county, hold employees hostage for 10 hours.

After fleeing the state and seeking asylum at places ranging from Indian reservations to the Soviet consulate in San Francisco, Hatcher and Jacobs are brought back, plead guilty to kidnapping charges, and are imprisoned.

FEBRUARY 2

1862

Private D. L. Day, Company B, 25th Massachusetts Volunteer Infantry, writes in his diary on Hatteras Inlet,

> A high wind prevailed this morning and the sea was somewhat rough; the boat had considerable motion, but the boys had their sea legs on, so it caused them very little trouble. Our company cooks, with commendable enterprise and industry and with an eye to our present well being, furnished us with baked beans and hot coffee for breakfast. This was a great treat and every man had all he wanted; a vote of thanks was given the cooks. For dinner, boiled beef was served, the first we have had since leav-

ing Fortress Monroe. I hope this kind of fare will hold out, but fear we shall have a relapse of the worst kind.

1943

President Franklin D. Roosevelt thanks Governor O. Max Gardner for his Christmas present—pajamas custom-made in New York from nylon parachute cloth manufactured at Gardner's textile mill in Shelby. "I hope when I wear them," he writes Gardner, "that I do not start counting ten and jump!"

Gardner's gift is intended to tout the value of synthetics research, which led to the invention of nylon for parachutes just in time to offset the Japanese monopoly on silk.

FEBRUARY 3

1865

Captain G. W. Booth responds to Governor Zebulon Vance's request for a report on conditions at the prison at Salisbury:

> About the 5th of November, 1864, a large number of prisoners of war, some 8,000, were suddenly sent here, the Government having no other place to send them. The grounds were enlarged and such preparations as could be made were arranged for their reception. A short time after their arrival tents were issued, and now they are all under shelter of some sort. The number of prisoners confined here has reached as high a figure as 10,000.
>
> The matter of food receives the earnest attention of the commanding officers. They [prisoners] regularly receive one pound of good bread, one pint of soup, besides small issues of

meat or sorghum. Sometimes small quantities of both. As to clothing, their condition is truly deplorable, most of them having been prisoners some six or nine months. The Confederate Government cannot issue clothing to them, and none has been received at this post from the North.

1870

The North Carolina General Assembly creates Dare County, the last of three counties in the state named in honor of women. Dare is named for Virginia Dare, the first child of English parents born in the New World; Wake is named for Margaret Wake, the wife of colonial governor William Tryon; Mecklenburg is named to honor Princess Charlotte Sophia of Mecklenburg-Strelitz, the wife of George III.

1930

After a month's rest at the Grove Park Inn in Asheville fails to halt his mental and physical deterioration, William Howard Taft submits his resignation as chief justice of the United States Supreme Court.

Taft, who earlier served as president, is 73 years old, weighs 300 pounds, and suffers from progressive heart disease. After sending his resignation ahead, he returns by train to Washington, where he will die barely a month later.

1949

Fort Bragg is the site of the nation's first court-martial in which enlisted men are eligible to serve as jurors.

FEBRUARY 4, 1834

Wake Forest Institute—later Wake Forest University—the state's first Baptist college, is founded in Wake County. Students are required to work in the fields three hours a day to help pay for their literary and religious studies, but enrollment falters and the labor scheme is later abandoned.

FEBRUARY 5

1895

The North Carolina General Assembly fixes the legal rate of interest at 6 percent.

FEBRUARY 6

1947

Former governor O. Max Gardner, appointed by Franklin D. Roosevelt as ambassador to the Court of Saint James, suffers a fatal heart attack on the morning he is to sail for England.

1975

Warner Brothers pays Charlotte musician Arthur Smith an estimated $200,000 for having appropriated his 1950s hit "Feudin' Banjos," renamed it "Duelin' Banjos," and used it without credit or payment in *Deliverance*. Smith says he is "highly satisfied and tickled" over the out-of-court settlement. The 1972 movie sparked a national rediscovery of banjo playing.

FEBRUARY 7

1889

Raleigh's board of aldermen, trimming the city budget, votes to eliminate "eighth-grade education in the graded schools at public expense."

1951

Linville Gorge is set aside for preservation in its natural state. Donated to the National Park Service by John D. Rockefeller, Jr., the 7,655-acre tract in Burke County is considered the wildest gorge in the eastern United States. It follows the Linville River, which the Cherokees knew as Eeseeoh—"River of Cliffs."

FEBRUARY 8

1862

A Union expedition led by General Ambrose Burnside captures Roanoke Island, takes 2,488 prisoners, and makes it even more difficult for Confederates to use state ports.

1869

The Philanthropic Society of Davidson College invites President Andrew Johnson to speak at commencement ceremonies: "Since the decline of the State University, Davidson is by far the most flourishing institution in North

Carolina. Our Chapel is said to be the largest in the South, and should you be pleased to honor us with your presence, we assure you that you will have as an audience, this chapel filled with the best and most intelligent of North Carolina's citizens."

Johnson, less than a month from leaving office after surviving impeachment, will send his regrets.

1927

The legislature designates "The Old North State," composed in 1840 by North Carolina Supreme Court justice William Gaston, as the official state song. The first verse:

> Carolina! Carolina! Heaven's blessings attend her,
> While we live we will cherish, protect and defend her,
> Tho' the scorner may sneer at and witlings defame her,
> Still our hearts swell with gladness whenever we name her.

Gaston, one of the state's major intellectual as well as political figures—he graduated at the top of his class at Princeton—apparently borrowed the melody from a troupe of visiting Swiss bell ringers. "The Old North State" was played in public for the first time at the state Whig Convention of 1840.

1950

Charlotte hires the state's first meter maids. Dubbed the "Skirt Squad" and the "Petticoat Patrol," their only duty is to issue parking citations. It will be 1967 before the city hires its first women as sworn police officers.

1950

In his regionally syndicated radio commentary, W. E. Debnam of Raleigh counters a recent "My Turn" newspaper column in which Eleanor Roosevelt cited "signs of poverty and unhappiness that will gradually have to disappear if [the South] is going to prosper and keep pace."

Debnam's bristling response—in which he reminds Mrs. Roosevelt of poverty in Harlem, the excesses of Reconstruction, and the success of Durham's black-owned North Carolina Mutual Life Insurance Company—strikes a chord with criticism-weary white Southerners. When he repackages it into a 50-cent booklet entitled *Weep No More, My Lady*, it sells more than 500,000 copies.

FEBRUARY 9

FEBRUARY 9, 1980

Lang Martin of Charlotte upgrades his listing in the *Guinness Book of World Records* by balancing seven new golf balls vertically without the use of adhesive. This beats his own 1977 record of six.

1790

George Washington appoints James Iredell of Edenton to the United States Supreme Court. Among Iredell's attributes, says Washington, is that "he is of a State of some importance in the Union that has given no character to a federal office."

The English-born Iredell proves to be one of the Supreme Court's sharpest minds until his death in 1799.

North Carolina's only other Supreme Court justice: Alfred Moore of New Hanover County, appointed by John Adams in 1800.

1874

The first of a series of earthquakes shakes Rumbling Bald Mountain in Rutherford County. Accounts of the more than 50 quakes over the next 10 weeks inspire French science-fiction pioneer Jules Verne to set *The Master of the World* (1904) atop a mountain near Morganton.

Verne, a prodigious researcher who never set foot in North Carolina, also describes a crazed French inventor's kidnapping from a New Bern asylum in *Facing the Flag* (1892).

1885

In the belief that they are descended from Sir Walter Raleigh's Lost Colony, Indians in Robeson County win designation from the legislature as "Croatan Indians."

A permanent identity, however, will prove elusive for these Indians, who have no treaties, no separate language, and no history that transcends speculation. In 1911, they become the "Indians of Robeson County," in 1913 the "Cherokee Indians of Robeson County," and in 1953 the "Lumbee Indians of Robeson County."

FEBRUARY 10, 1962

In a meet at the Los Angeles Sports Arena, Jim Beatty, a Charlotte native and University of North Carolina alumnus, runs the mile in three minutes, 58.9 seconds—the first time the four-minute barrier has been broken on an indoor track.

1958

The Reverend Martin Luther King, Jr., not yet 30 years old but already famous for leading the Montgomery, Alabama, bus boycott, pays his first visit to Greensboro.

The local NAACP has invited King, but only black Bennett College will provide him a hall. He addresses two overflow crowds—morning and night—at Pfeiffer Chapel. "We are breaking loose from the Egypt of segregation and moving into the promised land of integration . . . ," he says. "There are giants in the way, but it can be done."

Five years later, he will return to Greensboro for a ceremony honoring the students who ignited the sit-in movement at the Woolworth lunch counter.

FEBRUARY 12

1795

Hinton James of Wilmington becomes the first student to enroll at the University of North Carolina. He is welcomed by the school's two faculty members.

1865

Brigadier General Bradley T. Johnson, commander of Salisbury Prison, notifies Raleigh that a number of Confederate deserters have gathered along the Yadkin River and may be planning to attack the town. Western North Carolina, always a collecting ground for Union supporters, is becoming more bold as the Confederacy weakens.

1909

A petition to the legislature from 149 citizens of Rowan and Davidson Counties reflects the difficult adjustment of hunters and fishermen, who have historically enjoyed wide freedom, to the advent of state game- and fish-protection laws.

Restricting quail hunting to a "season," the petitioners argue, "would be to the great injury of our own citizens, in that no person would be allowed to kill a quail for his own use or in case of sickness, for the use of members of his family."

1970

The number of first-day visitors to SouthPark, a posh shopping mall carved from 104 acres of farmland on Charlotte's southeastern edge: 92,000.

SouthPark quickly becomes the hub of a thriving city within a city; downtown retailers report a 25-percent drop in sales the first year. By 1995, SouthPark will also include 2.9 million square feet of office space—far less than downtown Charlotte's 9.5 million square feet but just behind downtown Raleigh's 3 million square feet.

1991

The Herbert C. Bonner Bridge, the only link by which people on Hatteras Island can reach other bridges leading to the North Carolina mainland, reopens almost four months after a storm-tossed dredge broke loose from its moorings and knocked out a 369-foot span.

Despite the efforts of five ferries, Hatteras Island's tourist-fed economy suffered severe damage while the bridge was out.

FEBRUARY 13

1830

In *State v. Mann*, the North Carolina Supreme Court declines to investigate the circumstances of slavery.

Harriet Beecher Stowe will use the case as background for *Uncle Tom's Cabin*, her 1852 novel that energizes and broadens the abolitionist movement.

1911

Edward Bouton, who used Frederick Law Olmsted, Jr.'s, pioneering urban-design firm in developing the Roland Park section of Baltimore, writes Olmsted about "a very prominent man from Charlotte, N.C., who has some land which he wants to have laid out for the purpose of a suburban subdivision. I think he wants to do things rather well. This Mr. Latta is a man of considerable means. He owned the street car system at Charlotte for a number of years, and has . . . been in the suburban land business in an amateurish sort of way."

Edward Dilworth Latta does indeed hire Olmsted Brothers to design Dilworth, Charlotte's first suburb.

FEBRUARY 14

1849

With little enthusiasm, James K. Polk becomes the first president to have his picture taken in the White House.

In his diary, Polk complains about having had to deal with office seekers all morning: "I have great contempt for such persons and dispose of their applications very summarily. They take up much of my time. . . . I yielded to the request of an artist named [Matthew] Brady, of New York, by sitting for my daguerreotype likeness today. I sat in the large dining-room."

1973

Gospel Road, a feature-length documentary on the life of Jesus written, produced, narrated, and financed by Johnny Cash, makes its world premiere in Charlotte.

1987

"Bowing to convention," the *Charlotte Observer* begins referring to the city's central business district as "uptown" instead of "downtown." Charlotteans, as always, remain split on the issue.

FEBRUARY 15

1865

To avoid the approaching troops of General William T. Sherman, the Confederacy evacuates its prisoners of war being held in the former state asylum in Columbia, South Carolina.

In his memoir *Prison Life in the South*, A. O. Abbott, first lieutenant in the First New York Dragoons, later describes the POW train's stopover in Charlotte: "Disembarking in the mud and water, [we] marched three-quarters of a mile to a little pine grove, which was called by some 'Camp Necessity,' by others 'Camp Bacon,' for here we received the first meat we had had in over one hundred thirty days. . . .

"Here we had a few old 'A' tents for shelter, otherwise there was not the least convenience or preparation for our comfort. . . . The ground was soft and wet, and the water we drank was obtained from an old goose-pond."

1960

On *The Danny Thomas Show*, Sheriff Andy Taylor, played by Andy Griffith, arrests nightclub performer Thomas for speeding through sleepy Mayberry, North Carolina. The episode introduces the Taylor character and sets up television's first spin-off series, *The Andy Griffith Show*.

1960

On the nation's comics pages, the flat-bottomed swamp boat rowed by Pogo bears the label, "Ol' Terry Sanford—N.C."

The plug for the Fayetteville gubernatorial candidate grew out of cartoonist Walt Kelly's saloon-bred friendship with Sanford campaign aide Roy Wilder.

1995

After a 24-hour stakeout of a Raleigh apartment building, FBI agents capture Kevin Mitnick, "the most wanted computer hacker in the world."

Mitnick, 31, used his sophisticated skills to worm his way into the nation's telephone and cellular-telephone networks and vandalize government, corporate, and university computer systems. He first came to national attention at age 17 when, as a prank, he tapped into a North American Air Defense Command computer.

Mitnick's crucial mistake: breaking into the home computer of Tsutomu Shimomura, a San Diego computer security expert who became obsessed with tracking him down.

FEBRUARY 16

1865

Mary Boykin Chesnut, wife of a South Carolina plantation owner and high Confederate official, writes in her diary about fleeing to out-of-harm's-way Lincolnton:

> As we came up on the train from Charlotte a soldier took out of his pocket a filthy rag. If it had lain in the gutter for months, it could have been no worse. He unwrapped this cloth carefully and took out two biscuits of the species known as "hardtack." Then he gallantly handed me one and, with an ingratiating smile, asked me "to take some." Then he explained, "Please take these two—swap with me—give me something softer that I can eat—I am very weak still." Immediately, for his benefit my basket of luncheon was emptied—but as for his biscuits, "I would not choose any."
>
> Dirt—dirt—the Scripture states it plainly—cleanliness next to godliness.

1891

The legislature approves creation of the Soldiers' Home in Raleigh for the state's Confederate veterans.

1939

Federal art consultant Helen Appleton Read reports disapprovingly on a mural commissioned by the Treasury Department for the Morganton post office: "A competent enlarged illustration such as Dean Cornwell's *Sir Walter Raleigh* is cold and lacking in appeal when compared with murals in which the artist tries to give a personal interpretation of life or history as related to the community. . . . [But] the townspeople admired Cornwell's illustration."

Cornwell is a critically ignored magazine illustrator who, after winning a mural competition held by the Los Angeles Public Library, had to visit England to learn how to paint one. The Treasury Department's art program has shunted him off to North Carolina, where, as a future art historian will write, "whatever bombastic indiscretion he might see fit to commit in the local post office could be forgotten or chalked up to defective Southern tastebuds."

The Morganton mural is among several in the state resulting from federal programs designed to employ artists during the Depression. Among the other sites: Chapel Hill (where Cornwell did *Laying of the Cornerstone* for the post office), Raleigh, Siler City, Mooresville, Gastonia, Concord, Kings Mountain, and Lincolnton.

FEBRUARY 17

1865

Confederate inspector T. A. Hall reports to Richmond on conditions at Salisbury Prison: "The excessive rate of mortality among the prisoners . . . merits attention. . . . Since the 21st of October . . . 3,479 have been buried. Pneumonia and diseases of the bowels are the prevalent diseases. The prisoners appear to die, however, more from exposure and exhaustion than from actual disease."

1936

In a Charlotte warehouse, Bill Monroe, the father of bluegrass music, cuts his first recordings. It is during six Charlotte sessions over the next two years that Monroe will win acceptance for the mandolin as a lead instrument in country music.

One of the songs Monroe and his brother Charlie record that day—"What Would You Give in Exchange for Your Soul?"—sweeps the Carolinas and becomes one of the biggest country hits of the 1930s.

Six days a week, the Monroe Brothers do both a dawn show on WBT in Charlotte and a noon show on WFBC in Greenville, South Carolina. Evenings and weekends, they play schools and courthouses.

In all, they will cut about 60 songs in Charlotte, including the classic "Roll in My Sweet Baby's Arms," before splitting up in 1939.

1962

At halftime of the North Carolina State–Clemson basketball game at the original Charlotte Coliseum, engineers planning a mammoth arena in Houston fire two gunshots to test acoustics. "The Texans want to put an entire football field, complete with growing grass, inside their coliseum-to-be," reports the *Charlotte Observer*.

The Houston coliseum will turn out to be the trendsetting Astrodome. Its attempt at indoor grass fails and leads to the introduction of Astroturf.

1970

The pregnant wife and two young daughters of Dr. Jeffrey MacDonald are murdered at their Fort Bragg apartment.

MacDonald blames drug-crazed hippie intruders who chanted, "Acid is groovy, kill the pigs," but prosecutors contend it was he who clubbed and stabbed his wife and five-year-old in a fit of rage, then killed his two-year-old to cover up his crime. In 1979, a federal court in Raleigh will convict MacDonald on two counts of second-degree murder and one count of first-degree murder.

The case inspires *Fatal Vision*, a best-selling book and later a TV miniseries.

FEBRUARY 18

1915

President Woodrow Wilson and his cabinet view *The Birth of a Nation* in the East Room of the White House. Wilson's response—"Like writing history with lightning . . . so terribly true"—gives much-needed legitimacy to D. W. Griffith's controversial new silent movie based on *The Clansman*, a novel by Shelby native Thomas Dixon. Wilson is perhaps returning a favor; he and Dixon were classmates at Johns Hopkins, and early in Wilson's career, Dixon nominated him for an honorary doctorate at Wake Forest.

Another thumbs-up comes from North Carolinian Josephus Daniels, secretary of the navy, who arranges a later showing for the Supreme Court and Congress.

Set in a town based on York, South Carolina, the movie glorifies the Ku Klux Klan (and inspires its real-life revival), vilifies carpetbaggers, and caricatures blacks. Dixon's central villain closely resembles arch-Republican Thaddeus Stevens; Lincoln comes across as a well-meaning dupe.

FEBRUARY 19

1766

Stamp Act protesters in Wilmington, organized as the "Sons of Liberty," march to Brunswick and force a British officer to release two ships detained for lack of stamped papers.

1846

Lincolnton native James Pinckney Henderson is sworn in as the first governor of Texas.

The aristocratic Henderson—his Virginia grandfather commissioned Daniel Boone to cut the Wilderness Trail—studied law at the University of North Carolina. In 1835, he moved to Mississippi, where the Texas issue caught his passion. He recruited companies of men from Mississippi and North Carolina and was made a brigadier general in the army of the republic of Texas.

After Texas won its independence from Mexico, President Sam Houston made Henderson his attorney general, then secretary of state, then ambassador to Europe—all within less than a year of his arrival. At the age of 29, Henderson signed important treaties with England and France.

After defeating Mexico, the Texans were bewildered and embarrassed when the United States declined to annex them. (The North was reluctant to add another slave state.) In Washington, Henderson's skill and polish made him Texas's most effective spokesman for statehood.

Soon after Henderson takes office as governor, the United States and Mexico go to war over a boundary dispute. Henderson wins permission from the legislature to command Texas's troops in the field—he had arrived too late for the fighting a decade earlier—and after the war resumes the governorship.

1925

The North Carolina House rejects a resolution by Representative D. Scott Poole of Hoke County that would discourage public schools and colleges from teaching "any evolutionary hypothesis whereby man is linked in blood relationship with any lower form of life."

Among the resolution's opponents: Representative Sam Ervin of Burke County, who argues that it does nothing more than "absolve monkeys from all responsibility for the human race."

The vote is a setback for the state's antievolutionists, but they will continue to exert political power over the next several years, as a number of city and county school boards order teachers not to discuss Charles Darwin's theory.

1949

In one of a series of color advertisements on the back cover of *The New Yorker* magazine pairing Hollywood stars with North Carolina tobacco growers, actress Joan Fontaine says, "In my home, guests always insist on Chesterfields because they're so *mild*," while farmer Van W. Daniel of Ruffin in Rockingham County says, "Chesterfield buys the best sweet, *mild* cigarette tobacco. I have been a steady Chesterfield smoker for over 30 years."

FEBRUARY 20

1862

Winton in Hertford County becomes the first North Carolina town burned in the Civil War. Union forces set it afire in retaliation for a Confederate ambush there the day before.

1920

Nearing the end of a national tour, General John J. Pershing, commander of the United States Army during World War I, arrives in Asheville. Despite an influenza quarantine, hundreds are on hand to see Pershing's private rail car, attached to the Carolina Special, pull into the Biltmore station.

During his three-hour stay, he tours the Oteen Hospital for tubercular veterans and is greeted at the Grove Park Inn by Margaret Wilson, daughter of President Woodrow Wilson, who is trying to recover her voice after singing for Pershing's troops in Europe.

FEBRUARY 20, 1948

Piedmont Airlines, headquartered in Winston-Salem, inaugurates passenger service with a DC-3 flight from Wilmington to Charlotte to Cincinnati.

Over the next four decades, Piedmont will grow from what competitors dismiss as a "puddle jumper" to the nation's eighth-largest airline. In 1987, it is bought by Washington-based USAir for $1.6 billion.

1964

Richard Nixon, amateur pianist and former vice president, joins Arthur Smith and the Crackerjacks on their regionally syndicated country-music TV show. Nixon, making a "nonpolitical" tour of the state while building support for his successful 1968 presidential campaign, plays "Home on the Range" and banters with Smith. A staffer at Charlotte's WBTV, where the show is taped, calls Nixon "the life of the party" and says his comedic skills "would have turned Red Skelton green with envy."

FEBRUARY 21

1865

A. O. Abbott, first lieutenant in the First New York Dragoons, recalls the arrival in Goldsboro of a trainload of 700 fellow Union prisoners shipped from Salisbury and Florence, South Carolina:

> They had ridden all night in open flatcars, without a particle of shelter or fire. It was . . . a bitter cold, damp night, and, scantily clothed as they were, they had suffered beyond account. Three had died during the night, and were still on the train. Not one of them had a whole garment on, while nearly all were destitute of shirts or coats. A ragged or patched pair of pants, and a piece of an old blanket, constituted the wardrobe of the majority. Their faces were blackened by the pitch-pine smoke from the fires over which they had cooked their rations, while traces of soap and water were lost altogether. Hair and beard in their natural state. Yet all of this was nothing compared to their diseased, starving condition.
>
> In short, no words can describe their appearance. The sunken eye, the gaping mouth, the filthy skin, the clothes and head alive with ver-

min, the repelling bony contour, all conspired to lead to the conclusion that they were the victims of starvation, cruelty, and exposure to a degree unparalleled in the history of humanity.

Although conditions have been gruesome throughout the war for both Confederate and Union prisoners, most accounts attribute this more to a lack of resources than to intentional brutality.

1865

Troops commanded by General Braxton Bragg evacuate Wilmington, the Confederacy's last major port.

The city's fate had been sealed a month earlier with the fall of Fort Fisher, the key to the Cape Fear River defense.

1916

Though no match for the Charleston earthquake of 1886, the most severe earthquake recorded in 20th-century North Carolina shakes Skyland in Buncombe County. The shock is felt from Georgia to Virginia and as far west as Kentucky, but local damage is limited to broken crockery and cracked plaster.

FEBRUARY 22

1865

Freed in a prisoner exchange near war's end, 2,871 Union soldiers file out of Salisbury Prison.

Upon reaching Northern lines, an Iowa private will recall later, they "fell down by the side of the road and wept like children."

FEBRUARY 22, 1890

Thomas Edison is entertained at the home of Charlotte developer Edward Dilworth Latta. "A large number of citizens were present," reports the *Charlotte News*, "and it was a decidedly pleasant affair."

Within a year, Latta's "4-Cs" company will sign a $40,000 contract with Edison General Electric Company to install the city's first trolleys, linking downtown to Dilworth, the city's first suburb.

FEBRUARY 23

1862

Private D. L. Day, Company B, 25th Massachusetts Volunteer Infantry, writes in his diary on Roanoke Island, "The boys are amusing themselves making pipes from briar roots and fixing long stems of cane to them. Some of them are carved very handsomely and show much artistic skill. Washington's birthday was celebrated by salutes from the forts and a holiday in the camp."

1870

Hiram Revels, a Fayetteville native and one-time Lincolnton barbershop owner, is sworn in as the first black United States senator.

Revels served as a chaplain in the Union army and later settled at Natchez, Mississippi. He takes the seat vacated by Jefferson Davis, president of the Confederacy.

1893

Eager to tout their football team, students at the University of North Carolina start a one-page tabloid called the *Daily Tar Heel*.

Among its future editors: Thomas Wolfe (1920) and Charles Kuralt (1955).

1911

The North Carolina General Assembly establishes Avery County, the last of the state's 100 counties.

1948

Governor Gregg Cherry declines to join other Southern Democrats in threatening "secession" from the party in protest of President Truman's civil rights advocacy: "North Carolina has no Negro problem. We are going to keep our heads about this matter. We are going to meet our problems . . . as we come to them. We always have treated our Negroes fairly, and [they] enjoy the same educational advantages that the white people have."

The dissatisfied Democrats will break off into the "Dixiecrat" party and nominate Strom Thurmond, governor of South Carolina, for president. Thurmond carries four Southern states, but North Carolina sticks with Truman.

1951

Over opposition from Democrats who see it as an insult to the memory of Franklin D. Roosevelt—who was elected four times in succession—the North Carolina House ratifies by a nearly two-to-one margin a constitutional amendment limiting presidents to two terms. Representative Richard Sanders of Durham paints advocates as "ready to . . . crucify with a dagger a great man after his death—to discredit a man they couldn't defeat in life."

In less than a week, the 22nd Amendment will be ratified by the necessary 36 states.

1955

After being met at the railroad station by a white-suited Reynolds Price, Eudora Welty reads from her work at Duke University. The revered Mississippi fiction writer and the yet-unpublished undergraduate hit it off immediately, and Welty gives Price's career a boost by introducing him to her agent.

FEBRUARY 24

1868

The House of Representatives votes 128 to 47 to impeach President Andrew Johnson.

Radical Republicans in Congress wanted to deal severely with the South after the Civil War; Johnson resisted. When Johnson fired Secretary of War Edwin Stanton—violating a recently passed law prohibiting him from removing a Senate-confirmed official without Senate approval—the radicals seized their opportunity.

FEBRUARY 24, 1979

Responding to a badly missed shot by Rich Yonakor of the University of North Carolina, Duke fans chant, "Airrrr balllll." The taunt soon becomes a staple at basketball arenas across the country.

1986

After two weeks of intense debate, the county council of King County, Washington, votes five to four to replace county namesake William Rufus DeVane King with the Reverend Martin Luther King, Jr. "We won't have to reprint stationery or change road signs or anything like that," notes the council member who proposed the change.

When King County was formed in 1852, it was named in honor of the North Carolina–born vice president-elect; an adjacent county was named after President-elect Franklin Pierce. King died of tuberculosis just six weeks after taking the oath of office.

Seattle's Kingdome opened in 1976, giving King's name perhaps more prominence than it ever had when he was alive, though few made the association. But even that recognition proved fleeting for the man one historian has called "the least remembered . . . in American history."

1993

Hulk Hogan and other professional wrestlers convene in Ellerbe to scatter the ashes of "Andre the Giant" Roussimoff, perhaps the best-known wrestler in the world, at Roussimoff's 200-acre ranch.

Four weeks earlier, Roussimoff, 46, had died of a heart attack while in Paris for his father's funeral.

The French-born Roussimoff, who stood six-foot-10 and weighed 550 pounds, suffered from acromegaly, a growth-hormone disorder marked by progressive enlargement of the head, hands, feet, and chest.

In addition to wrestling, Roussimoff played the gentle giant Fezzick in the critically praised 1989 movie *The Princess Bride*.

FEBRUARY 25

1790

North Carolina makes the last major adjustment to its borders, ceding to the federal government the western lands that four years later will become the state of Tennessee.

The act of cession also includes what is perhaps the first written reference to the name *Smoky*, as in Great Smoky Mountains. A description of the state's new western boundary tells how it will pass "along the highest ridge of the said mountain to the place where it is called Great Iron or Smoky Mountain."

1820

During the lengthy debate over the Missouri Compromise, Congressman Felix Walker, whose district includes Buncombe County, rises to address his bored and weary colleagues. Because his constituents expect him to say something about Missouri, Walker explains, he is compelled to "make a speech for Buncombe."

The phrase "speaking for Buncombe"—abbreviated as "bunkum" or "bunk"—soon takes hold in the language.

1865

Confederates take the ironclad *Chickamauga* up the Cape Fear River to just below Indian Wells in Bladen County, where they attempt to scuttle her in a position to obstruct the river. The stream sweeps the ship parallel to the bank, however, and the channel remains clear for Union forces pressing inland.

FEBRUARY 26

FEBRUARY 26, 1825

After his party is stuck in the mud for an hour outside town, the Marquis de Lafayette arrives in Murfreesboro, where he spends the night at the Indian Queen Tavern. Lafayette, a Frenchman who served with distinction during the American Revolution, is received warmly in Murfreesboro and later in Halifax, Raleigh, and Fayetteville.

Returning from a World War II mission over Germany, a B-17 bomber piloted by Hugh G. Ashcraft, Jr., of Charlotte is riddled by flak and loses one engine. "Those who want to," Ashcraft tells his crew, "please pray."

The *Southern Comfort* makes it back to England, receiving wide attention and inspiring both a hit record and an enduring expression: "Coming in on a Wing and a Prayer."

In later life, Ashcraft will become president of the Harris Teeter supermarket chain.

FEBRUARY 27

1776

Patriot militia overwhelm Tory forces at Moores Creek Bridge in modern-day Pender County. By winning the first important Revolutionary War battle in the South, the patriots scuttle British plans to quickly overpower the Southern colonies and forestall other invasions for several years.

1896

The *Charlotte Observer* publishes one of the ear-

liest X-ray images made in America. Learning of Wilhelm Röntgen's experiments in Germany, Davidson College physics professor Henry Louis Smith has shot a bullet into the hand of a cadaver and made an X-ray of it.

A few weeks later, Smith will use an X-ray to locate a thimble lodged in a young girl's throat, making possible its surgical removal—the first clinical application of the X-ray.

The inventiveness of Smith, who will serve as president of both Davidson College and Washington and Lee College, later plays a role in hastening the end of World War I. Smith devises a small, self-deflating gas balloon which Allied forces load with propaganda and send over German lines. Some 27 million leaflets are dropped; at war's end, eight of 10 captured Germans carry Allied propaganda in their pockets.

FEBRUARY 28

1861

After the election of Abraham Lincoln leads South Carolina and six other states to secede and form the Confederate States of America, North Carolinians narrowly vote down a convention on secession. The statewide referendum, called by the North Carolina General Assembly, attracts almost 94,000 voters. The convention proposal fails by 651 votes, and North Carolina stays in the Union—for the time being.

1865

Prisoner of war A. O. Abbott, first lieutenant

in the First New York Dragoons, recalls the POW train's stop in Goldsboro en route to Wilmington:

> There was . . . a camp of enlisted men about a mile from us, and they were suffering all it was possible for them to suffer and live. Many of them did not live. Some of the "ladies," God bless them, loyal women of North Carolina, heard of the sufferings of these poor men, and, regardless of the "order" of the commandant of the post, visited them, ministering to their wants as best they could. Some of them came eight miles on foot, through the mud and wet. And one old lady and her two daughters . . . came in an ox cart, twenty miles, to do what they could.

1870

John Thomas Deweese, former Union soldier and self-described radical Republican, abruptly resigns as a North Carolina congressman. It will soon be revealed that Deweese accepted a $500 bribe in return for a recommendation to the United States Naval Academy.

He is uncontrite: "Hundreds have done the same thing before and will do it again."

1938

John Early, referred to in newspapers as "the nation's most famous leper," dies at the federal leprosarium in Carville, Louisiana.

Early, 64, was born near Weaverville. He contracted leprosy (otherwise known as Hansen's disease) while serving in the Philippines during the Spanish-American War. On his return, he was captured and quarantined; leprosy was widely feared though only slightly contagious. After the first of his many escapes, he took refuge on a small farm near Tryon. Neighbors objected, however, and he admitted himself to the Carville leper colony, then operated by the Catholic Church.

In 1921, he escaped to Washington, where he walked in on a startled congressional committee and spoke for a bill that would put the Carville facility under the United States Public Health Service. In large part because of his lobbying, the bill passed.

In 1927, Early again fled to Tryon. This time, his neighbors petitioned the surgeon general to suspend the federal law mandating segregation of lepers and to let him live in isolation on his farm. Their effort failed, however, and Early was returned to Carville for the last time.

FEBRUARY 28, 1960

Driving a Plymouth on a half-mile dirt track at Charlotte, 22-year-old Richard Petty wins his first stock-car race. "Dick Petty Wins Fairgrounds Race," headlines the *Charlotte Observer*.

1989

R. J. Reynolds Tobacco Company abandons its $350-million effort to change the way Americans inhale tobacco.

Five months earlier, Premier had been introduced as a "revolutionary breakthrough." Reynolds hoped that a cigarette that heated tobacco instead of burning it would sidestep bans on public smoking and appeal to smokers concerned about the feelings of nonsmokers.

Instead, those few smokers who tried Premiers complained that they smelled bad and tasted worse.

1964

A basketball game for the high-school championship of Harnett County goes 13 overtimes before Boone Trail defeats Angier 56–54. The game, played at Campbell College, is the longest ever in high-school, college, or professional competition.

Ignorance and neglect are the mainsprings of misrule.

Albion W. Tourgee

Carpetbagger Albion Tourgee [March 27]
was nothing if not opinionated.

March

Hungry women rampage in Salisbury
Turkey kills supreme court justice
Asheville fire claims Zelda Fitzgerald

1837

Presbyterians found Davidson College in northern Mecklenburg County.

Four years later, the school will give up its manual-labor requirement and announce plans to emulate the classical curriculum of Princeton.

1865

Prisoner of war A. O. Abbott, first lieutenant in the First New York Dragoons, recalls his release in Wilmington: "We laughed, cried, hurrahed, hugged, kissed, rolled in the sand, and rejoiced generally. Many declared it was the happiest day of their lives. . . .

"The 6th Connecticut was encamped on the bank of the [Cape Fear] river, and at the end of the pontoon bridge they had erected a bower of evergreens. In the centre of the arch was a card, surrounded by a beautiful wreath of evergreens, on which was printed, *Welcome, Brothers.*"

1971

Time magazine's cover: James Taylor, rock singer. "As a very little boy James was greatly affected by the Bible Belt religion he heard at school [in Chapel Hill]," the article says. "Mrs. Taylor remembers how he needed reassurance that he would not burn in hell for his sins."

Five months later, Taylor's "You've Got a Friend" will reach number one on *Billboard*'s top 40—the only number-one hit in his long career.

1975

"Chevy Van," written and sung by Charlotte native Sammy Johns, breaks into the *Billboard* top 40. It will reach number five—Johns's only hit record.

1977

Despite last-minute long-distance lobbying by President Jimmy Carter, the North Carolina Senate defeats the Equal Rights Amendment by a 26–24 vote.

It is the second time the ERA has failed in the Senate by that vote, each time falling victim to a switch by a Charlotte senator "committed" to voting yes.

The ERA will die in 1979, the deadline set by the United States Senate for winning ratification by the required three-quarters of the states.

MARCH 2

1923

Louis Graves, professor of journalism at the University of North Carolina, begins publishing the *Chapel Hill Weekly*.

MARCH 2, 1938

As the automobile industry struggles to free itself from the Depression, Governor Clyde Hoey asks North Carolinians to do their part during National Used Car Exchange Week:

The accumulation of used cars in the hands of automobile dealers throughout the United States has reached such proportions that it is difficult to sell new cars. . . .

It would be a very great stimulus to all kinds of business if the people of this State would cooperate very fully in the observance of this week set apart for exchanging used cars, in which they will discard the old cars which have about served their period of usefulness and replace them with some of the used cars which are available or a new car, as they may see fit.

1974

With only 17 seconds left to play at Carmichael Auditorium, the University of North Carolina overcomes an eight-point deficit to tie Duke 86–86 at the end of regulation. The Tar Heels win 96–92 in overtime.

The comeback ranks among the most stunning in college basketball history.

Interviewed 15 years later, University of North Carolina coach Dean Smith recalls, "Gosh, we were lucky, weren't we?"

Duke coach Neill McGeachy says only, "I think I've said everything that needs to be said about it. Thank you and good night."

1984

A Charlotte radio station drops talk-show host Morton Downey, Jr., after less than six months. "A great deal of it has to do with my having a negative rating in the community among some of the superliberals," he says. "The research indicates a lot of people probably listen to me because they hate me."

Four years later, Downey's syndicated TV talk show will become a short-lived national cause célèbre.

MARCH 3

1865

In Robeson County, the Confederate Home Guard captures and executes Allen and William Lowry, bushwhackers hiding in the swamps to escape conscription officers.

Leadership of the Lowry Band will pass to Henry Berry Lowry, Allen's son and William's brother. The 21-year-old Lowry quickly establishes a picaresque reputation that draws national attention—"Robin Hood come again," headlines the *New York Times.*

The Civil War ends, but the Lowry Band and the Home Guard, now known as the "County Militia," remain at odds. Lowry is captured, charged with a wartime killing, and jailed in Whiteville; he escapes and is declared an outlaw. He remains at large until 1868, when, with Republicans in charge of state government, he surrenders in Lumberton. He hears rumors he will be lynched, however, and again breaks out of jail. Rewards for the capture of Lowry and his half-dozen lieutenants reach an unheard-of $25,000, and Governor William W. Holden even sends in a battery of federal artillery.

In 1872, Lowry disappears amid conflicting reports of his death or escape. His body is never found; sightings are reported as far away as New York and California.

1915

At the urging of Governor Locke Craig, the legislature authorizes purchasing land for North Carolina's first state park. Mount Mitchell State Park includes not only the highest peak in eastern America but also the state's second-highest peak—which in 1947 will be named Mount Craig.

MARCH 4

1825

The Marquis de Lafayette, continuing his triumphant tour of the United States, thanks the citizens of Fayetteville for naming their town after him in 1783.

Lafayette recognizes the town's historic convention hall, where North Carolina ratified the United States Constitution, from a drawing that hangs in his bedchamber in France.

1835

In *State v. Will*, the North Carolina Supreme Court struggles with the legal relationship between masters and slaves while condemning brutality toward the helpless. The decision, establishing "a slave's right to defend himself against the cruel and unjust punishment of a master," will be cited by Justice Benjamin Curtis of the United States Supreme Court in his antislavery dissent in the controversial Dred Scott decision of 1857.

1845

James K. Polk, a native of Mecklenburg County, becomes the first president to have his inauguration reported by telegraph. Punching out the news is the inventor himself, Samuel F. B. Morse.

1853

Sampson County native William Rufus DeVane King, recuperating from tuberculosis in Cuba, is sworn in as vice president of the United States.

Educated at the University of North Carolina, King served as a congressman from North Carolina, as a senator from Alabama, and as minister to France. He and President James Buchanan, both bachelors, were inseparable companions for many years. Rumors flourished: Andrew Jackson dubbed the fastidious King "Miss Nancy."

Despite the rumors, King's lackluster record, and his ill health, the Democratic Convention of 1852 nominated him for vice president on the Franklin Pierce ticket. Mortally tubercular and unable to campaign, he tried to rest and regain his strength in Cuba.

He takes the oath of office in Havana—the only executive officer ever sworn in outside the country—but dies six weeks later without ever reaching Washington. His presence is so little missed that the vice presidency goes unfilled until the next election.

MARCH 4, 1943

The North Carolina House adopts the cardinal as the state bird.

In 1933, responding to the results of a contest sponsored by the State Women's Club, the legislature had awarded this designation to the Carolina chickadee. The act was repealed the following week, however, when concerns were raised that out-of-staters might latch onto the chickadee's more vulgar-sounding name and label North Carolina the "Tom-tit State."

MARCH 5

1913

Woodrow Wilson names Josephus Daniels, editor of the *News and Observer* of Raleigh, as his secretary of the navy. Daniels is the cabinet's first North Carolinian in 60 years.

The North Carolina Senate rejects Clarence Poe's plan for a "Great Rural Civilization."

Fearing that the migration of young people into the already crowded cities will undermine society, Poe—the influential editor of the *Progressive Farmer*—drafted a plan that strangely foreshadows Soul City, Floyd McKissick's federally financed "new community" that will fail to prosper in Warren County in the 1970s.

While visiting the British Isles in 1912, Poe had interviewed a white South African, who persuaded him that apartheid offered whites the best opportunity to help blacks.

Framed as an amendment to the state constitution, Poe's plan empowered voters in a rural district to prohibit land sales to persons of the minority race. Although this provision would not force anyone to leave, Poe believed that ultimately the countryside would be dotted with quiet, pastoral villages, either all white or all black.

Although Poe enlisted such influential allies as Josiah Bailey, later a United States senator, and Julian Carr, the Bull Durham magnate, his plan stirred a hornets' nest of protest across the South.

After the North Carolina General Assembly votes down the proposed amendment, the "Great Rural Civilization" will not be heard of again.

Once again assailing the Roosevelt administration on the floor of the Senate, rogue populist Huey Long of Louisiana points toward New Deal supporter Josiah Bailey of North Carolina. About the existence of poverty, Long asks rhetorically, "You will take my word for it, won't you?" Bailey stands and, as gasps echo from the galleries, replies, "I am utterly unwilling to take your word for that or anything else!" In the ensuing exchange, Long threatens to campaign against Bailey's reelection, and Bailey suggests that Long's interference in North Carolina politics would be met with tar and feathers.

Oddly, the two will remain friends. Long often drops by Bailey's Mayflower Hotel apartment for drinks, and Bailey invites Long on fishing trips from Morehead City. On one such expedition, Long, expounding his plans to become dictator-president, supposedly says his first move would be to have Bailey shot. Bailey is amused, but confides later that he thinks Long was perfectly serious. Long himself is assassinated on September 8, 1935.

Attributing their actions to "a bad case of spring fever," students at the University of North Carolina organize the American Streaker Society. More than 200 men remove their clothes and race across the campus and through the undergraduate library. Twenty women from Joyner Dormitory join the festivities. Three men stroll down Franklin Street wearing only shoes and socks.

Two days later, accompanied by the University of North Carolina Pep Band, more than 900 naked students will pass single-file through a roaring crowd of 6,000, including campus security guards who have sealed off the streets.

"Streaking" spreads across the nation before abruptly dying out, like such earlier college fads as goldfish swallowing and telephone-booth stuffing.

MARCH 6

1836

Dolphin Ward Floyd, born at an undetermined location in North Carolina, dies defending the Alamo. As a young man, he moved west and became active in the Texas independence movement. Floyd County, Texas, is named in his honor.

1933

Franklin D. Roosevelt, moving to avert a panic, declares a bank holiday, but word never reaches the remote Hyde County fishing village of Englehard. The Bank of Englehard continues doing business as usual.

The bank's violation is eventually reported, but the controller of the currency chooses to take no action.

1934

Charlotte fireman Joe Westnedge, riding the running board of an open fire engine, dies when it jumps a curb and pins him against a tree.

His death influences the department to buy the first enclosed-cab fire truck manufactured in the United States, with seats for 12.

1943

The *Charlotte Observer* editorializes about poetry and war:

One would hardly expect a poet to deliver himself of hard-headed statesmanlike utterances. A poet is often busy elsewhere. He's gazing in the brook or at the stars, busy with sonnet, ballad and roundelay. But Robert Frost, an American poet, speaking at the University of North Carolina, dealt in common sense. He thinks Americans are expecting too many drastic changes in internationalism after the war.

"Our concern right now is to win the war," he said. "Then the developments we hope for will come about naturally."

Many of the scientists, engineers and others who are supposed to deal only in realities might well ponder this. Instead they are dreaming of Utopia on a worldwide scale, starting the day after the war ends. The war, they think, will somehow win itself. It won't.

When America and her allies have defeated the devil nations, there will be time to rebuild the world, but that will have to come, as Mr. Frost says, naturally.

1961

Governor Terry Sanford proposes that the North Carolina General Assembly pay for improved schools and community colleges by ending a 20-year-old sales-tax exemption on groceries.

The state instituted a 3-percent general sales tax during the Depression, when it began taking responsibility for schools and roads. Food was exempted from the tax in 1941.

"I am well aware of the hardship of paying tax on necessary items by those whose income is so low that each penny counts," Sanford says. "But I am also aware of the greater hardship placed upon the children of these same people by inadequate school opportunities, and I have been able to devise no way that the poorest can be exempt from a general sales tax."

"Terry's Tax," as legislators are happy to label it, does benefit education, but it will also burden Sanford politically for the rest of his career.

1712

After nearly a month of fighting near what is now Grifton in Pitt and Lenoir Counties, colonial forces persuade the Tuscaroras to agree to a truce and a peace treaty.

The war will start anew, however, when Colonel John Barnwell begins selling Indian prisoners as slaves.

1727

Virginia and North Carolina commissioners drive a stake on the banks of Currituck Sound and begin surveying the dividing line between the two colonies.

1840

The Wilmington and Weldon Railroad is completed, providing Wilmington a long-sought link to Northern markets and making Weldon, on the Roanoke River in Halifax County, the state's rail hub. At 161 miles, the Wilmington and Weldon is the longest rail line in the world.

1914

George Herman Ruth, a rookie with the minor-league Baltimore Orioles, hits his first home run as a professional. The ball lands in a cornfield beyond right field at the Fayetteville Fair Grounds. It is only a spring-training scrub game; still, an account in the next day's *Baltimore American* is headlined, "Ruth Makes Mighty Clout."

It is also in Fayetteville that his teammates give Ruth, 20 years old and fresh out of St. Mary's Industrial School in Baltimore, the nickname "Babe."

1978

Addressing the 75th anniversary celebration of the North Carolina Historical Commission, John Hope Franklin recalls an unexpected benefit of being a black scholar (at the former North Carolina College for Negroes) at work in the whites-only State Archives:

> When I began to do research here in 1939, I could neither sit in the main search room nor have the services of the pages to bring me the materials that I wanted. Thus, armed with my own key, generously provided by [commission secretary] Christopher Crittenden, I entered the manuscript stacks whenever I pleased, browsed as long as I pleased and emerged with a library wagon piled high with all sorts of goodies which I took to my "private" search room.
>
> By the time that the other researchers protested my special privileges and I was relieved of my stack key, I had learned more about the manuscripts in the N.C. State Archives than any living person.

1982

The University of North Carolina edges Virginia 47–45 in the championship game of the lowest-scoring ACC Tournament ever.

With seven minutes and 34 seconds remaining,

UNC leads 44–43. Trying to lure seven-foot, four-inch Ralph Sampson from beneath the basket, Dean Smith orders the "Four Corners" slowdown. Virginia refuses to go along, and the rest of the game is slow-motion cat and mouse.

The top-ranked Tar Heels, star-laden with James Worthy, Sam Perkins, and freshman Michael Jordan, will go on to win the national championship. But the ACC title game in Charlotte is such a disappointment for fans that it leads to the NCAA's introduction of the shot clock and the three-point line.

MARCH 8

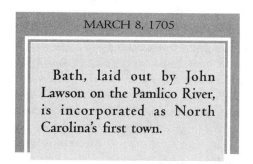

MARCH 8, 1705

Bath, laid out by John Lawson on the Pamlico River, is incorporated as North Carolina's first town.

1865

George W. Nichols, a major in Sherman's army, writes in his journal in Laurel Hill in Scotland County,

> The line which divides South and North Carolina was passed by the army this morning. . . . The real difference between the two regions lies in the fact that the plantation owners [in North Carolina] work with their own hands, and do not think they degrade themselves thereby. For the first time since we bade farewell to salt water I have to-day seen an attempt to manure land. The army has passed through thirteen miles or more of splendidly-managed farms; the corn and cotton fields are nicely plowed and farrowed; the fences are in capital order; the barns are well-built; the dwelling houses are clean, and there is that air of thrift which shows that the owner takes a personal interest in the management of affairs.

1881

Virginia inventor James Bonsack, not yet 21 years old, receives a patent on the first practical device for rolling cigarettes. Made of wood and fed manually, his "making" machine delivers 120,000 cigarettes per day—the output of 40 hand-rollers.

While James B. Duke's competitors are still insisting that smokers prefer hand-rolled cigarettes, he secretly arranges to install the Bonsack machine in his factory in Durham.

1890

Charles McNamee, manager of the grand estate George W. Vanderbilt is carving out of the mountains near Asheville, telegraphs landscape architect Frederick Law Olmsted that he has run into "trouble with the post office authorities in getting the name Bilton adopted on account of its similarity to Bolton, another place in this state."

Olmsted had originally proposed Broadwood, a name that would be "sonorous . . . fall trippingly from the tongue" and would not be "provocative of punning, sarcasm or ridicule. . . . French Broad [after the river] will not do." Vanderbilt rejected Broadwood, however, in favor of Bilton, derived from his family's ancestral home of Bildt, Holland.

Finally, stymied by the post office, Vanderbilt will settle on Biltmore.

1935

Scribner's publishes *Of Time and the River*, Thomas Wolfe's second novel. Wolfe is unhappy that his editor, Maxwell Perkins, cut short their intense collaboration and sent the manuscript to the printer while Wolfe was visiting the Century of Progress Exposition in Chicago.

Although the novel becomes a bestseller and mostly reinforces Wolfe's critical reputation, it marks the end of his relationship with editor and publisher. He is particularly wounded when Bernard DeVoto, writing in the *Saturday Review of Literature*, attacks his dependence on "Mr. Perkins and the assembly line at Scribner's."

1951

Samuel E. Bennett of Yancey County, North Carolina's last surviving Confederate veteran, dies at age 100.

Bennett, age 13, enlisted in the Black Mountain Regiment of the Confederate Home Guards along with his grandfather and four uncles. He was wounded in a dynamite blast while building earthworks near Richmond but recovered and served until the fall of the Confederacy.

1968

In an ACC Tournament game at Charlotte, North Carolina State uses the slowdown to defeat heavily favored Duke 12–10. "This is about as exciting as artificial insemination," opines play-by-play announcer Bill "Mouth of the South" Curry.

MARCH 9

1915

The legislature adopts election by Australian (secret) ballot. Until now, balloting has been by show of hands or other public means.

Also passed on the last day of the session: bills exempting Confederate veterans from jury duty and prohibiting white nurses from attending to black patients in North Carolina hospitals.

1954

Edward R. Murrow devotes *See It Now*, his weekly CBS half-hour, to exposing contradictions in Senator Joseph McCarthy's search for domestic Communists. The report is the media's first systematic dismantling of McCarthy's allegations, and it plays a major role in both the fall of McCarthyism and the rise of television journalism.

1966

University of North Carolina police prevent Herbert Aptheker, historian and member of the American Communist Party, from speaking on campus.

Aptheker first attempts to address students from the ledge of a campus landmark, the Confederate statue known as "Silent Sam." Thwarted, he steps a few feet away, crosses a low stone wall onto town property, and faces 2,000 students seated on the campus lawn. His speech proves less than incendiary; its main result is to focus national attention on the state's 1963 Speaker Ban Law.

Legislators had adopted the ban during a period of social unrest at the height of the Cold War. Secretary of State Thad Eure drafted the law "to regulate visiting speakers at state-supported colleges and universities." On the blacklist: any "known member of the Communist Party," anyone who advocates the overthrow of the state or federal constitutions, and anyone who has pleaded the Fifth Amendment about "subversive connections."

In 1968, a federal court will declare the Speaker Ban Law unconstitutional.

MARCH 10

1948

Zelda Fitzgerald is one of nine women killed in an early-morning fire at Highland Hospital in Asheville, where she was being treated for schizophrenia. Locked doors and barred windows stymie rescuers.

Dental records will identify the 47-year-old Fitzgerald, who with her late husband, novelist F. Scott Fitzgerald, had come to symbolize the excesses of the Jazz Age.

1991

After being whipped 96–74 by the University of North Carolina in the final of the ACC Tournament, Duke players angrily trudge onto the team bus. Coach Mike Krzyzewski bounds aboard and announces, "We're going to win the national championship."

Three weeks later, after defeating Nevada-Las Vegas and Kansas for the NCAA title, the players will cite Krzyzewski's comment as the origin of their dramatic reversal. In eight previous trips to the Final Four, dating back to 1963, Duke had come up empty.

MARCH 11

1879

Workers approaching from both sides complete the 1,832-foot Swannanoa Gap tunnel, the longest in western North Carolina. James Wilson, chief engineer of the Western North Carolina Railroad, wires Governor Zebulon Vance that "daylight entered Buncombe County today through the Swannanoa Tunnel. Grade and centers met exactly." Later the same day, however, a slide at the tunnel kills 21 laborers.

In all, some 400 workers, most of them convicts serving sentences for misdemeanors, will die in bringing the railroad through the mountains to Asheville.

1910

In Elizabethtown in Bladen County, Henry Spivey is executed for the murder of his father-in-law. His is the last public hanging in North Carolina.

1936

A bathing-suit publicity photo of CBS radio entertainer Nancy Flake appears in the *Greensboro Daily News* to advertise a touring burlesque show. She is incorrectly identified as "Mademoiselle Sally Payne, exotic Red Haired Venus." Three weeks later, the *Daily News* publishes a correction headed, "Error in Publication of Portrait in Advertisement," but Flake sues and wins a $6,500 judgment.

Although the North Carolina Supreme Court orders a new trial and a $1 settlement is negotiated, the case is the state's first to recognize the tort of invasion of privacy.

1956

Congressman Charles Bennett Deane of Rockingham effectively ends his political career by refusing to sign the so-called Southern Manifesto—a document pledging its signers to use "every lawful means" to resist the Supreme Court's school desegregation decision.

Deane, a five-term incumbent, will be turned out in the next election. "I do not have to remain in Washington, but I do have to live with myself," he says. "I will not sign my name to any document which will make any man anywhere a second-class citizen."

MARCH 12

1865

George W. Nichols, a major in Sherman's army, writes in his journal in Fayetteville,

Again we have made a capture of much greater importance than was at first supposed. The magnificent arsenal which our government built here contains millions of dollars' worth of machinery and material. The Rebels have used the work-shops in this city for the manufacture

of guns, fixed ammunition, gun-carriages, etc., to a much larger extent than was supposed. . . . Here are stored vast amounts of well-seasoned woods, weapons in all stages of completion, thousands of muskets; in short, every description of machinery and tools requisite for the manufacture and repairs of material of war. . . . We shall destroy it utterly.

Despite the crushing success of his march from Savannah, Sherman himself finds more reason for complaint than celebration. He writes General Alfred Howe Terry at Wilmington, "I want you to send me all the shoes, stockings, drawers, sugar, coffee, and flour you can spare; finish the loads with oats or corn. Have the boats escorted and then run at night at any risk. . . .

"We will load [three captured steamboats] with refugees, white and black, that have clung to our skirts, impeded our movements, and consumed our food. . . . I must rid my army of from 20,000 to 30,000 useless mouths."

1956

A subcommittee of the House Un-American Activities Committee convenes in Charlotte.

Two days of hearings will single out Bill McGirt, a poet working at a Winston-Salem fish market, as the state's top Communist, but he and 10 other subpoenaed witnesses refuse to testify, and little new information surfaces.

1973

H. R. "Bob" Haldeman, White House chief of staff, notes in his diary President Richard

Nixon's desire to distract Senator Sam Ervin back home in North Carolina: "He raised the point that he wanted . . . a candidate fielded and going against Sam Ervin, to give him some trouble in his district, to slow him down a little on his Watergate activities."

The ploy fails to materialize, however, and hearings held by Ervin's committee later expose Republican sabotage during the 1972 presidential campaign and the subsequent White House cover-up, paving the way for Nixon's resignation in 1974.

1991

The *National Examiner*, a supermarket tabloid, claims country-music star Randy Travis is secretly homosexual. Travis, a Marshville native, responds with an angry denial but adds, "I guess it could have been worse. They could've said I wasn't country."

Two months later, Travis, 32, marries longtime companion Lib Hatcher, 49. It was Hatcher who, while managing a Charlotte nightclub, picked 17-year-old Randy Traywick out of an amateur-night lineup and later became his legal guardian.

1994

Police arrest Henry Louis Wallace, suspected of being the state's most prolific serial killer.

Wallace, a 28-year-old fast-food worker, will be charged with murdering 10 Charlotte women over the previous 22 months.

1868

The impeachment trial of Andrew Johnson begins. The Senate is organized as a court; Chief Justice Salmon Chase presides. Johnson's lawyers request 40 days to prepare an answer to charges but are allowed only 10.

1966

University of North Carolina alumnus Robert Welch, president of the John Birch Society, tells a Chapel Hill audience that communists plan to transform the South into a "Negro Soviet Republic."

Since founding the John Birch Society in 1958, Welch has made headlines by calling Dwight D. Eisenhower a "conscious agent of the Communist conspiracy" and seeking to impeach Earl Warren, chief justice of the Supreme Court.

A native of Chowan County, Welch was a 12-year-old math whiz in short pants when he entered the university. Later, he attended the United States Naval Academy and Harvard Law School before becoming an executive for his brother's candy company in Boston.

1993

The "Blizzard of the Century" slashes its way up the eastern seaboard, spawning winds of 101 miles per hour on Flat Top Mountain in Buncombe County and immersing downtown Manteo in two feet of water, but sparing much of the state's midsection with only a few inches of snow and subfreezing temperatures.

1862

Union forces occupy New Bern, their first conquest on the North Carolina mainland.

1919

Professor Frederick Koch's Carolina Playmakers debut with a trio of short plays in the Chapel Hill High School auditorium. Leading the bill: *The Return of Buck Gavin, a Tragedy of the Mountain People*, written by Thomas Wolfe, who also plays the part of Buck.

Among Professor Koch's other notable early students: Paul Green, Jonathan Daniels, and Frances Gray (Patton). By 1928, Brooks Atkinson of the *New York Times* will write that "what Professor Koch has accomplished, not only in Chapel Hill, but through the state, is nothing short of extraordinary."

1938

In a brief ceremony at the Square, Charlotte decommissions its last electric trolley car, No. 85, while welcoming in the bus age.

"This is not a funeral," says the Reverend Luther Little of First Baptist Church, "but a resurrection marking the beginning of a new and better method of transportation that keeps time with the march of progress."

Less than 50 years later, however, many Charlotteans will be nostalgic enough about their old trolleys to begin discussing proposals for the modern equivalent: light rail.

In 1987, after a three-year search for an original Charlotte trolley car to restore—many wound up as far away as Bogota, Colombia—

No. 85 will be discovered only a few miles from its old route. It had served first as an Air National Guard office, then as a snack bar, and finally as a low-rent dwelling.

1767

Andrew Jackson, the seventh president of the United States, is born in the Waxhaws on the border between North Carolina and South Carolina. In later years, each state will vigorously claim him as a native.

1787

Darby and Peter, Duplin County slaves, are convicted of murdering their master with an ax. Darby is sentenced to be "tied to a stake on the courthouse lot and there burned to death and . . . his ashes strewd upon the ground." Peter, less severely punished because of his youth, is sentenced to have "one half of each of his ears cut off and be branded on each cheek with the letter *'M'* and to receive 11 lashes.

MARCH 15, 1930

Forty years after the late George W. Vanderbilt began construction, Biltmore House opens to the public. The Asheville Chamber of Commerce has persuaded his daughter, Cornelia, and her husband, John Cecil of England, to give tourists a look at the mansion's major rooms, gardens, and greenhouses.

1973

Henry Ward Oxendine of Robeson County becomes the first American Indian elected to the North Carolina General Assembly. Oxendine, a former eighth-grade teacher, is in his final year of law school at North Carolina Central University.

1985

Scouting along Little Peters Creek in Stokes County, botanist Steve Leonard rediscovers the small-anthered bittercress, a perennial herb considered extinct for more than a decade.

Leonard had made 15 springtime trips to Stokes and Forsyth Counties over 18 years, searching in vain near where Gladstone McDowell discovered the bittercress in 1939.

Leonard's discovery removes the plant from the extinct list and qualifies it for federal and state endangered-species lists.

MARCH 16

1960

Snow sweeps across the state for the third Wednesday in a row.

1984

James Hutchins, who killed three police officers after a domestic quarrel erupted at his Rutherford County home, becomes the first person in North Carolina executed by lethal injection. Previously, the state used the gas chamber, and before that, the electric chair.

1865

George W. Nichols, a major in Sherman's army, writes in his journal in Averasboro, where Confederate colonel Alfred Rhett, former commander of Fort Sumter, has just been captured,

Rhett [is] one of the "first family" names of which South Carolina is so proud. From the conversation of this Rebel colonel, I judge him to be quite as impracticable a person as any of his class. He seemed most troubled about the way in which he was captured. . . . One of [the Union soldiers], without any sort of regard for the feelings of a South Carolina aristocrat, put a pistol to the colonel's head and informed him in a quiet but very decided manner that if he didn't come along he'd "make a hole through him!" The colonel came; but he is a disgusted man. I made no doubt that [the soldiers] would have had but little scruple in cutting off one branch of the family tree of the Rhetts if the surrender had not been prompt.

MARCH 17, 1944

Actor Charlton Heston, who has just completed basic training at a nearby army camp, marries Lydia Marie Clarke in Greensboro.

1765

In the colonial town of Brunswick, two British naval officers engage in North Carolina's first known duel. Captain Alexander Simpson and Lieutenant Thomas Whitehurst, stationed aboard a warship in the Cape Fear River, are pursuing the same local woman. Whitehurst puts a bullet through Simpson's shoulder, but Simpson fells Whitehurst with a shot through the thigh, then fatally assaults Whitehurst with his pistol butt.

A Wilmington jury will find Simpson guilty of manslaughter. His punishment—"To be branded on the ball of the thumb with the letter M"—is carried out before the court; he then pays court costs and goes free.

1863

Hungry and unable to pay inflated prices, 75 Salisbury women, most of them wives of Confederate soldiers, arm themselves with axes and go in search of hoarded food.

The railroad agent turns them away from the depot, claiming he has no flour. They break into a warehouse and take 10 barrels, then find seven more at a store. After coming up empty at a government warehouse, they collar a suspected speculator and relieve him of a bag of salt.

The women then return to the depot, storm past the uncooperative agent, and claim 10 more barrels of flour.

Soon afterward, a farmer arrives at the station with a wagonload of tobacco for shipment. According to a contemporary account, when the agent tells him about the rampaging women, the farmer hurriedly drives off, "fearful that they would learn to chew."

1910

Walter Morrison, Robeson County rapist, becomes the first person executed by electrocution in North Carolina. From colonial times until 1910, when the state takes over authority for capital punishment, counties have carried out their own executions, typically by hanging.

The execution does not go smoothly. Even after Morrison receives three shocks of 1,800 volts, physicians at Central Prison are uncertain he is dead, and a fourth shock must be administered.

1943

The Bank of Black Mountain fails. It will be the last North Carolina bank to go under until First Hanover Bank in Wilmington in 1991.

1961

In Louisburg in Franklin County, an aide reads a speech by Governor Terry Sanford in observance of Confederate Centennial Day. One hundred years earlier, he says, Major Orren Randolph Smith and his neighbors were the first North Carolinians to fly the Confederate flag.

Smith, a Confederate quartermaster, claimed credit for designing the Stars and Bars, the first flag of the Confederate States of America. His campaign, vigorously carried on by his daughter after his death in 1913, resulted in recognition by the United Confederate Veterans and the North Carolina General Assembly; several monuments were also erected to him. In reality, however, Smith's claim was only one of an immense number. The best evidence suggests that credit for the Stars and Bars rightly belongs to Nicola Marschal, an artist in Marion, Alabama.

MARCH 19

1917

James McConnell of Carthage in Moore County, one of 38 volunteer American pilots making up the famed Lafayette Escadrille of World War I, is shot down. McConnell, 30, is buried where his Nieuport biplane fell, on the edge of a French village.

Carthage later erects a monument praising McConnell for having "fought for Humanity, Liberty and Democracy, lighted the way for his countrymen and showed all men how to dare nobly and to die gloriously."

1971

Congress passes the Public Health Cigarette Smoking Act, banning cigarette advertising on TV and sending R. J. Reynolds Tobacco Company looking for new ways to spend its advertising dollars.

When RJR executives approach racing great Junior Johnson about sponsoring a stock car, he suggests a bigger opportunity. Thus will be born NASCAR's Winston Cup series, one of the most fruitful unions in sports-marketing history.

RJR's money fuels stock-car racing's rise to a new level of national popularity and inspires in NASCAR fans a lucrative brand loyalty to Winston cigarettes.

MARCH 20

MARCH 20, 1793

Samuel Spencer, justice of the state supreme court, dies as a result of wounds inflicted by a turkey gobbler.

Spencer was sitting on the porch of his home near Wadesboro in Anson County when he became sleepy and began to nod; his bobbing red cap apparently provoked the turkey to attack. The 59-year-old judge was thrown from his chair and suffered numerous scratches, which became fatally infected.

1862

Disguised as a man, Malinda Blalock enlists with her husband, Keith, and becomes North Carolina's only known female Civil War soldier.

Keith, a Unionist, enlists with the intention of deserting to Northern lines. Malinda, who has cut her hair, donned men's clothing, and assumed the name "Sam," will tent with her "brother" at a regimental camp near Kinston. For the next four months, according to an early account, she does "all the duties of a soldier" and proves "very adept at learning the manual and drill." She passes up opportunities to skinny-dip with her comrades.

Frustrated by the lack of opportunity to desert, Keith wins a discharge by rubbing his body with poison oak or poison sumac and creating a severe rash. Malinda reveals herself as a woman. After Keith's ploy is discovered, he is sought as a deserter. The Blalocks subsequently share their Grandfather Mountain hut with other deserters, skirmish with conscription officers, and take part in the ongoing guerrilla raids and vendettas that mark the war in the mountains. After Keith's stepfather is slain by Confederate sympathizers, Keith kills the man he thinks responsible. He is apprehended but pardoned before trial by Republican governor William W. Holden. Afterward, the Blalocks settle on a Mitchell County farm. Malinda dies at age 61 in 1901; Keith moves to Hickory and is killed in a handcar accident on a mountain railroad in 1913 at age 75.

1865

Bentonville is the site of the bloodiest battle ever fought on North Carolina soil. General Joseph E. Johnston manages to surprise Sherman's larger force, but Union reinforcements arrive and turn the battle. Confederate losses total 2,600, Union losses 1,600.

1922

St. Agnes Hospital at St. Augustine's College in Raleigh, perhaps the only well-equipped hospital for blacks between Washington and New Orleans, sends out a fund-raising letter under the headline, "A critical situation. A most urgent need. A plea for St. Agnes Hospital that we may continue to serve."

Among those responding: the Ku Klux Klan, which donates $100.

MARCH 21

1524

Italian adventurer Giovanni da Verrazano, sailing for the French government, looks across the Outer Banks and mistakes Pamlico Sound for the Pacific Ocean. Nevertheless, Verrazano is the first European known to have reached the shores of the future North Carolina.

1945

Byron Nelson defeats Sam Snead in a playoff to win the Charlotte Open at Myers Park Country Club. It is Nelson's second consecutive PGA victory; the next week, he will win the Greensboro Open at Starmount Country Club, and the week after that, the Durham Open at Hope Valley Country Club. Before he is finished, Nelson will win 11 tournaments in a row, a record considered among the most unapproachable in sports.

1963

Bob Ingle, the son of a small grocer, puts together enough borrowed money to open his first supermarket in Asheville. By the mid-1990s, Ingles Markets will have grown into a five-state, 172-store chain.

MARCH 22

1871

William W. Holden becomes the nation's first governor to be removed from office by impeachment.

Conservatives in the Reconstruction legislature, long at odds with Republican Holden, have been galvanized by his use of troops to quell racial disturbances during the Kirk-Holden War in Alamance and Caswell Counties. After a seven-week trial, Holden is convicted of six charges and removed.

1960

At Morehead City, Hatteras Yacht of High Point launches a 41-foot yacht—the largest fiberglass-hull boat ever built.

A year later, when Hurricane Carla devastates Galveston, Texas, a widely published wire-service photo of a boathouse full of splintered wooden yachts—and a battered but intact Hatteras—speeds the industry's switch to fiberglass.

MARCH 23

1713

Colonial forces, including a large number of Indians from South Carolina, destroy Fort Nohoroco, a Tuscarora stronghold near modern-day Snow Hill in Greene County. More than 900 Tuscaroras are killed or captured, bringing to an end their war with the settlers.

Most Tuscaroras will eventually move to New York, opening choice interior lands to white settlement.

1865

George W. Nichols, a major in Sherman's army, writes in his journal in Goldsboro, "Our army [requires] not only to be reclothed, but to gain the repose it needs. Mind, as well as body, requires rest after the fatigues of rapid campaigns like these. These ragged, bareheaded, shoeless, brave, jolly fellows of Sherman's legions, too, want covering for their naked limbs."

1957

At the Final Four in Kansas City, the University of North Carolina knocks off a supposedly invincible Kansas team led by Wilt Chamberlain. The 54–53 victory gives the Tar Heels a 32–0 record.

It is the second straight night that coach Frank McGuire's team has won in triple overtime—and the first time a state team has brought home the national title.

1976

North Carolina Republicans, urged on by Senator Jesse Helms, resuscitate Ronald Reagan's failing presidential campaign. After five defeats, Reagan scores his first primary victory over President Gerald Ford.

Although Reagan will fail to wrest the nomination from Ford, his late-blooming primary victories establish him as the GOP front runner in 1980.

1989

University of Utah electrochemist Stanley Pons, a native of Valdese, and British colleague Martin Fleischmann rock the science world with the announcement that they have achieved "cold fusion"—nuclear fusion at room temperature. Experts had believed that the fusion of atoms—which could provide cheap, safe, and virtually inexhaustible energy—was feasible only at extremely high temperatures.

In the coming months, however, other scientists will be unable to duplicate the Utah experiment, and the Pons-Fleischmann claim is widely discredited.

MARCH 24

1663

King Charles II awards a new charter for the vast tract later known as Carolina.

The Lords Proprietors—eight noblemen who helped return the English throne to the monarchy in 1660—are granted broad feudal governing powers, but the colonists are given the same rights as Englishmen.

1863

Confederate major general Daniel Harvey Hill responds by letter to Union major general John Gray Foster, who had censured Hill for the burning of Plymouth during battle:

> You forget, sir, that you are a Yankee and that Plymouth is a Southern town. It is no business of yours if we choose to burn one of our own towns. A meddling Yankee troubles himself about everybody's matters except his own and repents of everybody's sins except his own. We are a different people. Should the Yankees burn a Union village in Connecticut or a codfish town in Massachusetts we would not meddle with them but rather bid them God speed in their work of purifying the atmosphere.
>
> Your second act of forgetfulness consists in your not remembering that you are the most atrocious house-burner as yet unhung in the wide universe.

1865

George W. Nichols, a major in Sherman's army, writes in his journal in Goldsboro, where the troops are being resupplied with provisions that "bummers" have taken from the eastern North Carolina countryside,

> We found food for infinite merriment in the motley crowd of "bummers." These fellows were mounted upon all sorts of animals, and were clad in every description of costume; while many were so scantily dressed that they would hardly have been permitted to proceed up Broadway without interruption. Hundreds of wagons, of patterns not recognized in army regulations, carts, buggies, barouches, hacks, wheelbarrows, all sorts of vehicles, were loaded down with bacon, meal, corn, oats, and fodder, all gathered in the rich country.

1915

Anna Morrison Jackson, the widow of General Stonewall Jackson, dies in her native Charlotte at age 83. All stores and government offices close, schools hold memorial services, and Elizabeth College cancels classes.

During her 52 years of widowhood, she was recognized as the "first lady of the South"—on their visits to Charlotte, Presidents Theodore Roosevelt and Woodrow Wilson both called at her gabled brick home on West Trade Street.

In a funeral car furnished by Southern Railway, Mrs. Jackson is taken to Lexington, Virginia, where she is buried with full military honors beside her husband.

1965

Guy Owen's comic novel *The Ballad of the Flim-Flam Man*, narrated by apprentice grifter Curley Treadaway, is reviewed appreciatively in the *New York Times*. "Curley is a grand raconteur," writes Orville Prescott, "and his literary style is a joy—occasionally so deep-fried in Carolina colloquialisms that it can't be understood; but most of the time exuberant, ribald, startling and fun."

Owen, born near Clarkton in Bladen County, teaches literature and creative writing at North Carolina State. His *Flim-Flam Man* will become even better known through a 1967 movie version starring George C. Scott.

MARCH 25

MARCH 25, 1920

Sportscaster Howard Cosell is born in Winston-Salem.

His father is an accountant for a credit clothing chain. Later, the family moves to Raleigh, then to Brooklyn, all before Howard turns three.

"It is a piece of biographical data I now find curious," Cosell says in his autobiography. "No one thinks of me as a Southerner."

1974

In Moscow, George Hamilton IV becomes the first American country singer to perform behind the Iron Curtain.

Hamilton, who grew up in Winston-Salem, got his start in 1956 as a student at the University of North Carolina, when his locally recorded "A Rose and a Baby Ruth"—a ballad of teenage love written by John D. Loudermilk of Durham—sold more than a million records. Later, Hamilton's interest turned toward country and folk music. His "Abilene," also written by Loudermilk, was the number-one country song of 1963.

1974

In a Final Four played at the Greensboro Coliseum, North Carolina State, led by David Thompson, knocks off Marquette 76–64 in the championship game. But the Wolfpack's most notable feat in winning the title was eliminating UCLA—winner of the past seven championships—in the semifinals.

MARCH 26

1830

Meeting in Greenville, Missionary Baptists form the North Carolina Baptist State Convention after a split with Primitive Baptists, who oppose educated ministers and the establishment of Wake Forest Institute.

1852

Fayetteville physician William Mallett performs one of the first Cesarean sections in the South in which the mother survives. Mrs. Taylor, as she is referred to in Mallett's journals, is 17 years old and in labor with her first child. She refuses chloroform and ether for religious reasons; Mallett gives her opium to relieve the pain.

The child is delivered dead, but Mrs. Taylor recovers fully and later bears several more children.

1952

In Seattle, Kansas defeats St. John's 80–63 to win the NCAA basketball championship. Playing the last 29 seconds: Kansas sub Dean Smith.

"I should've fouled," Smith laments decades later. "Then I would've been in the box score."

MARCH 27

1705

Newly appointed Deputy Governor Thomas Cary, son-in-law of a Quaker, disappoints North Carolina Quakers by refusing to change a policy that effectively bars them from holding public office.

By 1711, however, Cary will ally with the Quakers and undertake a bizarrely inept armed rebellion against the government. He is arrested and sent to England, only to be released there for lack of evidence.

1867

Black and white delegates from 56 counties convene in Raleigh to formally launch the Republican Party of North Carolina. The new party comprises small farmers and Unionists ("scalawags" to their enemies), blacks enfranchised by the Republican Congress, and fortune-seeking Northerners ("carpetbaggers").

Carpetbagger Albion Tourgee sniffs that the chief characteristics of his fellow party members are "ignorance, poverty and inexperience."

1920

Without warning, women show up at all Democratic precinct meetings in Raleigh and read statements demanding they be allowed to participate. Elsie Riddick, assistant executive secretary to the North Carolina Corporation Commission, contends that since 35 states have already ratified the 19th Amendment, "and it is a certainty that we will vote in the next election . . . we have [the] right, therefore, to vote in this precinct meeting—just as any young man would who will become 21 years old prior to the next election."

"The unexpectedness of the stroke gave the male Democrats no time to formulate any answers," according to the *News and Observer*, and the women are allowed to vote.

MARCH 28

1928

The University of North Carolina Newsletter reports that since 1920, the number of horses in the state has fallen from 171,000 to 105,000, while the number of mules has risen from 257,000 to 282,000. The automobile is rapidly replacing the horse on the road and in the field, but the mule has not yet succumbed to the tractor.

1938

Slammin' Sammy Snead wins the inaugural Greater Greensboro Open by five strokes.

Snead will go on to win a record 81 PGA tournaments—including eight of the first 26 GGOs. His final GGO win, in 1965 at age 52, makes him still the oldest player ever to win a PGA tournament.

1977

Marquette, coached by Al McGuire, defeats the University of North Carolina 67–59 to win the Final Four in Atlanta.

In its semifinal game, Marquette used a last-second tap-in to edge an upstart team from the University of North Carolina at Charlotte—making its only Final Four appearance—by a 51–49 score.

After the title game, McGuire, a Brooklyn native, tearfully retires from a coaching career that began with a seven-year stint at Belmont Abbey College in Belmont.

1984

In one of the region's worst weather disasters, at least two dozen tornadoes cut across North Carolina and South Carolina, killing 69, injuring more than 1,300, and leaving more than 3,000 homeless.

MARCH 29

1982

In New Orleans, freshman Michael Jordan sinks a 16-foot jump shot and James Worthy intercepts a misdirected pass to lock up the University of North Carolina's 63–62 victory over Patrick Ewing and Georgetown. Perhaps most notably, the championship is coach Dean Smith's first in seven trips to the Final Four.

MARCH 30

MARCH 30, 1792

Joel Lane sells 1,000 acres of his Wake County plantation as the site for North Carolina's permanent capital, Raleigh.

The location, a compromise between new settlements in the west and established ones in the east, is arrived at after 15 years of rancorous legislative debate.

MARCH 31

1865

Confederate captain J. Louis Smith reports on the recent movement and exchange of Union prisoners: "Loud complaint has been made in [Greensboro] by the officers of the post and prominent citizens to the inefficiency of the officers and the looseness of discipline exercised over the prisoners marched from Salisbury. . . . Prisoners were allowed to straggle over the country and town, to purchase liquor, and to annoy the citizens."

1973

Carowinds, the Carolinas' first major theme park, opens on the South Carolina border near Charlotte.

1988

For exposing misuse of funds by the PTL television ministry of Jim and Tammy Bakker, the *Charlotte Observer* receives the Pulitzer Prize for public service. During 1987, a reporting team led by Charles E. Shepard published more than 600 stories about PTL.

In 1989, Jim Bakker will be convicted of fraud and sentenced to prison.

The *Observer* won its first public-service Pulitzer in 1981 for a series on brown lung, a breathing ailment suffered by textile workers after prolonged exposure to cotton dust.

1995

The Goody's Headache Powders factory in Winston-Salem, a red-brick landmark for more than half a century, closes its doors.

The new owner of Goody's, Block Drug, will transfer production to its Memphis plant, which already makes archrival BC powders. (Stanback powders, made in Salisbury since 1924, ranks number three in sales.)

Goody's originated in 1932 at the Winston-Salem drugstore of Martin "Goody" Goodman, who two years later sold his formula to entrepreneur Thad Lewallen.

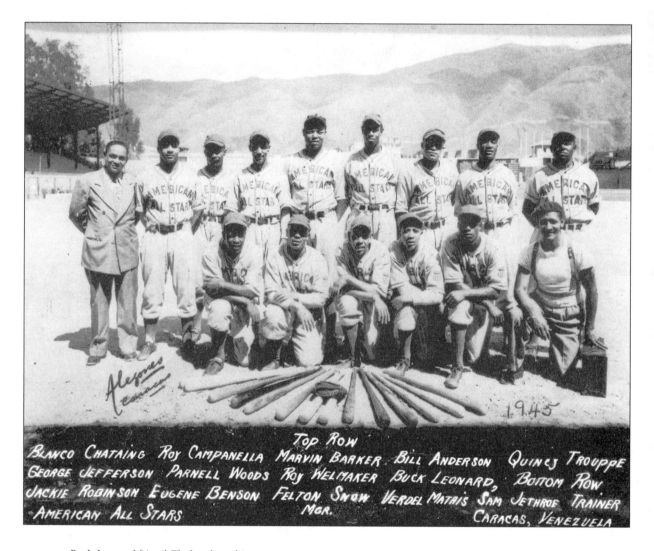

Top Row

BLANCO CHATAING ROY CAMPANELLA MARVIN BARKER BILL ANDERSON QUINCY TROUPPE
GEORGE JEFFERSON PARNELL WOODS ROY WELMAKER BUCK LEONARD, Bottom Row
JACKIE ROBINSON EUGENE BENSON FELTON SNOW VERDEL MATHIS SAM JETHROE TRAINER
AMERICAN ALL STARS   MGR.   CARACAS, VENEZUELA

Buck Leonard [April 7] played on this team
of Negro League stars barnstorming
in South America in 1945.
That's Leonard at top right; among
his teammates are Jackie Robinson and Roy Campanella.

North Carolina Museum of History

April

22-pound nugget unearthed in Cabarrus
Babe Ruth suffers world-class bellyache
Charlie Chaplin puckers up for war bonds

APRIL I

1907

By act of the legislature, black passengers must now sit in the back of North Carolina streetcars.

Between 1900 and 1907, blacks had staged boycotts of Jim Crow streetcars in cities across the South, including Charlotte and Wilmington, but to no avail.

1930

A throng estimated at more than 30,000 is on hand for Charlotte's first airmail delivery. The carrier is Eastern Air Transport, later to become Eastern Air Lines. Begins the story in the next day's *Charlotte Observer:* "Roaring out of the darkness of the south, Gene Brown, intrepid air flier of the night skies . . ."

1949

Mayor Herbert Baxter throws the switch on a machine that ostensibly begins pumping fluoride into Charlotte's water supply. In reality, the media event is a ruse designed to flush out anti-fluoridation hysteria. Indeed, complaints quickly begin pouring in about hair falling out and pet fish dying.

A month later, the city reveals the truth, and Charlotte really does become the first city in the South and the 14th in the nation to fluoridate.

1950

Dr. Charles Drew, the black surgeon who developed the blood bank, dies after a traffic accident near Burlington.

Drew, 45, and three other doctors from Howard University left Washington about 2:15 A.M. en route to an annual clinic at Tuskegee Institute in Alabama. About 7:30 A.M., Drew fell asleep at the wheel. The car left the road, throwing him out and crushing him when it rolled over.

A persistent story, perpetuated by a *M*A*S*H* TV episode built around it, has Drew dying in the then-segregated Alamance General Hospital emergency room after being refused treatment. In fact, according to both his widow and another black doctor who was at the hospital that night, white doctors made every effort to save Drew's life.

APRIL 2

1891

William Lawrence Saunders, North Carolina secretary of state, dies at age 56. On his tombstone: "I decline to answer," his response to a congressional committee investigating the Ku Klux Klan.

Saunders, severely wounded during the Civil War, allegedly acted as the Klan's chief strategist in the state.

1968

Charlotte dentist Reginald Hawkins receives a telegram from the Southern Christian Leadership Conference in Atlanta informing him that the Reverend Martin Luther King, Jr., must postpone his North Carolina appearances on behalf of Hawkins's gubernatorial campaign. The telegram says that King will stay in Memphis to support striking sanitation workers and that "we will be in touch with you in the next two weeks regarding the new tour schedule."

Two days later, King is assassinated in Memphis.

1981

Three days after shooting President Ronald Reagan, John Hinckley, Jr., arrives at the Federal Correctional Facility in Butner for mental examinations.

Hinckley is determined fit to stand trial, but a jury finds him not guilty by reason of insanity, and he is confined to a Washington mental hospital.

APRIL 3

1730

At the site of present-day Franklin in Macon County, Sir Alexander Cuming persuades seven young Cherokee men to accompany him to London.

During their four months in England, they will have their portraits painted by William Hogarth, kiss the hand of King George II, and sign a treaty of alliance.

Ty Cobb hits a home run in the first game played at Asheville's McCormick Field, but the Detroit Tigers lose the exhibition to the Asheville Skylanders 18–14.

By 1991, when the stadium is razed, it is the oldest minor-league park in the country.

1946

Thomas Dixon, author of the novel that became *The Birth of a Nation*, dies in Raleigh, broke and forgotten.

By the 1930s, Dixon's books, which had brought him millions in royalties and made Doubleday a top publishing house, no longer sold well. Among his more curious flops: *The Inside Story of the Harding Tragedy*, a rebuttal to *The Strange Death of President Harding*, which his sister, May Dixon Thacker, had based on the testimony of Cabarrus-born hoaxer Gaston B. Means.

Dixon, a compelling speaker as well as a writer, made two fortunes but was caught in both the panic of 1907 and the crash of 1929. In 1937, Judge Isaac Meekins, a Wake Forest classmate, appointed him clerk of the United States District Court in Raleigh. Two years later, still hoping his autobiography-in-progress would generate a third fortune, Dixon suffered a disabling stroke.

He is buried in his native Shelby a few feet from W. J. Cash, author of *The Mind of the South*.

1948

Playing before 1,300 fans at North Carolina State, Yale first baseman George Bush goes three for four with a triple, a double, three RBIs, two runs scored, a sacrifice, and a stolen base. Yale, on a Southern tour that also includes the University of North Carolina, Duke, and Wake Forest, wins 9–6.

APRIL 4

1959

Actress Debra Paget is crowned queen of Wilmington's annual Azalea Festival. Emceeing her coronation: Ronald Reagan, host of TV's *General Electric Theater*.

1983

Lorenzo Charles turns teammate Dereck Whittenburg's too-short 35-footer into a buzzer-beating slam dunk, giving underdog North Carolina State a 54–52 victory over Houston in the NCAA championship game in Albuquerque. Coach Jim Valvano races around the court looking for someone who isn't already being hugged.

1819

President James Monroe, making a tour through the South, is honored at a ball in the upstairs courtroom of the Chowan County Courthouse in Edenton.

The elegant brick courthouse, adorned with cupola, clock, and weather vane, was built in 1767 after William Byrd, the acerbic Virginia aristocrat, likened the county's 50-year-old wooden courthouse to "a common tobacco barn."

1897

Wilmington is visited by what may be the state's first UFO. According to the *Wilmington Messenger*, which headlines its account, "Was It an Air Ship?" hundreds of citizens spotted the "remarkable . . . brilliantly lighted" object as it floated above the city, creating "a sensation among all classes of people."

1917

President Woodrow Wilson's declaration of war on Germany—"The world must be made safe for democracy," he says—meets resistance from Representative Claude Kitchin of North Carolina, Democratic majority leader.

Acknowledging that he is walking the path of opposition "barefoot and alone," Kitchin emotionally tells a packed House that he is "unwilling for my country by statutory command to pull up the last anchor of peace in the world and extinguish during the long night of a worldwide war the only remaining star of hope for Christendom."

The war resolution passes 373 to 50.

Some North Carolinians call for Kitchin to resign and label him a member of the "petticoat brigade." He survives, however, and plays a major role in pushing through legislation to finance the war effort.

1980

An eight-foot-tall bronze statue of the Reverend Martin Luther King, Jr., is unveiled in Charlotte's Marshall Park.

The statue is coolly received by the King family, which would have preferred that the privately raised $68,000 be spent on its own projects, and by the public, which strains to find any facial resemblance to the assassinated civil rights leader.

"I put down what I felt more than what I saw," says sculptor Selma Burke, a 79-year-old native of Mooresville. "If anything, that strengthens the statue."

Burke won the King commission in part because her résumé claimed credit for the profile of Franklin D. Roosevelt on the dime. The United States Treasury, however, denies she was involved in the project.

1982

Writing in *The New Yorker*, John Updike praises Anne Tyler's ninth novel, *Dinner at the Homesick Restaurant*, for reaching "a new level of power and [giving] us a lucid and delightful yet complex and sombre improvisation on her favorite theme, family life."

Tyler was born in Minneapolis but graduated from Broughton High School in Raleigh and Duke University, where she studied under Reynolds Price. Price later recalls that Tyler, as a 16-year-old freshman, instinctively understood the nature of fiction—"as if a kind of perfect pitch had been inserted into her head by God."

Tyler's *Breathing Lessons* will win a Pulitzer Prize in 1989.

1990

Bryan "Chainsaw Ted" Williams of Cherryville makes his national debut on *The Tonight Show*, imitating a chain saw, motorcycles, and (with his head in a bucket of water) an outboard motor. Cherryville, he tells Johnny Carson, is a town of 5,280, or "a mile of people."

APRIL 6

1800

The Mecklenburg Declaration of Independence is purportedly destroyed in a fire that levels the home of signer John McKnitt Alexander.

In the endless debate that follows, defenders maintain that the "Meck Dec" was read from the courthouse steps in Charlotte on May 20, 1775—America's first official act of independence from the British, a full 14 months before the Continental Congress in Philadelphia drafted its own declaration. The North Carolina Constitutional Convention of 1861 will emblazon the date May 20, 1775, on the state flag.

Among the skeptics: Thomas Jefferson, who in 1819 will write John Adams that "the pa-

per from Mecklenburg County, of North Carolina" is spurious, and most 20th-century historians.

Undisputed, however, are the Mecklenburg Resolves of May 31, 1775, which rejected the king's authority and declared any future agent of the British to be "an enemy to his country." Royal Governor Josiah Martin attacked the resolves as "most traitorously declaring the entire dissolution of the Laws [and] Government."

1865

More than 1,000 soldiers and several cannon are involved in the five-hour Battle of Asheville, but with the end of the Civil War in sight, fighting is less than fierce. No deaths are reported.

1995

Having Our Say opens on Broadway. The production is adapted from the best-selling memoir—subtitled *The Delany Sisters' First 100 Years*—of Raleigh-born Sadie and Bessie Delany.

Vincent Canby of the *New York Times* calls the two-woman play "a grand narrative that at one minute reaches back to the beginning of the 19th century and, not long afterward, leaps forward to the 1990s . . . a panorama of particular times and places, of racism, sexism and indomitable will."

The sisters grew up on the campus of St. Augustine's College, where their father, who later became the nation's first black Episcopal priest, was vice principal.

After graduating from St. Augustine's, they moved in 1916 to New York, where they earned graduate degrees from Columbia University and became charter members of the Harlem Renaissance of intellectuals, artists, and musicians. Bessie was among the first black women to practice dentistry in New York; Sadie was the first black woman to teach "domestic science" in a white New York City high school.

APRIL 7

1847

Stephen A. Douglas, Illinois congressman and future debater of Abraham Lincoln, weds Martha Martin at her family's plantation home in Rockingham County. The two had met through North Carolina congressman David Reid, the bride's cousin.

1925

When the New York Yankees, making an exhibition swing through the South, pull into the Asheville train station, they find their star player suffering from what will become known as "the bellyache heard round the world."

"I'm going home even if I have to take an airplane," says Babe Ruth, stricken with cramps and fever. "I don't give a damn if the thing falls."

Moments later, he collapses on the platform. Teammates help him into a taxi and take him to the Battery Park Hotel, where a local physician prescribes rest. Ruth usually sleeps in the nude, but the doctor insists he stay warm, so a Yankee scout scours Asheville for a pair of size-48 pajamas. The largest he finds are size 42, in pink. He makes the top wearable by slitting the back, but the bottom stands no chance on the 270-pound Ruth.

While his teammates continue to Greenville, South Carolina, for their next game, Ruth boards a train for New York. When his arrival is delayed, rumors of his death spread. That false report is quickly squelched, but the one attributing his attack to gorging on hot dogs becomes part of his legend.

In New York, Ruth undergoes successful surgery for an intestinal abscess, but he misses much of the season.

1947

Before 1,500 fans at Griffith Park, Buck Leonard has three hits to lead the Homestead Grays to a 17–0 exhibition victory over the hometown Charlotte Black Hornets.

First baseman Leonard, a Rocky Mount native, began his career with the Rocky Mount Black Swans in 1925. He is best known for his 17 seasons playing for the Homestead (Pa.) Grays. The Grays are the New York Yankees of the Negro National League, and Leonard and teammate Josh Gibson are the league's Babe Ruth and Lou Gehrig.

In 1972, Leonard, despite having being barred from the major leagues by segregation, is inducted into the Baseball Hall of Fame.

APRIL 8

1926

Babe Ruth visits Charlotte for a spring-training exhibition and sets the town on its ear.

Before the game, he gives the local press a brief hotel-room interview. Reclining nude beneath a sheet and smoking a large cigar, he remarks on Southern women ("All they were cracked up to be") and the demands of celebrity ("Not exactly annoying. One gets used to it. Doesn't one?").

A crowd of 4,000 jams Wearn Field to see the potent Yankees toy with the Brooklyn Robins (later Dodgers). To give Ruth's legion of admiring kids a better look, the Yankees move him from right field to left; the kids swarm out of the stands and spill into the outfield.

In the seventh inning, Ruth grants the crowd its wish. In the words of *Charlotte Observer* sports columnist Jake Wade, "Ruth had previously singled, but that only whetted the appetite of the hungry mob. They had come from miles around to see Babe Ruth knock a home run. Nothing else would satisfy them.

"The Bambino took his stout stand at the plate. With the air tense with excitement, he slammed one . . . out of the park, bringing home [Ben] Paschal and [Lou] Gehrig ahead of him. Immediately after the smash of the Bam, the crowds began to file out of the grandstand. Everybody was happy."

1948

In the first integrated game at McCormick Field, Jackie Robinson of the Brooklyn Dodgers goes hitless against the minor-league Asheville Tourists. Robinson, who the previous season broke major-league baseball's color barrier, is booed by some of the 10,000 fans but cheered by most.

The Dodgers had chosen Asheville as an exhibition site after cancelling games in Atlanta and Jacksonville out of fear of racial violence.

APRIL 9

1585

Manteo and Wanchese, the first American tourists to visit Europe, leave England with a ship of colonists bound for North Carolina.

The two Carolina Algonquian Indians were invited to London by explorers commissioned by Sir Walter Raleigh. Manteo was made Lord of Roanoke while in England, but Wanchese was alienated by the Europeans and will be absorbed back into his tribe.

Manteo and Wanchese become the namesakes of communities on opposite ends of Roanoke Island.

1896

Barely three feet under the topsoil, a 22-pound nugget is discovered at Reed Gold Mine in Cabarrus County. The nugget, valued at $4,800, will be the last great find at the historic mine, which set off the nation's first gold rush. Just a day before the discovery, depressed by the mine's meager output, one of the partners had offered to sell out for $5.

Reed Gold Mine grew out of a discovery in 1799 by 12-year-old Conrad Reed, who took home a strange rock he found while fishing in Little Meadow Creek. His father, John Reed—not knowing it was gold—used it as a doorstop until 1802, when he offered it to a Fayetteville jeweler for $3.50. When Reed learned the 17-pound nugget was worth 1,000 times that, the gold rush was on.

Prior to the California gold rush of 1849, North Carolina provided all the native gold coined by the United States Mint; at one point, gold ranked second only to agriculture among the state's top industries. But by the end of the Civil War, Reed Gold Mine was largely exhausted.

The 1896 nugget proves to be an aberration, and future attempts to revive the state's gold industry fail.

1918

Governor Thomas Bickett makes a sales pitch for Liberty Bonds, which help finance World War I: "They will yield more solid comfort for the inner man than possum and potatoes, and more juicy sweetness than the apples for which our first ancestor threw Paradise away."

1942

Three hundred parking meters go into use in downtown Charlotte. A penny buys 12 minutes, a nickel an hour. Even before their use is mandatory, the newly installed meters take in more than $100.

APRIL 10

1901

The Brooklyn Dodgers cap their week-long spring-training stay in Charlotte with a 30–13 exhibition victory over Raleigh of the Carolina-Virginia Inter-State League. Brooklyn right fielder Wee Willie Keeler, a future Hall of Famer, manages only a single in six at-bats.

Despite its less-than-tropical Aprils, turn-of-the-century Charlotte has provided spring training for both the Dodgers and the Philadelphia Phillies. *Sporting Life* magazine notes that "the place offers so many natural advantages for such work and there is such an absence of temptation in that inland city that Manager William Shettsline thinks the Quaker team could not do better than return to the Queen City."

After the Dodgers' first day in town, the *Charlotte Observer* claimed that the Brooklyn players "have already learned that if they signal a street car between blocks and want to get on it, they have got to race for it. And that is about as good as running bases."

APRIL 10, 1922

WBT in Charlotte becomes the South's first commercial radio station and the nation's fifth.

1959

In New Bern, the reconstructed Tryon Palace, the former home of colonial governor William Tryon, opens to the public. It is North Carolina's first state historic site.

Fifteen years earlier, Maud Moore Latham had undertaken a campaign to purchase and have the state restore Tryon Palace, which was completed in 1771 but burned to the ground in 1798.

1899

North Carolina Mutual Life Insurance Company is founded by 39-year-old John Merrick.

Merrick, born to a slave mother in Sampson County, worked his way up from bootblack to owner of a chain of Durham barbershops, then built houses for black workers attracted by the city's burgeoning tobacco industry.

North Carolina Mutual will become the largest black-owned business in the United States and lead to Durham's reputation as the "Capital of the Black Middle Class."

1918

In Charlotte, a 10-minute speech by visiting movie star Charlie Chaplin raises more than $20,000 for Liberty Bonds to finance World War I.

Chaplin promises to kiss any woman in the audience who signs up for $5,000 in bonds. There are no takers, but several $1,000 pledges are made.

Chaplin also tours Camp Greene, shaking hands and—to call attention to the need for money to feed the troops—posing for a photo with a plate of dollar bills. He departs in his famous stage waddle.

1960

Time magazine's cover: Bowman Gray, chairman of R. J. Reynolds Tobacco Company. "Gray smokes four packs of Winstons a day (and an occasional Salem)," says *Time*. Gray joins Edward R. Murrow and Humphrey Bogart—as Captain Queeg—among the handful of *Time* cover subjects depicted smoking cigarettes. The background for his portrait is a wallpaper-like field of smoking cigarettes.

1776

Delegates to the Fourth Provincial Congress adopt the Halifax Resolves, instructing North Carolina's delegation to the Continental Congress "to concur with the delegates of the other Colonies in declaring Independency."

1844

Henry Clay, senator from Kentucky and Whig presidential candidate, arrives in Raleigh to visit Congressman Kenneth Rayner, a longtime ally.

Clay sets up a small table beneath a white oak in Rayner's yard and composes a letter to the *National Intelligencer* in Petersburg, Virginia. Annexing Texas without Mexico's consent, Clay writes, would be "compromising the character of the nation, involving us certainly in war with Mexico and probably with foreign powers, dangerous to the integrity of the Union, inexpedient to the financial condition of the country and not called for by any general expression of public interest."

The letter will manage to alienate both sides in the slavery debate and will probably be responsible for swinging the election to Mecklenburg native James K. Polk, a Democrat.

Clay, unrepentant, insists his position is faithful to the doctrine of the Whig Party. "I had rather be right," he adds in words that will long outlive the issue, "than be president."

1865

Sherman's army, en route from Goldsboro to Raleigh, celebrates the news of Lee's surrender.

1956

Bob Raiford, a disc jockey on Charlotte's WBT, is fired for "taking an unauthorized stand on a controversial issue." His stand: denouncing on the air the racial beating of Nat King Cole during a concert two days earlier in Birmingham, Alabama.

1990

The *Washington Daily News*, circulation 10,700, wins the Pulitzer Prize for public service.

The *Daily News* revealed that the town's water supply had nine times the safe level of a cancer-causing chemical and that town officials hadn't told the public because federal law didn't require disclosure in towns of fewer than 10,000 people. The stories led to a state law requiring all towns, including those too small under the federal regulations, to test for and report levels of trihalomethanes.

APRIL 13

1865

As Raleigh awaits Sherman, Union lieutenant George Round is sent ahead to set up a Signal Corps flag station. Scaling the eerily empty State Capitol, Round makes a crucial misstep: "I . . . leaped gently to what I supposed to be the solid top of the dome," he writes later. "I heard a sudden crash, and the top of the dome gave way beneath my feet. I had actually jumped into the circular glass skylight. . . .

"The next instant I found myself grasping at railing and stonework and heard the broken glass of the skylight ring sharply on the stone floor of the rotunda one hundred feet below me."

Round's fall is broken by a wire net, and he survives with only "a terrible fright, a lacerated wrist and, on the next day, a lame shoulder."

1936

Richard Nixon is installed as president of the Duke University Student Bar Association. The banquet program features a caricature by fellow student David Henderson captioned, "Our New Prexy 'Nose' All."

1945

The body of President Franklin D. Roosevelt passes through Charlotte en route from Warm Springs, Georgia, to Washington. Thousands gather at the Southern Railway station to glimpse the flag-shrouded coffin in the last coach.

At one end of the station, a white church choir sings "Onward, Christian Soldiers" and "My Faith Looks up to Thee"; at the other end, a black group sings spirituals. "For Negroes were there, too," reports the *Charlotte Observer*, "hundreds of them, paying their tribute to the man whom they looked upon as the best friend they ever had in the White House."

The Lions Club's display of flowers is afterward sent to young polio patients, for whom FDR was a special hero. "They made sure each of us got a bouquet or a rose bud," state treasurer Harlan Boyles recalls almost 50 years later. "I still have mine. . . . I'll never forget it."

1947

In a Chapel Hill incident that foreshadows the Freedom Rides of the early 1960s, black activist Bayard Rustin and three companions are roughed up and arrested for testing a state law requiring segregated seating on buses.

For his part in the "Journey of Reconciliation," Rustin will spend 22 days on an Orange County chain gang. In 1955, however, he makes his point on a grand scale, as the organizer of the Reverend Martin Luther King, Jr.'s, landmark bus boycott in Montgomery, Alabama.

1955

I. Beverly Lake, assistant attorney general of North Carolina, argues before the United States Supreme Court that the state should be given no deadline to desegregate its schools: "Race consciousness is not race prejudice. It is not race hatred. It is not intolerance. It is a deeply ingrained awareness of a birthright held in trust for posterity. . . .

"The majority of North Carolinians have been taught from infancy, and they understand, how it came about that Israel became a great nation, while Edom faded into oblivion, and they agree with the great Disraeli, who said: 'No man will treat with indifference the principle of race, for it is the key to history.'"

1961

Charlie Sifford, the first black to play in a PGA tournament in the South, leads the opening round of the Greater Greensboro Open with a three-under-par 68.

The next day, however, Sifford's game is thrown off by racial taunts and threats from the gallery. He will finish the tournament in a tie for fourth.

Sifford, sometimes called "golf's Jackie Robinson," was born and reared on Charlotte's west side. He caddied at the Carolina Golf Club (25 cents for nine holes) before dropping out of high school and moving to Philadelphia in 1939. Because of his late start on the PGA tour—he was a rookie at age 37—Sifford's career resembles Satchel Paige's as much as Robinson's.

APRIL 14

1865

Greensboro briefly serves as the capital of the collapsing Confederacy. Retreating from Richmond, Jefferson Davis and his cabinet stop for five days. Davis declines offers to stay at local homes out of fear they will be torched afterward by Union troops. Instead, he remains in his railroad car, where he drafts a letter to General Sherman arranging for the surrender of Confederate troops.

APRIL 14, 1879

In the state's first long-distance telephone call, Western Union's Raleigh manager raises his counterpart in Wilmington. "Hello, old man Specs!" he exclaims.

1909

A fire that the *Asheville Citizen* calls the "most thrilling in the city's history" and likens to the "eruption of a mighty volcano" quickly devours the Gothic-style Kenilworth Inn. A strong wind feeds the 2 A.M. blaze, which casts the "glare of noonday" on the countryside for miles around. Many guests barely escape, but only owner Joseph Gazzam loses his life.

The hotel, rebuilt in the Tudor style, later becomes a medical facility and, most recently, Appalachian Hall.

APRIL 14, 1912

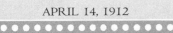

Former governor Charles Brantley Aycock, whose administration pushed the state's schools decades ahead, drops dead of a heart attack during a speech in Birmingham, Alabama. He is 52. His last word: "Education."

1980

Sally Field wins the best-actress Oscar for *Norma Rae*, based on the union-organizing efforts of Roanoke Rapids textile worker Crystal Lee Sutton.

Despite the movie's commercial and critical success, Sutton criticizes its accuracy and threatens to sue for invasion of privacy. Replies director Martin Ritt, "She's obviously no longer the free spirit of my movie. She's turned into a middle-class bourgeois woman who doesn't want anyone to know about her life."

APRIL 15

1861

Two days after the fall of Fort Sumter, President Lincoln asks that North Carolina contribute two regiments to a force of 75,000 to coerce the seceded states.

Governor John Willis Ellis will reply by telegram that Lincoln can expect "no troops from North Carolina."

1865

Confederate diarist Mary Boykin Chesnut, awaiting the war's end in Chester, South Carolina, comments on a friend's gloomy observation: "[He] said he knew the thing was up when he saw how anxious the Charlotte people were for the Yankees to come.

"I hope they will get enough of them and take our share, too."

Four days later, Chesnut receives word of Lee's surrender at Appomattox Courthouse.

1902

In Charlotte, J. Luther Snyder dispenses the first Coca-Cola bottled in the Carolinas. Until now, Coke has been available only at soda fountains.

As Snyder later recalls, business is mediocre until the arrival of Prohibition in 1905: "Eighteen saloons, two breweries . . . I had a terrible time selling soft drinks with that kind of competition."

1910

"I'm back in New York after a six months' stay in the mountains near Asheville, North Carolina," short-story master O. Henry writes a friend in Chicago. "I was all played out—nerves, etc. I . . . didn't pick up down there as well as I should have done. There was too much scenery and fresh air. What I need is a steam-heated flat with no ventilation or exercise."

Less than two months later, O. Henry—born William Sydney Porter in Guilford County—will be dead of alcoholism at age 47.

1972

"The First Time Ever I Saw Your Face," sung by Roberta Flack, a native of Black Mountain, hits number one on the *Billboard* pop chart.

APRIL 16

1846

George Donner, born in Davidson County, leads a California-bound wagon train out of Springfield, Illinois.

The Donner party will be caught in a weeks-long snowstorm in the Sierra Nevadas. Many die, and some resort to cannibalism.

In what is later known as the Donner Pass, a bronze statue commemorates the bravery of all the pioneers who went west.

1865

Catherine Ann Devereux Edmondston, wife of a Halifax County planter, writes in her journal after hearing the news from Appomattox,

> How can I write it? How find words to tell what has befallen us? Gen. Lee has surrendered! Surrendered the remnant of his noble Army to an overwhelming horde of mercenary Yankee knaves & foreigners. . . .
>
> For the past few days our constant employment [has been] burning our private papers. . . . The thought of seeing them in Yankee hands, of hearing them read in vile Yankee drawl amidst peals of vulgar Yankee laughter, or worse still, of knowing them heralded abroad in Yankee sensational newspapers, restrained me [from saving any letters]! This has been the fate of thousands of my fellow countrywomen, for the Northern journals teem with private papers stolen from Southern Households and published to a vulgar curious world as specimens of Southern thought, Southern feeling, and Southern composition. When I thought of all this . . . turning to Mr. Edmondston, I buried my face in his lap and fairly wept aloud!

APRIL 17

1853

A 129-mile plank road, touted as the world's longest, links Fayetteville with Salem and Bethania in Forsyth County.

Numerous other plank roads, often referred to as "farmers' railroads," are built, but maintenance is expensive, and they eventually give way to railroads.

1865

Union cavalry enters Chapel Hill. Officers' mounts are stabled in the University of North Carolina's library, prompting Sherman to call them the best-educated horses in the army.

Union general Smith B. Atkins will fall in love with Eleanor Swain, daughter of the university president, causing a major scandal. When they eventually marry, the college bell tolls in protest.

1968

An early-morning riot at Central Prison in Raleigh leaves six inmates dead. Seventy-eight inmates are wounded, along with three guards and two state troopers.

The incident began when inmates, angry over the administration's efforts to eliminate extortion from their leather-goods business, staged a sit-down strike in the yard and presented a list of grievances. When guards tried to move them back into their cells, inmates hurled torches at them; the guards responded with shotgun fire.

APRIL 18

1784

The North Carolina General Assembly convenes to create Sampson County, at 963 square miles the state's largest county. (The smallest: Chowan, at 234 square miles.)

1865

Jefferson Davis, fleeing south from Richmond, is offered shelter in Charlotte by Lewis Bates, the superintendent of Southern Express Company. On his arrival at the Bates house, Davis makes a brief speech, during which he is interrupted by the delivery of a telegram with news of Lincoln's assassination. "Can this be true?" he says. "This is dreadful, horrible! Can it really be true?"

1983

Claude Sitton, editor of the *News and Observer* of Raleigh, wins the Pulitzer Prize for commentary.

Sitton made his reputation as chief Southern correspondent for the *New York Times* during the civil rights movement. His peers appreciated his inventing the "Sitton notebook," a cut-down version that didn't revealingly jut out of a hip pocket at a Klan rally.

In 1968, he moved to Raleigh to continue the liberal tradition of the paper Josephus Daniels bought at auction in 1894 to serve as an organ of the Democratic Party.

1986

Pulitzer Prize–winning novelist William Styron returns to accept an honorary degree from Davidson College, whence he fled more than four decades earlier after a "miserable" freshman year. "My innate sinfulness," he recalls, "was in constant conflict with the prevailing official piety. . . .

"Some say the 1940s were the period when America lost its innocence. I lost my innocence at seventeen, to a professional woman in a sec-ond-floor walk-up in Charlotte at the Green Hotel."

Styron, who eventually graduated from Duke, made good use of his experiences at the Green Hotel in *Sophie's Choice*.

APRIL 19

1864

In one of the Confederates' few North Caro-lina victories, Plymouth is recaptured from the Union with the assistance of the *Albemarle*, an ironclad ram with an 18-foot prow and a lo-comotive engine.

The *Albemarle*, designed by 19-year-old Gil-bert Elliott of Elizabeth City, was built in a cornfield beside the Roanoke River in Halifax County.

It is still unfinished when called upon to make its debut at Plymouth, but it rams and sinks one Union steamer and sends another fleeing.

1935

The North Carolina General Assembly, giv-ing in to state employees who want to attend the annual baseball game between cross-county rivals North Carolina State and Wake Forest, declares Easter Monday a state holiday.

Although Wake Forest later relocates to Win-ston-Salem and the big game fades, Easter Monday will survive until the 1987 session, when legislators switch the holiday to Good Friday to accommodate the state's banks, which have complained about being out of step with the rest of the nation.

1952

Collier's magazine profiles Grady Cole as "Mr. Dixie." Cole, a homespun announcer who wakes up the Piedmont every morning on WBT, has been Charlotte's premier celebrity since 1929.

"Cole says he's still not a professional radio man," *Collier's* notes. "But he snows under all rivals, and his droll news and weather reports bring him $100,000 a year." His share of the Charlotte audience: 71 percent.

Governor Kerr Scott is credited with the state's massive rural road-building program of the early 1950s, but it was Cole who generated popular support with his long-running "Get Farmers out of the Mud" campaign.

APRIL 20

1864

Captain Conley (first name unknown) of the 101st Pennsylvania Volunteers writes in his journal after being taken prisoner at Plymouth,

> After our capture we were marched to Hamilton. . . . The 17th N.C . . . was marched out along the road, where they halted, opened ranks, and faced inward. The prisoners were then required to form in two ranks and march through. This, we soon learned, was done to pick out the "Buffaloes" as they called them; that is, North Carolinians who had either de-serted from their own regiment, or were known to them to be deserters, or who had fled to avoid the general conscription.
>
> As we passed through, they picked out five or six. I shall never forget the look of hopeless despair depicted on the countenances of those

when thus picked out. But most of them escaped unrecognized. I afterwards learned that all of those arrested were court martialed and executed.

APRIL 20, 1960

Cartoonist Al Capp, creator of "Li'l Abner," provokes hisses from a Chapel Hill symposium with his support of the University of North Carolina's speaker ban: "Why insist on burdening the university with some character the university simply doesn't want to invite into its home? If anyone is determined to hear these pearls of wisdom, they can hear them anywhere else."

Student: "Mr. Capp, you detest us, so why are you speaking at Chapel Hill?"

Capp: "For 3,000 bucks, and I wouldn't spend an hour with a bunch like you for a nickel less."

1989

Lieutenant Governor Jim Gardner calls for a North Carolina Senate vote on a resolution to make the Plott hound, a native of Haywood County known for its bear-hunting prowess, the state dog: "All in favor will howl."

The measure passes.

APRIL 21

1865

Sergeant Lucius W. Barber, 15th Illinois Volunteer Infantry, writes in his journal near Goldsboro after hearing of Lincoln's assassination, "Now, while the nation is rejoicing with unspeakable joy at its deliverance, it is suddenly plunged into the deepest sorrow by the most brutal murder of its loved chief.

"We are now continually passing paroled men from Lee's army on their way to their homes, or to where their homes were. Many found blackened ruins instead, and kindred and friends gone, they know not whither. Oh, how much misery treason and rebellion have brought upon our land!"

1941

Mayor Fiorello La Guardia of New York speaks at the dedication of Charlotte's Douglas Airport.

1956

Margaret Truman, only child of the former president, marries Clifton Daniel, Zebulon native, University of North Carolina alumnus, and *New York Times* foreign correspondent.

The wedding so engages the nation's fancy that it even bumps that of Grace Kelly and Prince Rainier from the cover of *Life* magazine.

1964

Winston-Salem beats out tepid competition from Charlotte, Raleigh, and Greensboro to become home for the fledgling North Carolina School of the Arts. Governor Terry Sanford envisions a conservatory to rival the best in the Northeast; critics envision a "toe-dancin' school."

1965

At a Democratic Party benefit at the Charlotte Coliseum, Judy Garland struggles through "He's Got the Whole World in His Hands," "When You're Smiling," and "Over the Rainbow." Though billed as "America's greatest entertainer," she is in sad and obvious decline. "Can you people hear?" she asks the skimpy crowd of 4,000. "Trouble is, I can hear, too, and it isn't too good."

Her performance contrasts sharply with one she had given at the coliseum four years earlier, a vigorous warmup for her triumphant Carnegie Hall concerts. During that visit, she had also helped speed demolition of the run-down Southern Railway passenger station, remarking that it was "a helluva station. . . . What happened to it?"

Garland, 47, will die of a drug overdose in 1969.

1985

Surgeons at Duke University Medical Center perform North Carolina's first successful heart transplant. The patient is 55-year-old Thomas Harrison, a Durham plumber.

1941

Charlottean W. J. Cash writes Margaret Mitchell to explain a reference to her *Gone With the Wind* in his *The Mind of the South*:

> About that "sentimental" crack: thinking it over, I have an idea that what inspired that carelessly thrown-off judgment was the feeling that your "good" characters were shadowy. On reflection, I think the feeling may have proceeded less from themselves than from the fact that they were set beside that flamboyant wench, Scarlett. There were good women all over the place in the South, of course. But Scarlett is a female to go along with Becky Sharp [in William Thackeray's *Vanity Fair*], wholly vivid and convincing. Beside her everybody else in the book, including even Butler, seems almost an abstraction. I hope you don't mind my saying it; I know how stupid the judgments of others on his creation sometimes seem to a writer. Indeed, I am often madder at the critics who are trying to be kind than at those obviously out to do me dirt.

1976

Near Asheboro, Governor Jim Holshouser turns the first shovelful of dirt for North Carolina Zoological Park—the nation's first state-owned zoo.

1971

At Duke University's Wallace Wade Stadium, the Grateful Dead make their first North Carolina appearance. Not yet a cult juggernaut, they share a "Joe College Weekend" bill with the Butterfield Blues Band and the Beach Boys.

APRIL 25

1908

Egbert Roscoe Murrow is born near Greensboro. Young Egbert hates his name—his older brothers teasingly call him "Egg." While a student at Washington State College, he goes by Ed.

In 1944, by now a household name on CBS radio, he files a delayed birth certificate (none was filled out at birth) certifying himself as Edward R. Murrow.

1927

Effie Hutchins, 32-year-old wife of a Burnsville lawyer and mother of two children, claims the unofficial title of women's national hiking champion by walking from Burnsville to Asheville—a distance of 40 miles—in seven hours, 38 minutes.

Such record attempts are a 1920s phenomenon, like flagpole sitting and dancing the Charleston. The same week, two Raleigh men announce plans for a Manteo-to-Murphy automobile endurance run, and a Kinston youth unsuccessfully attempts to navigate the Neuse River in a washtub. "The hiking fad," observes one Asheville account, "is sweeping the country like influenza."

Hutchins's walk is heavily reported in Boston, the home of socialite Eleanora Sears, whose previous record—44 miles in just under 10 hours—Hutchins has bettered by more than two minutes a mile.

Although her record proves short-lived—fellow Yancey Countian Mae Brewer breaks it the next week—Hutchins will earn another turn in the public eye. In 1934, she wins election to the North Carolina House, becoming the state's sixth female legislator.

APRIL 25, 1984

In the latest development in the eternal battle for barbecue supremacy, *New York Times* food writer Craig Claiborne declares North Carolina pork superior to Texas beef: "I will state unequivocally that the chopped barbecue pork sandwich served in [Lexington and Goldsboro] is by far my favorite kind of barbecue."

"Totally ludicrous," responds a spokesman for the Texas Department of Agriculture.

APRIL 26

1825

The *Catawba Journal*, published weekly in Charlotte, views with alarm the debut in New York of the nation's first Sunday newspaper: "If Sunday newspapers are tolerated here, we may look next for the introduction of Sunday theatres, and other fashionable vices of Europe."

1865

While Confederate general Joseph E. Johnston is surrendering to Sherman at the Bennett house, troops from both sides ransack John Ruffin Green's bright-leaf smoking-tobacco factory in Durham.

The seeming disaster will turn into a bonanza for Green. The soldiers find they prefer smoking to chewing, and after they return home, Green begins receiving orders from around the country. To take advantage of the region's growing reputation, he names his bright-leaf product Durham Smoking Tobacco and adopts the Durham Bull trademark, a symbol his successors will make known worldwide.

1876

In Murfreesboro, Dr. Walter Reed marries Emily Blackwell Lawrence.

The 24-year-old Reed spent part of his youth in Murfreesboro and Harrellsville, Hertford County towns where his father held Methodist pastorates.

Reed will achieve medical fame in 1900 by discovering that yellow fever is carried not by water but by mosquitoes; he is the namesake of Walter Reed Army Medical Center in Washington, D.C.

APRIL 27

1940

John F. Kennedy, on the verge of graduating from Harvard and writing the best-selling *Why England Slept*, visits Charlotte for the wedding of an old girlfriend. Frances Ann Cannon, a member of the well-known textile family, marries John Hersey, the future author of *Hiroshima*.

Kennedy dated Cannon for a year and may even have asked to marry her. She was Protestant and he Catholic, however, and her family took her on an around-the-world tour to discourage the romance.

The wedding is at White Oaks, the James B. Duke mansion.

Beforehand, Kennedy wrote a friend that "I would like to go but I don't want to look like the tall slim figure who goes out and shoots himself in the greenhouse half-way through the ceremony."

1952

In North Carolina's first reported visit from a "manned" UFO, a saucer-shaped craft about 10 feet in diameter strikes the chimney of the home of Lumberton businessman James Allen, then lands in his yard. The occupant, about three feet tall, emerges, fails to respond to Allen's inquiries, and returns to the craft, which departs with an intense whistling sound.

APRIL 28

1940

First Lady Eleanor Roosevelt stays at the Hotel Charlotte after speaking at Winthrop College in Rock Hill, South Carolina. Her breakfast, as recalled 40 years later by headwaiter Chauncey Mann: "First, half a grapefruit.

Cereal—Cream of Wheat. One poached egg on whole wheat toast. No bacon. And coffee, no cream, no sugar."

1993

Jim Valvano dies at Duke University Medical Center after a 10-month battle with bone cancer that he turned into a national crusade.

The month before his death, he established the Jimmy V Foundation for Cancer Research and accepted the Arthur Ashe Award for Courage. "Cancer can take away all my physical abilities, but it cannot touch my mind, it cannot touch my heart and it cannot touch my soul," he said. "Those three things are going to carry on forever."

Valvano, 47, coached basketball at North Carolina State from 1980 to 1990. His 1983 team won the national championship.

APRIL 29

1856

The State Hospital for the Insane—later renamed for Dorothea Dix, crusader for the mentally ill—opens in Raleigh.

1956

Driving a car he assembled from motley parts, Phil Styles beats out three dozen Jaguars, MGs, and other conventional sports cars to win the first Chimney Rock Hill Climb. Styles, a Burnsville garage owner, completes the 3.2-mile, 18-turn course in three minutes, five seconds.

The final hill climb at Chimney Rock Park will be held in 1995.

APRIL 29, 1963

The incorrigible Ernest T. Bass throws his first rock through a window on *The Andy Griffith Show*. Over the course of the series, Ernest T. will throw a total of 21 projectiles, five of which have notes attached.

APRIL 30

1953

Concerned about travel demands and public exposure, the North Carolina legislature severely restricts girls' high-school basketball tournaments. The most prominent casualty: an unofficial state invitational held at Southern Pines.

By 1972, girls will compete for an official state title, this time sponsored by the North Carolina High School Athletic Association.

1963

Angie Brooks, Liberian representative to the United Nations, is refused service at the S & W Cafeteria and the Sir Walter Hotel restaurant in Raleigh. An S & W lawyer dismisses the incident as "a phony thing designed to embarrass the United States in the eyes of the world," but the State Department apologizes to the Liberian government.

The episode, staged by master activist Allard Lowenstein, a University of North Carolina alumnus and an assistant professor of social studies at North Carolina State, energizes the civil rights movement in Raleigh. Two blacks are arrested trying to eat at the legislative cafeteria; more than 500 demonstrators drown out a performance of the North Carolina Symphony at the governor's mansion with their singing of freedom songs.

By the end of June, local restaurants and theaters will have desegregated.

Graham Martin, the last United States ambassador to South Vietnam, coordinates the chaotic helicopter airlift of Americans as Saigon falls to the North Vietnamese.

Martin, a Mars Hill native and Wake Forest graduate, will be sharply criticized for his handling of the evacuation, in which thousands of Vietnamese who worked for the United States and hundreds of classified documents are left behind.

President Lyndon Johnson,
promoting his "War on Poverty,"
visits a Rocky Mount tobacco farm [May 7].

May

Coal mine explosion near Sanford kills 53
"Air conditioning" enters language
Gaylord Perry loads up first spitter

MAY 1

1868

Tom Dula, convicted of stabbing to death his pregnant girlfriend, is hanged in Statesville.

The lurid trial drew reporters from as far away as New York and London. Even before his execution, a ballad about the case was being sung in Wilkes and Watauga Counties:

> Hang down your head, Tom Dula
> Hang down your head and cry;
> You killed poor Laura Foster
> And now you're bound to die.

In 1958, the Kingston Trio will win a Grammy for its revival of "Tom Dooley."

1928

In honor of Greensboro's becoming the first city in the state with airmail service, some 200 residents dine at the King Cotton Hotel, then drive to the Tri-City Airport to watch a Richmond-bound plane take on 23,000 pieces of mail from the Greensboro post office.

MAY 2

1771

In one of the colonies' first acts of violent resistance—two years before the Boston Tea Party—nine men blacken their faces, dress as Indians, and blow up a British munitions train headed for Hillsborough, where North Carolina's Regulators are rebelling.

The Cabarrus Black Boys, as they later become known, are put under sentence of death and hunted by British patrols for four years, but are never caught.

| MAY 2, 1892 |

Operating the new electric arc furnace at his father's aluminum plant in Spray, John Motley Morehead III stumbles onto a new chemical compound, calcium carbide, which releases a gas—acetylene—when placed in water.

The aluminum operation goes bankrupt before uses can be found for its new products. But Morehead's discovery will soon lead to the formation of the industrial giant Union Carbide, of which he is the major stockholder.

1934

Illustrating a new three-cent stamp "in memory and in honor of the mothers of America" is James Abbott McNeill Whistler's famous portrait of his mother, Wilmington-born Anna McNeill Whistler.

1986

New York architect Robert A. M. Stern, the host of PBS's *Pride of Place* series, tours downtown Charlotte and pronounces it "the ugliest collection of third-rate buildings in America. Charlotte has defined a type unto itself—a town that has grown very fast in a very mediocre way. There's no place like Charlotte."

MAY 3

1958

Poet e. e. cummings, returning from a series of North Carolina readings, writes his sister about his remarkably favorable impressions: "What a surprise—to enter a peacefully homogeneous community where money is never mentioned, where no racial tension exists either on or under any surface; & where instead of colliding with indoctrinated automata, one meets courteous individuals! For the first time I realize what 'America' might have been."

1971

The *Winston-Salem Journal* and *Sentinel* win the Pulitzer Prize for public service.

The sister dailies intensified their environmental coverage after northwestern North Carolina was threatened with strip mining.

1991

In Person: An Evening with Burt Reynolds, the Laughs, the Loves, the Lies, the Legends, the Lies (Not Necessarily in That Order) debuts at the Flat Rock Playhouse. A national tour follows.

MAY 4

1953

The Pulitzer Prize for public service goes to

the *Whiteville News Reporter* and the *Tabor City Tribune*—the first weekly newspapers ever to win a Pulitzer.

From 1949 to 1952, owner Horace Carter campaigned against the Ku Klux Klan, which had grown strong in Columbus County and across the South Carolina border. Carter's editorials led to threats, loss of revenue—and the conviction of 62 KKK members.

1994

"One for the Road with Charles Kuralt and Morley Safer" tops off Kuralt's 37 years with CBS News.

Kuralt, 59, is best known for his "On the Road" dispatches and for *Sunday Morning*, which he has anchored since its premiere in 1979. He has won 11 Emmys.

Born in Wilmington and reared in Charlotte, Kuralt wrote for the *Charlotte News* before leaving for CBS in 1957.

Ten years later, he talked the network into letting him roam the country and tell the stories of ordinary people and places: "At a time when America was in a little bit of crisis, we reminded people that the whole country wasn't in flames and that most people lived in peace with their neighbors and that there are a lot of good people in the country."

MAY 5

1992

Mel Watt, born poor in rural Mecklenburg County but educated at Yale Law School, wins the Democratic nomination in the newly created, mostly black 12th Congressional District.

Victory in the general election will make Watt and Eva Clayton of Warren County the state's first black members of Congress since 1901, when former slave George Henry White of Tarboro resigned his seat after the North Carolina General Assembly disfranchised blacks.

MAY 6

1865

Near Waynesville, General James B. Martin surrenders the last Confederate forces in the state.

1969

Howard Lee of Chapel Hill becomes the first black to be elected mayor of a predominantly white Southern town.

1972

In the state's first presidential primary, North Carolina Democrats dash the hopes of native son Terry Sanford by resoundingly endorsing Governor George Wallace of Alabama. The defeat effectively ends the campaign of Sanford, Duke University president and former governor.

Barely a week later, a gunman will seriously wound Wallace at a Maryland shopping center, forcing him to withdraw. The Democratic nomination eventually goes to Senator George McGovern of South Dakota.

1991

The New Yorker reflects on provincialism while praising Charlotte's nightlife: "New Yorkers don't want to be prejudiced when they go to the boonies. They just can't help themselves. Like calling Charlotte, North Carolina, the boonies. How disconcerting to find that the city's nearly 400,000 people don't live in lean-tos."

MAY 7

1836

Uncle Joe Cannon of Illinois, legendarily autocratic Speaker of the House, is born in a log house in Guilford County.

Years later, he returns for a visit, and the house is pointed out to him. "I'll be damned," he says with a cursory glance. "Let's go."

1930

By a 41–39 vote, the United States Senate rejects Supreme Court nominee John J. Parker. Born in Union County and living in Charlotte, Parker would have been the first North Carolinian on the Supreme Court in 120 years.

Parker, a Republican who had run unsuccessfully for governor, was serving on the Fourth United States Circuit Court of Appeals when nominated by President Herbert Hoover. Senate debate centered on a 1920s case in which the judge had ruled with management about a "yellow dog" contract. Though the Supreme Court later upheld Parker's decision, the anti-union label proves fatal to his nomination.

Parker remains on the bench and in 1945 will sit as an alternate judge at the Nuremberg war-crimes trials. He dies in 1958 at age 72 from a heart attack suffered shortly after dining at Washington's Mayflower Hotel. His dinner companion: Clement Haynsworth, the Greenville, South Carolina, judge whose own Supreme Court nomination will be rejected by the Senate in 1969.

1964

President Lyndon Johnson publicizes his "War on Poverty" with a visit to the home of tenant farmer William David Marlow.

In the aftermath of the media event, the Marlows' yellow clapboard house outside Rocky Mount will become a tourist attraction, and neighbors will make wisecracks about "the poorest folks in the world."

"We didn't ever feel like we were in poverty," says Doris Marlow. "We've been talked at, talked about and throwed off on."

By August, the Marlows have had enough. William David Marlow, leaving most of his tobacco crop in the field, moves into town to become a house painter.

1980

Home, based on life in playwright Samm-Art Williams's hometown of Burgaw in Pender County, debuts on Broadway. Williams's script is nominated for a Tony, and *Time* magazine names *Home* one of the year's 10 best plays.

MAY 8

1875

Susan Dimock, North Carolina's first native daughter to practice medicine, dies when the steamship *Schiller* wrecks on a granite reef off the English coast.

Dr. Dimock was born in Washington, North Carolina, where a local physician became her mentor, but moved to Massachusetts with her widowed mother at age 17. When Harvard's medical school turned her away because she was a woman, she went abroad and in 1871 received a degree with honors from the University of Zurich. She practiced for three years at a Boston hospital before asking for leave to revisit Europe.

She is 28 years old at her death.

1937

British novelist Aldous Huxley, spending several days at Black Mountain College while driving cross-country, tells an Asheville reporter that he finds western North Carolina "wonderful country," the rise of Duke University "most extraordinary," and the South "livening up."

1953

The Atlantic Coast Conference, destined to become the nation's premier college basketball league, is founded in Greensboro. The original members are the University of North Carolina, Duke, Clemson, Maryland, Wake Forest, North Carolina State, and South Carolina.

1961

The "Freedom Riders," headed from Washington, D.C., to Jackson, Mississippi, to challenge the South's segregated bus facilities, incur their first arrest during an overnight stop in Charlotte.

Joe Perkins, a 27-year-old New Yorker, refuses to leave after being denied a shoeshine in the bus station's whites-only barbershop and is jailed for trespassing.

"We had expected this sort of thing in the Deep South," says James Farmer, executive director of the Congress on Racial Equality, "but not in Charlotte."

The Freedom Riders will experience much worse treatment, starting with beatings in Rock Hill, South Carolina, and ending with bread-and-water imprisonment in Mississippi. Their mission, however, not only brings the bus system into compliance with the law but also arouses widespread public sympathy and paves the way for more civil rights workers to come south.

MAY 9

1942

Patrolling off Cape Lookout during World War II, the Coast Guard cutter *Icarus* sinks the German submarine *U-352* with a barrage of depth charges.

Fifty years later, a dozen U-boat crewmen will visit Morehead City to meet the Americans who sank and then rescued them.

MAY 10

1863

General Thomas J. "Stonewall" Jackson, the Confederacy's master tactician, dies of pneumonia eight days after being mistakenly shot by troops from the 18th North Carolina Regiment.

He was shot at nightfall while scouting ahead of the line near Chancellorsville, Virginia. His men mistook him for the enemy. As he lay wounded, doctors amputated his maimed arm.

"He has lost his left arm," Robert E. Lee will lament, "but I have lost my right arm."

1926

One hundred forty-two home economics club members from cotton mills in Charlotte and Gastonia shake hands with President Calvin Coolidge at the White House and present him with "samples of cloth woven by their own hands."

The young women had spent the previous year raising money for the three-day train excursion by selling candy and movie tickets and putting on skits.

According to an account in the *Charlotte Observer*, "Those who call President Coolidge 'cold and silent' have never seen him meet a group of lovely and guileless young girls. He may be as cold and remote as the North Star when dealing with callous reporters and wary politicians, but his stolid personality surely melted to kindly radiance as he responded to the little speeches and tokens shown from these young daughters of industry."

1949

Morehead Planetarium, the world's first university-based planetarium, opens at the University of North Carolina. Among its unanticipated future uses: training astronauts in celestial navigation.

1864

On the eve of the Battle of Spotsylvania Court House in Virginia, Confederate colonel Thomas Miles Garrett of Bertie County, frustrated at being passed over for promotion, vows to "come out of the fight a brigadier-general or a dead colonel."

Garrett will indeed die in battle. The next day, a dispatch arrives from Richmond conveying the promotion he so coveted.

1898

Ensign Worth Bagley of Raleigh becomes the first American officer killed in the Spanish-American War. Bagley is executive officer of the torpedo boat *Winslow* when it is hit by enemy fire in the harbor of Cárdenas, Cuba.

In 1907, Bagley will be honored with a statue, paid for by public contributions, on Capitol Square in Raleigh.

The six-month war claims only one other North Carolinian—army lieutenant William Shipp of Charlotte, who dies in the Battle of San Juan Hill.

1915

Despite declining health, trapshooting great George Lyon of Durham hits 147 of 150 targets at the Southern Handicap in Memphis, Tennessee, his last major contest.

Eight months later, he will die of tuberculosis in Albuquerque, New Mexico.

Lyon, the scion of two tobacco-manufacturing families, was world champion in 1911 and 1912 and coached the United States trapshooting team to victory at the 1912 Stockholm Olympics.

Lyon's Park in Durham, the site of many of his trapshoots, is named for him.

1935

The North Carolina General Assembly approves local-option liquor sales, ending a quarter-century of prohibition in the state.

1977

Owner Ted Turner, frustrated by the Atlanta Braves' 16-game losing streak, sends Dave Bristol home to Andrews in Cherokee County and takes over as manager himself.

Turner adds another game to the streak before baseball commissioner Bowie Kuhn returns him to the stands and Bristol to the dugout.

1985

The Reverend Sun Myung Moon, founder of the Unification Church, receives an honorary degree from Shaw Divinity School in Raleigh.

Although school officials cite Moon's humanitarianism, his résumé also includes $60,000 in donations. "Anyone who makes a contribution has a right to be honored," one board member contends.

Moon's wife accepts the degree in his behalf; her husband is serving time in federal prison for tax evasion.

MAY 12

1918

Future senator Sam Ervin, in infantry training, writes his mother,

Today is "Mother's Day," and according to orders from General Pershing it is to be most fittingly observed by each member of the Amixforce wiring a letter to his mother. No order heretofore given has, in my humble opinion, contained so vast a store of true wisdom. . . .

My hope and prayer is that I may be spared to come back in honor and safety in order that I may repay a small part of the great debt that I owe to you. No one can be under a greater obligation than I, for my mother is the most beautiful and self-sacrificing mother in the world.

1953

Fred Chappell, a junior at Canton High School in Haywood County, hitchhikes 250 miles to Duke University to hear his hero, Irish poet Dylan Thomas.

Chappell will soon enroll at Duke and study under renowned writing professor William Blackburn, whose students over the years also include Reynolds Price, William Styron, Josephine Humphreys, and Anne Tyler.

Later, as one of the state's most accomplished writers and teachers (at the University of North Carolina at Greensboro), Chappell recalls Thomas's reading: "They poured him onstage over at Page Auditorium. And you thought, 'Oh geez. This is not going to happen.' And he gave a magnificent reading. An impossible reading. And then they poured him offstage."

MAY 13

1865

On his 35th birthday, Zebulon Vance, the

state's Civil War governor, is arrested at his home in Statesville and taken to Washington.

After being held on unspecified charges in the Old Capitol Prison for two months, Vance will go free and open a law practice in Charlotte. In 1876, he is again elected governor, marking the end of the state's Republican-dominated Reconstruction government.

1976

Forsyth County's last remaining clamshell-shaped Shell gas station—a choice, if battered, example of 1930s "roadside" architecture—is entered in the National Register of Historic Places.

The tiny station at the corner of Peachtree and Sprague Streets in Winston-Salem, one of eight built by Quality Oil Company, was most recently used as a small-engine repair shop.

MAY 13, 1990

Muppets creator Jim Henson, feeling under the weather, cuts short a Mother's Day visit to Ahoskie in Hertford County to return to New York City.

Three days later, he will die of a fast-spreading form of bacterial pneumonia.

Henson, 53, often visited Ahoskie, where his mother, Barbara Henson, retired in the early 1980s.

1771

Colonial governor William Tryon, fearing civil war, sends 1,452 militiamen to restore order in the western Piedmont.

Two days later in what is now Alamance County, the rebellious Regulators will be soundly defeated in the Battle of Alamance.

1932

In the first performance of the North Carolina Symphony, composer Lamar Stringfield conducts 48 volunteer musicians from 16 communities at Hill Hall on the University of North Carolina campus.

A decade later, the North Carolina General Assembly will give the symphony a crucial boost, passing a "horn tootin' bill" that makes North Carolina the first state to provide continuing financial support for an orchestra.

1965

Life magazine profiles Andrew Wyeth, the nation's preeminent realist painter. Bob Timberlake, a Lexington businessman, reads the story and finds himself overwhelmed by a long-dormant desire to become an artist.

Soon, Timberlake is painting full-time. He visits Wyeth in Chadds Ford, Pennsylvania, and receives encouragement.

Within a few years, he will become known as "the Southern Wyeth"; by the 1990s, he is a one-man arts-and-crafts conglomerate—paintings, prints, books, postage stamps, quilts, furniture.

1978

Clyde Edgerton, associate professor of education at Campbell College, listens to Eudora Welty read her short story "Why I Live at the P.O." on public television and decides to start writing fiction the next day.

The result is *Raney*, a 1985 novel that wins appreciative reviews for its droll depiction of life in eastern North Carolina. It does not please officials at the Baptist college, however, and Edgerton ultimately resigns and takes a position at St. Andrew's College.

1981

Cedric Maxwell, a Kinston native who took the University of North Carolina at Charlotte to its only NCAA Final Four, is named the Most Valuable Player of the NBA championship series.

Maxwell broke out of his role as a defensive specialist to score 90 points in the last four games of the Boston Celtics' 4–2 series victory over the Houston Rockets.

MAY 15

1942

Wartime gasoline rationing goes into effect in North Carolina and 16 other Eastern states. The maximum purchase per week: three gallons.

MAY 16

1936

Outlaw baseball arrives in North Carolina. The Carolina League—in no way connected to the later league of the same name—will last three seasons. It is an odd offshoot of the Depression (the country is full of baseball players whose leagues have folded) and blue laws (the Charlotte Hornets have been forced out of the Piedmont League because their parent organization, the Boston Red Sox, demanded they schedule Sunday games).

Organized baseball blacklists the Carolina League for signing players who are under lifetime contracts to major-league teams, but its rowdy style of play proves appealing in such towns as Shelby, Concord, Kannapolis, Landis, and Valdese.

1938

Time magazine's cover: Frank McNinch, Federal Communications Commission chairman.

"President Roosevelt—to whom radio means a lot—sent over his acute and large-eared little trouble shooter, 65-year-old Frank Ramsay McNinch," *Time* reports. "Chairman McNinch comes from Charlotte, N.C., a thriving city of which he was twice mayor. A small but fearless Presbyterian elder, Mr. McNinch is against liquor (he keeps a vacuum jug of milk on his desk)."

MAY 17

1906

In a speech to the Southern Cotton Manufacturers' Association convention in Asheville, Charlotte industrialist Stuart Cramer introduces the term *air conditioning* into the language.

In 1905, Cramer, an engineering genius who

held 60 patents, installed a pioneer air-conditioning system in the Gray Manufacturing plant in Gastonia. Until he came along, textile mills had to resort to crude methods—such as pouring boiling water on the floor—to provide the humidity necessary to process cotton.

1981

Poet A. R. "Archie" Ammons, a 55-year-old native of Whiteville in Columbus County, receives one of the inaugural round of 25 John D. MacArthur "genius" fellowships. Over the next five years, he will receive a total of $264,000 to spend as he likes.

Despite winning the 1972 National Book Award, Ammons until now has had to work at salaried jobs—as a principal at Hatteras Elementary School, a glassware sales executive in New Jersey, a professor at Cornell University—to support his poetry.

MAY 18

1954

Although the Supreme Court struck down school segregation just the day before, President Dwight D. Eisenhower makes no reference to the decision during a Mecklenburg Declaration of Independence—"Meck Dec"—celebration in Charlotte.

"Until we have peace," Eisenhower tells a sunburned crowd of 60,000 at Freedom Park, "we cannot march forward to attain the dream that was held by the men of Mecklenburg."

1959

Charlotte-born Wilbert Harrison, an obscure blues and beach musician, sees his slow-shuffling "Kansas City" hit number one on the pop charts.

After five years in the navy, Harrison won an amateur-hour contest in Miami (singing Frankie Laine's "Mule Train") and began performing as a one-man band at clubs along the East Coast.

The sudden success of "Kansas City" will not carry over. In fact, it lands Harrison in the midst of a costly, career-crippling legal dispute between record companies. His only other hit comes in 1970, when "Let's Work Together (Part I)" reaches number 32.

MAY 19

1862

The *Fayetteville Observer* reports on an appearance by Blind Tom at Camp Mangum, the Civil War training camp outside Raleigh:

> The blind negro Tom has been performing here to a crowded house. He is certainly a wonder. . . . He resembles any ordinary negro boy 13 years old and is perfectly blind and is an idiot in everything but music, language, and imitation, and perhaps memory. . . .
>
> He has never been instructed in music or educated in any way. He learned to play the piano from hearing others, learns airs and tunes from hearing them sung, and can play any piece on first trial as well as the most accomplished performer. . . . One of his most remarkable feats was the performance of three pieces of music at once. He played Fisher's Hornpipe with one

hand and Yankee Doodle with the other and sang Dixie all at once. I could distinctly hear and understand each. He also played a piece with his back to the piano and his hands inverted. . . .

This poor blind boy is cursed with but little of human nature; he seems to be an unconscious agent acting as he is acted on, and his mind a vacant receptacle where Nature stores her jewels to recall them at her pleasure.

Future neurologists such as Oliver Sacks will cite "Blind Tom"—Thomas Greene Bethune, raised a slave in Georgia and taken on world tour by his master—as one of the earliest documented idiot savants.

MAY 19

1995

One of the 1,700 workers at the Philip Morris cigarette factory in Cabarrus County notices an unusual odor, setting in motion the tobacco industry's first product recall.

After tests find filters contaminated by the insecticide methyl isothiocyanate, Philip Morris begins pulling 8 billion cigarettes—including Marlboro, the world's best-selling brand—from retail shelves.

MAY 20

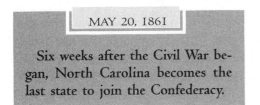

MAY 20, 1861

Six weeks after the Civil War began, North Carolina becomes the last state to join the Confederacy.

1909

President William Howard Taft visits Charlotte for Meck Dec Day and the dedication of the 12-story Realty Building, the Carolinas' first steel-frame skyscraper.

Just as a parade past Taft's reviewing stand ends, a sudden downpour sends thousands running for cover. The president's speech, moved indoors, opposes partisan politics in the federal judiciary. But it will be the "Taft rain" that Charlotteans remember.

Later, at what will become Johnson C. Smith University, Taft sits in a chair custom-built to accommodate his 325 pounds and urges blacks to continue pulling themselves up by their bootstraps.

1914

The North Carolina Equal Suffrage League enters a float in the Meck Dec Day parade in Charlotte. It is the first time suffragists have marched in the state.

1916

Woodrow Wilson visits Charlotte for Meck Dec Day. "A hearty cheer greeted the president as he left the train, and he smiled warmly and doffed his silk hat in response," the *Charlotte Observer* reports. "Southern crowds are not much on cheering except when 'Dixie' is played; they usually prefer to gaze in silence, but the president and Mrs. Wilson were greeted with vocal demonstrations wherever they went."

Wilson, however, is soon overshadowed by Mayor T. L. Kirkpatrick, who takes the speakers' platform to introduce Governor Locke Craig. Undeterred by the sight of spectators and soldiers fainting in the steamy heat, Kirkpatrick offers a 40-minute review of Mecklenburg history. When the mayor at last yields, Craig introduces President Wilson in a single sentence.

Kirkpatrick, who will suffer considerable teasing about speaking more than twice as long as the president, always insists that Wilson told him he was not feeling well and to stretch his remarks. The mayor's speech makes such an impression on First Lady Edith Wilson that she scathingly recalls it in her memoirs.

1931

The world's only actual-size replica of the Parthenon, constructed in Nashville in 1896 to celebrate the Tennessee centennial, reopens after extensive renovation and additions.

Now depicted on a pediment is eight-year-old Randall Jarrell, who posed for the sculpture of Ganymede, cupbearer to the gods. Reads the inscription, "To Randall—our most interested and interesting visitor—the sculptors: Belle Kinney—L. F. Scholz, June 1925."

As an adult, Jarrell will become more widely celebrated as literary critic for *The Nation*, poetry editor of the *Yale Review*, and teacher at Woman's College in Greensboro.

At age 51, he is fatally struck by a car while walking along a dark road in Chapel Hill.

MAY 21

1870

When white Democrats meet in the Caswell County Courthouse in Yanceyville, John W. "Chicken" Stephens—a "scalawag" Republican state senator in the Reconstruction government—attends and takes notes.

The next morning, Stephens will be found in a courthouse storeroom, strangled and stabbed to death.

Numerous Ku Klux Klan suspects are arrested, but none confesses. Convinced that a jury would never convict, Governor William W. Holden sends in George Kirk, a former Union army officer, to enforce martial law in Alamance and Caswell Counties—an episode known as the Kirk-Holden War. A federal judge ultimately frees the defendants, however, under provisions of the 14th Amendment—passed to protect the rights of black people.

The murderers are never brought to justice. In 1935, however, the facts come out with the death of John Lea, at age 92 the last surviving member of the Klan execution ring. In a sealed statement he gave state officials in 1919 to be read posthumously, Lea confesses that Stephens was lured into an unoccupied office, seized, disarmed, tied, gagged, and thrown onto a woodpile. The Klansmen had planned to hang him that night on the town square, but fear of discovery led them to choke and stab him instead.

1927

Charles Lindbergh touches down at a Paris airfield, concluding the first solo nonstop flight across the Atlantic Ocean.

Lindbergh christened his single-engine plane the *Spirit of St. Louis*—but only because Durham-based American Tobacco Company, leery of a possible crash, passed up his proposal to sell the right to name it the *Lucky Strike*.

1980

Charlotte Motor Speedway makes the mistake of scheduling a Waylon Jennings concert on qualifying day for the World 600 stock-car race. Eight people are injured, three are arrested, and 175 riot police are called out.

"We just got the wrong mix of people," says speedway president H. A. "Humpy" Wheeler. "We had God-fearing, flag-waving, red-white-and-blue folks out there with the motorcycle boys."

MAY 22

1926

President Calvin Coolidge signs a bill creating three national parks, the largest of which will straddle the North Carolina–Tennessee line and eventually cover more than 520,000 acres. Great Smoky Mountains National Park is slow to develop, however, until John D. Rockefeller, Jr., contributes funds for land purchases.

By 1941, Great Smoky Mountains National Park will be the first national park to draw more than a million visitors in one year.

MAY 23

1775

Colonial governor Josiah Martin orders the mounted cannon on the Tryon Palace grounds in New Bern carried away for fear patriots will use them against him.

A week later, his government collapsing, Martin flees, eventually taking refuge on a British warship in the Cape Fear River.

MAY 24

1964

Glenn "Fireball" Roberts, the first Southern stock-car driver to get national attention—including the cover of *Sports Illustrated*—suffers severe burns in a crash in the World 600 at Charlotte Motor Speedway.

Roberts, a 35-year-old Florida native, will die of those burns 39 days later in a Charlotte hospital. Soon afterward, NASCAR orders fire-prevention research that leads to rubber fuel cells (replacing fragile metal tanks) and fire-retardant clothing.

MAY 25

1673

In what is now Perquimans County, Ann Durant represents a seaman in his successful suit for wages due. She is the first woman known to have appeared as an attorney in a North Carolina court.

1933

Senator Josiah Bailey of North Carolina takes the floor to note that "even the mules in the South wear shoes."

Bailey's is one of many indignant responses to Secretary of Labor Frances Perkins's characterization of the South as "an untapped market for shoes. . . . A social revolution will take place if you put shoes on the people of the South."

1963

In Chapel Hill's first large-scale civil rights demonstration, about 350 people, half of them black, protest segregated businesses. They march from St. Joseph Christian Methodist Episcopal Church up Franklin Street, over to Rosemary Street, and back to the town hall.

MAY 26

1908

After a vigorous campaign by the Anti-Saloon League, North Carolina votes to become the first Southern state to adopt statewide prohibition. The tally: drys 62 percent, wets 38 percent.

MAY 27

1925

A coal-mine explosion at Coalglen, near Sanford, kills 53 men.

As bodies are slowly removed from the Carolina Coal Mine, the atmosphere turns part funeral, part carnival. "The crowd is a North Carolina crowd," notes the *News and Observer* of Raleigh. "It has been fine, save for an indecent exposition of the picnic spirit by a truckload of heedless students who came over from the University."

The Coalglen disaster will hasten the decline of the state's once-active coal industry, which dates back to 1775.

1791

President George Washington, en route to Salisbury on the return leg of a Southern tour, stops overnight at Cook's Inn in Charlotte, a community with a population of fewer than 500.

In his haste to depart, Washington will leave behind his wig powder box. Afterward, the town's young women line up for Mrs. Cook to dust their heads with Washington's powder.

In his diary, the president dismisses Charlotte as "a trifling place."

1917

Black business leaders C. C. Spaulding and Dr. Aaron McDuffie Moore tell the Durham Chamber of Commerce that 1,500 to 2,000 blacks have left the city in the previous 90 days.

The exodus of black Southerners to the North, begun during Reconstruction, has accelerated since 1900, when white supremacists resumed legal and political dominance.

1942

In Hollywood, Roy Acuff records "The Wreck on the Highway," based on a real-life accident in Rockingham.

The melancholy song will become a country-music classic and a staple of Acuff's long career, but it was first recorded (as "Crash on the Highway" or "I Didn't Hear Anybody Pray") in Charlotte in 1938 by the Dixon Brothers.

Many years later, the Reverend Dorsey Dixon, Jr., will recall, "My father wrote this song in

1936, when the '36 Fords came out with a V-8 engine and began to kill people all over the nation. The wreck took place at the Triangle Filling Station. . . . Dad went down and seen the wreck, seen the whiskey, blood and glass on the floor of the car."

Dixon and his brother Howard, both long-time mill workers, specialized in what have been called "did-wrong-and-got-caught songs." In the 1930s, the Dixon Brothers often performed on WBT radio under the sponsorship of Crazy Water Crystals. They also made several records at RCA Victor's makeshift Charlotte studio.

MAY 29

1831

In the nation's most destructive urban fire to date, Fayetteville loses 600 homes, 125 businesses, several churches, and the State House, where the 1789 Constitutional Convention voted to make North Carolina the 12th state.

1888

William Henry Belk opens his first store, the New York Racket, on Main Street in Monroe.

A century later, the family-owned Belk retail empire will include more than 300 stores in 14 states.

1893

Twenty-nine immigrant farmers from the Cottian Alps in Italy step off the train in Burke County. Waldensian Protestants, they faced persecution and economic hardship in their homeland.

At first, handicapped by rocky soil and an ill-conceived communal concept, the new settle-ment nearly fails. By the 1920s, however, the town of Valdese will be thriving with textile mills and the regionally renowned Waldensian Bakery.

1911

At the urging of Teddy Roosevelt's "trustbusters," the United States Supreme Court declares the American Tobacco Company a monopoly in restraint of trade and orders it broken up into such former competitors as Liggett and Myers, R. J. Reynolds Tobacco Company, and Lorillard Tobacco Company.

The decision is a blow to James B. Duke, who will increasingly turn his attention to bringing hydroelectric power to the Piedmont portion of the Carolinas through what becomes Duke Power Company.

MAY 29, 1942

Charlotte-born John Scott Trotter conducts the orchestra for Bing Crosby's rendition of Irving Berlin's "White Christmas." The record will sell more than 30 million copies—the best-selling single in history.

Trotter, the roly-poly son of a wholesale grocery salesman, launched his career as a pianist and arranger in fellow Charlottean Hal Kemp's band at Chapel Hill. In 1936, he left for California, where he began his long association with Crosby by scoring the movie *Pennies from Heaven*.

1893

A railroad car carrying the remains of Jefferson Davis, former president of the Confederacy, stops for several hours in Raleigh. The train is on its way from New Orleans, where Davis died four years earlier, to Richmond, his final burial site.

In Raleigh, thousands pay tribute as a horse-drawn hearse carries Davis's brass-trimmed coffin down Fayetteville Street to a memorial service at the State Capitol.

1911

The University of North Carolina presents an honorary degree to Governor Woodrow Wilson of New Jersey the year before he wins the presidency.

Although Wilson spent his freshman year at Davidson College—before transferring to Princeton—he will never receive an honorary degree from that school.

1935

America's Town Meeting of the Air, conceived and moderated by George Vernon Denny, debuts on NBC radio with the subject, "Which Way, America—Fascism, Communism, Socialism or Democracy?"

More than 3,000 listeners write to praise *America's Town Meeting*, which soon becomes a Thursday-night fixture.

Denny, born in Washington, North Carolina, and educated at the University of North Carolina, begins each program by ringing a town crier's bell and saying, "Good evening, neighbors."

1977

After more than a decade of contention among environmentalists, city officials, residents, developers, and government agencies, engineers begin blasting a wedge out of Asheville's Beaucatcher Mountain to make way for a six-lane expressway.

I-240 is designed to relieve the daily traffic jams caused when four lanes squeeze into the two-lane, half-century-old Beaucatcher Tunnel, but opponents see it as a visual and historical insult—in *Look Homeward, Angel*, Thomas Wolfe described the mountain as a barrier that hemmed him off from the world's adventures.

The completion of Beaucatcher Pass—290 feet deep, 820 feet wide at the top—will require five years and nearly 4 million pounds of explosives.

1918

The troop transport *President Lincoln*, returning from Europe with 700 aboard, is hit by a German torpedo. Although the ship sinks within 18 minutes, the death toll is only 26, thanks to the extraordinary emergency drill system put in place by commander Percy Wright Foote, a native of Roaring River in Wilkes County. To keep up his men's spirits, Foote leads them in singing "Keep the Home Fires Burning" and "Where Do We Go from Here, Boys?"

Foote will receive a special commendation

from Secretary of the Navy Josephus Daniels, but more important his emergency procedures are adopted for the entire Troop Transport Service.

1964

The San Francisco Giants and the New York Mets play the longest game in major-league history—seven hours, 23 minutes—and Gaylord Perry, a native of Williamston in Martin County, loads up his first illegal pitch. Clinging to a spot on the Giants' roster, reliever Perry hesitates only briefly before unveiling his new pitch.

"I was 25 years old, and I had spent most of my first six seasons in the minors . . . ," he recalls later. "I thought of my wife, Blanche, our very young children, and Mama and Daddy back on the farm, all counting on me. And me taking home only $9,500 a year."

Perry and the spitter combine for 10 scoreless innings, and the Giants quickly install him in their starting rotation. Next stop: the Baseball Hall of Fame.

1992

At Dover Downs in Delaware, Harry Gant of Taylorsville in Alexander County extends his record as the oldest driver ever to win a Winston Cup stock-car race. He is 52 years old.

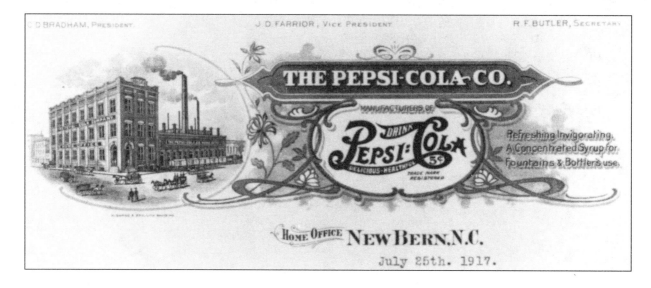

An early billhead shows
the original Pepsi-Cola plant
in New Bern [June 16].

June

Careless roofer burns down State Capitol
Revenue agents nab Junior Johnson (on foot)
Sam Ervin says he's "just an old country lawyer"

JUNE 1

1859

Concluding a tour of the state in which he has repeatedly spoken for the preservation of the Union, President James Buchanan delivers the commencement address at the University of North Carolina.

1888

George W. Vanderbilt, age 25, purchases the first of 661 parcels of land that will ultimately become his 125,000-acre Biltmore Estate. He is the youngest of the eight children of railroad tycoon William Henry Vanderbilt, reputedly the world's richest man.

1930

Undeterred by the Depression, Montaldo's moves into its new location in downtown Charlotte. In the coming years, the store will undergo extensive expansion, establishing itself as "queen" of the New York–based women's wear chain.

Founder Lillian Montaldo wants "guests" to feel at home in a "French country" house furnished with Louis XV and Louis XVI antiques, marble mantels, and plaster moldings. Well-heeled shoppers are greeted by a doorman who parks their cars and are then taken to living-room-sized dressing rooms, where the season's new fashions are laid out before them.

The North Tryon Street store closes in 1992. In 1995, the chain, now down to mall stores in Charlotte, Greensboro, and Richmond, goes bankrupt.

At one time, North Carolina accounted for five of the 10 Montaldo's stores.

1956

Federal agents staking out a 20,000-gallon moonshine still hidden in the woods of Wilkes County apprehend the owner's son after a 400-yard chase that ends at a barbed-wire fence.

"I wouldn't have been any more surprised if I had caught Gen. MacArthur," agent Joseph Carter recalls many years later. "I guess the pinnacle of my career is I'm the only person who ever caught Junior Johnson.

"But I have to say, it was on foot. There was never an agent of the law who could ever catch the great Junior Johnson in a car."

1963

The Wake County towns of Fuquay Springs, named for early settlers David and Stephen Fuquay, and Varina, named for the wife of the first local postmaster, merge into Fuquay-Varina.

The new town will prosper, but in 1978 some residents petition for a less distinctive name. "Our name needs more dignity. We need a name people can relate to," says Wake County commissioner Waverly Akins. "Is Fuquay-Varina a name we want to live with the rest of our lives?"

The movement falters, and Fuquay-Varina lives on.

JUNE 1, 1991

North Carolina enacts tougher penalties for poachers of Venus's-flytrap, a carnivorous plant that occurs naturally only within a 75-mile radius of Wilmington.

Poaching has already shrunk by half the range of the prized houseplant—described by Charles Darwin as "the most wonderful little plant in the world."

JUNE 2

1802

A cryptic message about a planned uprising is found in a Bertie County slave cabin. It triggers a widespread conspiracy panic—in Bertie County alone, 11 slaves are executed.

1913

Governor Locke Craig gives the main address as the United Daughters of the Confederacy dedicate a monument in honor of University of North Carolina students who fought for the South.

The statue will become known on campus as "Silent Sam."

JUNE 3

1933

The State, a weekly magazine touting North Carolina's industries, tourist attractions, and lifestyle, debuts in Raleigh.

Publisher Carl Goerch, a New York native who eventually becomes the state's most tireless promoter, will sell out in 1951, but the magazine continues to be published, most recently as a monthly.

1937

Author Thomas Wolfe writes from New York to his mother in Asheville,

> Yes, I suppose there are more modern and up-to-date places around Asheville with electric lights, new beds, etc. but I did not have time to look for them and I honestly thought that the Whitson cabin was . . . the best place that I saw. . . .
>
> As to your own fears of loneliness—and not liking to be alone out in the country at night—I know of no way in which you can get peace and seclusion, and not get it, at the same time. What I need desperately at the present time is to get away from the noise and tumult of New York, to get away from towns and cities and,

for a few weeks at least, to get away from too many people.

1972

Robert Harrell, "the Fort Fisher Hermit," dies on the beach at age 79.

Harrell moved to the desolate spit of land south of Wilmington in 1955. He camped in an abandoned World War II bunker, living off the land, the sea, and spare change from curious beachgoers. He let his hair and beard go uncut and typically wore only a bathing suit and a ratty straw hat.

He had a history of mental illness but talked impressively to visitors about politics, religion, and the coast. "I came here to write a book, my think-book on humanity," he once said. "I'm here for the same reason Dr. Schweitzer went to Africa. There's no difference in our goals. His was medicine and missionary work. Mine is psychology."

After his death, Harrell's body is returned to his native Shelby for burial. In 1989, however, friends and relatives will rebury him at his beloved beach. His tombstone reads, "He made people think."

1985

Fritz Klenner, his cousin Susie Newsom Lynch, and her two sons die as a Chevrolet Blazer loaded with guns, poison, and a bomb explodes on a highway outside Greensboro.

Four years later, *Bitter Blood*, Jerry Bledsoe's account of the family's far-ranging killing spree that left nine dead, will reach number one on the *New York Times* paperback bestseller list.

1835

A state convention in Raleigh modifies the 1776 constitution to balance eastern and western representation; more than half the state's 738,000 citizens now live in the west. Roman Catholics win the right to hold office, but free blacks lose the right to vote.

1929

Charlotte's new Armory Auditorium opens just in time to host the annual four-day reunion of the United Confederate Veterans.

"Sixty years ago we were beaten and prostrate . . . ," Governor O. Max Gardner tells the veterans. "Our struggle began a victory of the spirit."

The event climaxes with a parade of bands, military units, and visiting veterans in cars. The *Charlotte Observer* estimates the crowd at 150,000—"30,000 more than followed Sherman to the sea."

Afterward, 11 Confederate generals issue a statement declaring the Charlotte reunion "the best in every way of the preceding 38 reunions."

1940

Houghton Mifflin publishes Carson McCullers's first novel, *The Heart Is a Lonely Hunter*, begun in Charlotte and completed in Fayetteville.

McCullers lived in North Carolina during the late 1930s while her husband, Reeves, was working as a credit investigator. During her stay in Fayetteville, she also wrote *Reflections in a Golden Eye*.

1941

Charlotte, which has lagged behind many other Southern cities in doing away with blue laws, passes an ordinance permitting Sunday movies and outdoor sports.

1954

Duke University faculty members block a degree proposed for Vice President Richard Nixon, a Duke law-school alumnus.

For weeks, the campus has buzzed with tension and intrigue, before the nomination finally dies a polite parliamentary death.

By 1961, however, faculty feelings about Nixon's politics and ethics will have moderated, and Duke approaches him about accepting an honorary degree.

He rejects the offer.

1967

Frances Bavier wins an Emmy for her portrayal of Aunt Bee on *The Andy Griffith Show*.

Bavier, who was born in New York City, will retire from show business in 1972 and move to a two-story house in Siler City, a town she learned about from occasional mentions on the show. She lives there almost reclusively until her death in 1989 at age 86.

At an auction of her estate, two fans from Denton in Davidson County pay $20,000 for her 1966 Studebaker.

1984

Surgeons find a malignant, inoperable, pencil-sized tumor in the spine of Reynolds Price, Duke University's renowned writer and teacher.

At age 51, Price is midway through his sixth novel, *Kate Vaiden*.

Radiation treatments will leave him a paraplegic, in constant pain, restricted to a wheelchair. But Price's creativity responds mightily. In the next decade, he will complete 14 books—more than he wrote over the previous 22 years—including the 1994 memoir *A Whole New Life*.

JUNE 5

1928

Asheville hosts the first official Mountain Dance and Folk Festival.

The founder is Bascom Lamar Lunsford, popularizer of clogging and composer of "Good Old Mountain Dew." Initially, the festival, the first of its kind in the country, is part of the annual Rhododendron Festival. Later, it will claim the first weekend in August as its own.

JUNE 6

1765

Schoolmaster George Sims of Granville County, on trial for failure to pay a small debt, issues the "Nutbush Address." His attack on corruption and unfair taxation is one of the opening volleys of the rebellious Regulator movement.

1931

To mark the opening of its first Charlotte drugstore, Walgreen offers 50 customers free rides in a Sikorsky twin-engine amphibian: "See Charlotte from the air. . . . You'll get a great thrill—you'll feel supremely safe—and you'll enjoy an experience that you will talk about for months to come. . . . This is the same type plane used by the Prince of Wales on his South American trip."

1944

On the home front on D-Day, Canadian paratroop sergeant Harold Russell loses his hands when a defective fuse explodes a charge of TNT he is holding as he instructs a demolition squad at Camp Mackall, in Richmond and Scotland Counties.

Russell will learn to use prosthetic hooks. Two years after the accident, he wins an Academy Award for best supporting actor for his portrayal of a handless sailor in *The Best Years of Our Lives*. He receives a second Oscar for "bringing aid and comfort to disabled veterans through the medium of motion pictures."

As a career, however, Russell chooses public relations.

In 1992, at age 78, he will sell his acting Oscar for $60,500 to pay his wife's medical bills.

JUNE 7

1929

During a confrontation with strikers at Gastonia's Loray Mill, Police Chief O. F. Aderholt is fatally shot.

On questionable evidence, Fred Beal, a union organizer from Lawrence, Massachusetts, and six other strike leaders are found guilty of murder and sentenced to 20 years at hard labor. They skip bail and flee to Russia. After an unhappy year, Beal escapes back to the United States and begins writing against communism.

In 1938, still a fugitive, he asks the governor of Massachusetts to arrange for his extradition to North Carolina. He serves several years in state prisons before being paroled in 1942.

1930

In the state Democratic primary, United States senator Furnifold Simmons, a five-term incumbent, loses to Josiah Bailey.

Two years earlier, Simmons had come out against Democratic presidential nominee Al Smith—a "wet," a Catholic, and a New Yorker. Simmons's defection helped Herbert Hoover become the first Republican to take North Carolina since 1872, but it cost him crucial support among Democratic Party loyalists.

1944

The department store J. B. Ivey and Company takes out a full-page ad in the *Charlotte Observer* the day after the Allies' D-Day invasion of France:

> Your time has come, Mr. Shicklegruber. This Is The Knockout.
>
> Your "stars" failed you this time, Adolf. . . . And your swastika is not going to help you any more now than it did when your army came face to face with the Russians on the Eastern front.

We're on your Western front now and we mean business! We're going to run you and your foul gang out of Germany but not so you can set up your little business of trying to run the world from another city. When we've finished with this invasion, you'll be through forever!

The bombings of Berlin, Bremen, Frankfurt and Hanover don't add up to half the price you will pay for the lives you have taken and the suffering you have caused. Did you think we were going to let you get away with ruthless murder?

You should have known, Adolf, that we would catch up with you. You thought you were smarter than Mussolini. . . . Maybe you were. But you were not as wise as the United Nations. We don't expect you to take your punishment "like a man," because if you were a man you never would have started this outright slaughter.

Over many long months of blood, sweat and tears, we have painstakingly laid plans for this invasion. You, yourself, have said there can be only one victor . . . so back up against the wall, Mr. Shicklegruber, we're about to deliver the knockout blow.

Back The Invasion. . . . Buy Extra War Bonds.

JUNE 8

1945

Helen Keller, advocate of the disabled, arrives in Asheville for a five-day tour of service hospitals.

A *Citizen-Times* interviewer notes that Miss Keller's secretary and companion, Polly Thomson, "turned to her and translated the reporter's first question by touching the palm of Miss Keller's hand with the tips of her fingers and speaking at the same time. The amazingly alert brain, behind eyes that have been sightless since she was two years old and shut in by ears that have detected no sound for the same period, was like a thirsty sponge, grasping so eagerly for the question that only a few key words were necessary to carry the complete thought."

JUNE 8, 1964

Jim Hunter of Hertford in Perquimans County signs with the Kansas City A's.

Flamboyant owner Charles O. Finley, dismayed that his $75,000 "bonus baby" has no nickname, will concoct a story about Hunter's running away from home at age six and being discovered fishing. Hence, "Catfish" Hunter.

JUNE 9

1978

The North Carolina House approves local-option liquor by the drink.

The bill appeared dead earlier in the week but was revived with the help of five opponents who departed the chamber shortly before a motion to reconsider.

1861

At the Battle of Big Bethel, Henry Lawson Wyatt of Edgecombe County becomes the first Confederate soldier killed in action in the Civil War. The skirmish northwest of Newport News, Virginia, leaves 19 dead—all but Wyatt on the Union side.

After the war, the state will claim the distinction, "First at Bethel, farthest at Gettysburg, last at Appomattox." (Two North Carolina regiments headed General George Pickett's charge up Cemetery Ridge at Gettysburg, and North Carolina troops under Captain David Allen were among the last to surrender at Appomattox.)

During the war, North Carolina provides more men and loses more men—40,275—than any other state in the Confederacy. (By comparison, the Vietnam War will claim 1,596 North Carolinians.)

1880

Outfielder Charley Jones of the Boston Braves, the first North Carolina native to play in the major leagues, becomes the first player to hit two home runs in one inning.

Jones, born Benjamin Wesley Rippay in Alamance County, made his big-league debut in 1876 and will conclude his playing days in 1888.

1946

Jack Johnson, perhaps the greatest heavyweight champion of all time, is fatally injured in a car wreck 25 miles north of Raleigh.

Almost 70 years old and reduced to sideshow appearances, Johnson is en route to New York after an engagement with a small Texas circus. Notorious as a heavy-footed driver, he has always gotten by on his superb reflexes.

About 3:30 P.M., approaching Franklinton on U.S. I, he takes his Lincoln Zephyr into a gentle curve, loses control, and crashes into a power pole.

The emergency-room staff at St. Agnes Hospital in Raleigh fails to recognize him until an older doctor says, "That's Jack Johnson." Before nightfall, he dies of internal injuries.

JUNE 11

1918

Governor Thomas Bickett warns wartime slackers that "I have instructed our police officials to rigidly enforce vagrancy laws. All men . . . who refuse to work five days in the week, after having been given notice by the County Council of National Defense, should be prosecuted . . . the idle rich as well as the idle poor."

1941

Reacting to Charles Lindbergh's opposition to United States involvement in the war against Germany, Charlotte's city council changes the name of Lindbergh Drive to Avon Terrace.

A property owner had complained to the city that "judging from the man's stand in regard to his country, he does not deserve to have a street in Charlotte named for him."

1954

Sam Ervin, appointed to the United States Senate to fill the unexpired term of the late Clyde Hoey, is sworn in by Vice President Richard Nixon.

JUNE 11, 1988

Bull Durham, a romantic comedy based loosely on the local Durham Bulls minor-league baseball team, premieres at the Carolina Theater.

The producer is Durham native Thom Mount, and many scenes were shot at quaint and cramped Durham Athletic Park, built in 1939.

Bull Durham, which stars Kevin Costner and Susan Sarandon, will score big at the box office, accelerating the nation's rediscovery of minor-league baseball. One negative effect: the Bulls become such a hot ticket that in 1995 they desert Durham Athletic Park for a new stadium with more seats.

JUNE 12

1868

Fred G. Roberts of Edenton writes President Andrew Johnson,

Permit me, a North Carolinian to the manor born, to congratulate you & the whole Country upon your triumph over the impeaching Committee in particular & the Republican party in general.

The character of your family must be beyond reproach or the Keen Scented Butler [Republican representative Benjamin Butler of Massachusetts] with his unscrupulous followers, would not have hesitated to bring the most trivial offence to light, that you might become the but & ridicule of the Country. . . .

I feel proud that you was born in the old North State—that you are not ashamed of it, that you do not shrink from proclaiming to the world you are a working man.

Johnson has just survived his impeachment trial in the Senate, as radical Republicans fell one vote short of the necessary two-thirds majority. The tally: 35 for conviction, 19 for acquittal.

1875

Harper's Weekly, reporting on the recent centennial celebration of the Mecklenburg Declaration of Independence, speaks favorably of "an enterprise that will in time make Charlotte a centre of considerable trade and manufacture."

It adds, however, that "a grand cock-fight between North Carolina and South Carolina birds . . . might better have been omitted from the programme."

JUNE 13

1903

A. J. Tomlinson, a preacher and book salesman for the American Bible Society, climbs to the top of a mountain near Murphy in Cherokee County. In prayer, he envisions the Church of God of Prophecy, a Pentecostal denomination.

The church that grows from Tomlinson's vision will one day count more than 72,000 members in the United States and congregations in some 60 countries worldwide.

In 1943, the church builds a biblical theme park on the site. Among its attractions: a carving of the Ten Commandments that covers an entire mountainside, a reproduction of Christ's tomb, and Tomlinson's revered "Place of Prayer."

1972

In one of the most memorable phrases of the Watergate hearings, Senator Sam Ervin of North Carolina refers to himself as "just an old country lawyer."

Senator Edward Gurney, a Florida Republican, has accused Democrat Ervin of harassment in his persistent questioning of Maurice Stans, chief fund-raiser for President Nixon's reelection campaign.

"I'm just an old country lawyer," Ervin replies. "I have to do things my way."

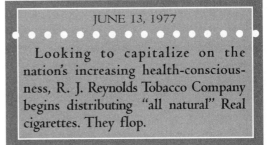

JUNE 13, 1977

Looking to capitalize on the nation's increasing health-consciousness, R. J. Reynolds Tobacco Company begins distributing "all natural" Real cigarettes. They flop.

1995

Eighty-four-year-old Mother Teresa, winner of the Nobel Peace Prize, visits Charlotte. She opens a four-nun convent to serve the poor, then holds a service at the Charlotte Coliseum.

JUNE 14

1787

On a site in the future city of Asheville, James M. Smith becomes the first child of European descent born in North Carolina west of the Blue Ridge Mountains.

1897

President William McKinley, en route to Washington by train, arrives in Asheville for an overnight stay at Biltmore House.

George W. Vanderbilt is out of the country and has left E. J. Harding in charge. Harding precipitates a minor flap by briefly refusing entrance to the White House press. "Mr. Vanderbilt does not like newspaper notoriety," he explains, "and neither do I."

1961

Carl Sandburg, in Beverly Hills, writes his biographer, Harry Golden, in Charlotte, "Your book is going to be a nice hayride. I am ready anytime to read proofs or to welcome your good face out here. I am not sure I understand it, but long ago I met some mathematician saying, 'Make the sign of infinity and pass on.'"

1964

Charlottean Walter Maxwell, fishing off a pier at Cherry Grove, South Carolina, lands a 1,780-pound tiger shark—still a world record.

1965

Surgeons achieve the nation's first successful reattachment of a severed hand.

Robert Pennell, a 26-year-old prisoner from Hickory, was clearing highway right of way in Surry County when he stepped into a hole and lost his balance. Trying to right himself, he reached for a fallen oak—and into the path of another prisoner's bush ax. Pennell was taken to a Mount Airy hospital, where doctors sent back for the detached left hand, put it in a bucket of ice, and rushed it and Pennell to Winston-Salem. At North Carolina Baptist Hospital, a team led by Dr. Jesse Meredith worked for eight hours reconnecting bones, arteries, veins, tendons, and nerves.

After months of painful physical therapy, Pennell, serving time for burglary, will be paroled. Less than a year and a half after the reattachment, he is injured in a car wreck. Again he is taken to Baptist Hospital, but this time there is no miracle. He dies on Thanksgiving Day 1966.

JUNE 15

1940

The New Yorker begins an unprecedented six-part series in which Charlotte-born St. Clair McKelway painstakingly demonstrates that fully half the items in Walter Winchell's gossip column are false.

Furious, Winchell responds by having editor Harold Ross barred from the Stork Club.

McKelway, *The New Yorker*'s first managing editor, will spend 47 years at the magazine. "He lived his life in a dream," *The New Yorker* notes in its 1980 obituary, "but it was, on the whole, a benevolent dream. . . . He seemed constantly on the way to his club."

1959

In one of the state's most violent labor disputes, three Textile Workers Union officials and five union members are indicted for conspiracy to dynamite a Carolina Power and Light substation and to destroy two mill buildings.

Boyd Payton, the union's Southern director, had gone to the town of Henderson in Vance County to assist in negotiations at Harriet-Henderson Mills. After the entire work force walked out, the company used strikebreakers to reopen. In the next month, 16 bombings were reported, more than 150 arrests were made, and Payton himself was assaulted. Governor Luther Hodges, who called out the North Carolina Highway Patrol and the National Guard to protect the strikebreakers, unsuccessfully tried to mediate the dispute, which he later describes as "a blot" on the state "in which just about everyone was at fault."

The government's conspiracy case rests almost entirely on testimony from a paid informant of the State Bureau of Investigation, but the jury brings in a guilty verdict.

In 1961, after hearing pleas from such diverse figures as Billy Graham and Harry Golden, Governor Terry Sanford will reduce the sentences of the eight defendants. In 1964, on his last day in office, he pardons Payton.

1970

The Land of Oz, a theme park based on *The Wizard of Oz*, opens atop Beech Mountain.

The park, conceived by Charlotte artist Jack Pentes, proves too low-tech, too small, and too remote—and the weather is often dreary. Attendance is 250,000 the first year but only 60,000 in 1980, when the park closes.

A residential development will eventually supplant the abandoned Oz; artifacts such as the Yellow Brick Road wind up in Boone's Appalachian Cultural Museum.

1981

Doug Marlette's "Kudzu" debuts.

Marlette, the *Charlotte Observer*'s editorial cartoonist, sets his comic strip in Bypass, North Carolina. Key players: Kudzu Dubose, Mama Dubose, Veranda, Uncle Dub, Maurice, Nasal T. Lardbottom, and the Reverend Will B. Dunn, who bears considerable resemblance to Nashville preacher Will Campbell.

In 1988, Marlette will win a Pulitzer Prize for his editorial cartoons.

1986

Raymond Floyd of Fayetteville shoots a final-round 66 to win the U.S. Open at Shinnecock Hills Golf Club in Southampton, New York. Floyd, 43, is the oldest U.S. Open champion ever.

He also won the Masters in 1976 and the PGA in 1969 and 1982.

JUNE 16, 1903

The United States Patent Office registers "Pepsi-Cola" as the trademark for a beverage concocted by Caleb Bradham at the soda fountain of his New Bern drugstore.

By 1911, Bradham will have franchised some 300 bottlers in 24 states. But World War I causes disastrous fluctuations in the sugar market, and in 1922, he is forced into bankruptcy.

The Pepsi-Cola formula and trademark survive, but Bradham receives no benefit. Back at his drugstore, he fills prescriptions until his death in 1934 at age 67.

JUNE 17

1864

General Gabriel Rains of New Bern, whose use of land mines to stymie pursuing Union forces has created outrage in the North, is appointed chief of the Confederacy's newly created Torpedo Bureau. Under his supervision, a variety of "torpedoes"—explosive devices he has patterned after a design by Samuel Colt—will be manufactured at Richmond, Wilmington, Mobile, Charleston, and Savannah.

Confederate naval mines will sink about 58 Union vessels; some 1,300 land mines will be buried in the defense of Richmond; and two of Rains's agents will detonate a bomb at the wharves of Ulysses S. Grant's supply base at City Point, Virginia, causing numerous casualties and $4 million in damages.

1986

Singer Kate Smith, 79, dies of respiratory failure in Raleigh.

Smith, known since the 1930s for her rousing rendition of "God Bless America," moved to Raleigh in 1979 to be near her sister and two nieces.

Because of a dispute between executors and cemetery over the size of her mausoleum, nearly 18 months will pass before her burial in Lake Placid, New York, her longtime summer home.

Inscribed in pink granite: "This is Kate Smith. This is America."

JUNE 18

1840

Lamenting that his congregation has succumbed to such vices as dancing, whist games, the theater, circuses, parties, and clothing adorned with satin, lace, ribbons, and feathers, George Washington Freeman resigns as rector of Christ Episcopal Church in Raleigh. "A new spirit has arisen," he notes, "and the Pastor and his flock are no longer of one mind."

1907

University of North Carolina professor Archibald Henderson arrives in England to meet George Bernard Shaw, whose biography he is writing. Aboard ship, Henderson has struck up a friendship with Mark Twain, who is en route to Oxford to accept an honorary degree.

For a moment, Henderson will recall, he glimpses a rare opportunity: "There was the world's greatest wit and the world's greatest humorist, meeting face to face." Alas, "nobody said anything funny. . . . They stood there and lied to each other. Each man told the other that they had read everything the other had written, that they were greatly influenced by the other's writing. . . . It was the greatest disappointment in my life."

Henderson, a Salisbury native, will write three biographies of Shaw—and one of Mark Twain. Although his primary field of scholarship is mathematics, Henderson's interests stretch from history to literature to physics. He writes extensively about the theory of relativity proposed by his friend Albert Einstein.

JUNE 19

1771

Six Regulators taken prisoner by Royal Governor William Tryon's militia are hanged in Hillsborough. Among them is Benjamin Merrill, who was sentenced at court-martial to be hanged, disemboweled, decapitated, and drawn and quartered. No evidence survives, however, that he suffered anything more than hanging.

1939

Governor Clyde Hoey dedicates the state's ex-

hibit at the New York World's Fair with a speech claiming that "everyone in North Carolina lives long and well and has a good time."

JUNE 19, 1949

The infant National Association for Stock Car Auto Racing—future sports giant NASCAR—holds its first major event, at New Charlotte Speedway, a half-mile dirt track.

Jim Roper, who drove his 1949 Lincoln from Kansas to Charlotte, finishes in second place, three laps behind, but an inspection of the first-place Ford finds that the rear springs have been illegally altered. The $2,000 winner's purse goes to Roper, and the disqualified driver unsuccessfully sues NASCAR.

1959

The first unit of a UNIVAC 1105 computer—a 19-ton behemoth foreshadowing the era of laptops and the Internet—arrives at the University of North Carolina. Its first task: tabulating the 1960 census.

1995

In the biggest United States bank merger ever, First Union Corporation pays $5.4 billion for First Fidelity Bancorporation of New Jersey.

The deal makes First Union the nation's sixth-largest bank and Charlotte—also home to number-four NationsBank—the nation's largest banking center except for New York City and, arguably, San Francisco.

JUNE 20

1960

Less than a year after losing his title to Ingemar Johansson, Floyd Patterson knocks out Johansson in the fifth round in New York. Patterson, born in Waco in Cleveland County, becomes the first heavyweight champion ever to regain his title. He first won the title in 1956, knocking out Archie Moore in the fifth round in Chicago.

In 1962, Patterson will lose the title for good, in a first-round knockout at the hands of Sonny Liston.

1984

Michael Jordan of the University of North Carolina is chosen third in the National Basketball Association draft, behind Akeem Olajuwon and Sam Bowie. Rod Thorn, general manager of the Chicago Bulls, warns fans that "Jordan isn't going to turn this franchise around."

1831

In Raleigh, a workman who goes to breakfast in the midst of soldering leaks in the zinc roof accidentally burns down the State Capitol.

Backers of Fayetteville, a larger town with livelier commerce, will lobby unsuccessfully to have the capital relocated there.

1913

Georgia "Tiny" Broadwick, a native of Henderson in Vance County, becomes the first woman to parachute out of an airplane, jumping from a biplane over Griffith Park in Los Angeles.

Broadwick's interest in aircraft began in 1908, when a carnival with a hot-air balloonist played the state fair in Raleigh. She was 15, already a mother and widow, accustomed to working 12-hour days in a cotton mill. "When I saw that balloon go up . . . ," she later recalls, "I knew I would never be the same."

JUNE 22

1776

Four men believed to be army deserters terrorize the Moravian village of Salem. Arguing over their tavern bill, they strike a Moravian with a gun barrel and threaten to kill everyone on the premises.

They are eventually subdued, tried, and sent to the prison in Salisbury, but the incident persuades the peaceful Moravian men "to keep a good club within reach."

1892

Entrepreneur John Blue, seeking a way to get his timber and turpentine to market, begins his own railroad and names it after two communities on the line—the Aberdeen & Rockfish.

A century later, the A & R, still family-owned, operates eight locomotives and 72 miles of track in southeastern North Carolina and northeastern South Carolina.

JUNE 23

1917

Boston Red Sox pitcher Babe Ruth, not yet a famous outfielder, walks the Washington Senators' leadoff batter and is ejected from the game for arguing with the umpire. Ernie Shore, a native of East Bend in Yadkin County and a graduate of Guilford College, comes on in relief. The base runner is thrown out attempting to steal, and Shore retires the next 26 batters in order.

After considerable debate, baseball officials credit Shore, who later in life will become sheriff of Forsyth County, with a rare perfect game.

1970

Tom McMillen of Mansfield, Pennsylvania, billed on the cover of *Sports Illustrated* as "The Best High School Player in America," notifies coach Dean Smith that he will play basketball for the University of North Carolina.

His family is unhappy with his choice, however, and two months later, the six-foot-11 McMillen changes his mind and enrolls at the University of Maryland.

He will become an All-American at Maryland and play 11 seasons in the NBA before winning election to Congress as a Maryland Democrat.

JUNE 24

JUNE 24, 1749

In New Bern, James Davis begins operation of the first printing press in North Carolina.

Provincial officials, embarrassed by frequent errors in their hand-copied laws, had offered Davis a five-year contract to move to New Bern from Williamsburg, Virginia.

Two years later, the colony's first newspaper, the *North Carolina Gazette*, will come off Davis's press.

1950

In one of the state's watershed political events, United States senator Frank Porter Graham loses the Democratic primary runoff to Raleigh lawyer Willis Smith.

Governor Kerr Scott had appointed Graham, president of the University of North Carolina, to succeed the late senator J. Melville Broughton. To keep that seat, Graham, a liberal academician, entered his first political race. He easily led the primary but failed to win a majority. In the runoff campaign, Graham was depicted as a "race mixer" and communist sympathizer; on principle, he refused to counterattack.

Smith wins by almost 20,000 votes.

JUNE 25

1824

In an ad in *The Star* of Raleigh, tailor James J. Selby offers a $10 reward for the return of two apprentices:

> *Ran away* from the Subscriber, on the night of the 15th instant, two apprentice boys, legally bound, named *William* and *Andrew Johnson*. The former is of a dark complexion, black hair, eyes, and habits. They are much of a height, about 5 feet 4 or 5 inches. The latter is very fleshy, freckled face, light hair, and fair complexion. . . . They were well clad—blue cloth coats, light colored homespun coats, and new hats, the maker's name in the crown of the hats, is Theodore Clark. I will pay the above reward to any person who will deliver said apprentices to me in Raleigh, or I will give the above Reward for Andrew Johnson alone.
>
> All persons are cautioned against harboring or employing said apprentices, on pain of being prosecuted.

In 1865, Andrew Johnson will succeed the assassinated Abraham Lincoln as president of the United States.

1885

Woodrow Wilson and the former Ellen Louise Axson, married the previous day in Savannah, Georgia, arrive at their honeymoon cottage in Arden.

They will spend about two months in the four-room clapboard house while he prepares to begin his teaching career as a professor of history at Bryn Mawr College. She compiles the index for a new edition of his acclaimed *Congressional Government, a Study in American Politics.* They read and take long walks through the rhododendron-crowded mountains.

1983

Deneen Zezell Graham, a 19-year-old dancer from North Wilkesboro, becomes the first black Miss North Carolina.

JUNE 26

JUNE 26, 1913

High Point, hub of the state's furniture industry, hosts its first semiannual market. Exhibitors cover 30,000 square feet in eight buildings.

By 1921, the market has its own 249,000-square-foot facility.

By the 1990s, the Southern Furniture Market will become the International Home Furnishings Market—the world's largest furniture trade show—and take up more than 7 million square feet in more than 150 buildings in High Point and nearby Thomasville.

1956

Elvis Presley, 18 years old and only days away from his epochal appearances on the Tommy Dorsey and Ed Sullivan TV shows, performs at Charlotte's Carolina Theater with Mother Maybelle and the Carter Sisters.

JUNE 27

1857

Dr. Elisha Mitchell falls to his death from a 40-foot waterfall while scaling Black Mountain in the Blue Ridge.

In 1835, 1838, and 1844, Mitchell, a Presbyterian minister and University of North Carolina math professor, measured the mountain and declared it the highest point in the United States east of the Rocky Mountains.

In 1855, however, Senator Thomas Clingman claimed Mitchell had erred. Stung, the 63-year-old Mitchell returned to the mountain to justify his measurements.

In 1882, the United States Geological Survey will uphold Mitchell's measurement and officially rename the peak Mount Mitchell, as it has been known locally since the 1840s.

Mitchell is buried atop the mountain he died on.

1905

With the Giants leading the Dodgers 11–1 in the eighth inning at the Polo Grounds, New York manager John McGraw substitutes Fayetteville native Archie "Moonlight" Graham in right field for the half-inning that will constitute Graham's entire major-league career—but lead to posthumous fame.

The Giants go on to the pennant, and Graham, who was 29 before a hot spring training gave him his brief moment in the big leagues, goes on to medical school and a long career as a small-town doctor in Chishom, Minnesota.

Graham, older brother of academician Frank Porter Graham, dies in 1972 at the age of 92.

A decade later, a character based on him will play a central role in Ray Kinsella's novel *Shoeless Joe*, later made into the movie *Field of Dreams*.

JUNE 28

1969

Spiveys Corner, a community in Sampson County, hosts the first National Hollerin' Contest.

1989

Richard Nixon, driven from office 15 years earlier by the Watergate scandal, addresses a fund-raiser for Governor Jim Martin at Winston-Salem's Benton Convention Center. It is the 76-year-old Nixon's final appearance in North Carolina, a state that twice gave him its presidential electoral votes.

"When I was in Washington, D.C., a couple days ago, I saw one of my friends in the press," he tells the crowd of 300 campaign contributors. "The other one was out of town."

JUNE 29

1986

United States senator John East, plagued by depression and illness, is found dead in the garage of his Greenville home, the victim of self-inflicted carbon monoxide poisoning.

JUNE 30

1665

After the Lords Proprietors complain that their original charter failed to include the already-settled Virginia frontier, Charles II amends the charter to extend Carolina's northern border to the modern-day Virginia line.

More important to international relations, however, Carolina's southern boundary now stretches well past the Spanish town of St. Augustine, Florida. Thus, England warns Spain of its intent to dominate North America.

1939

Because voters have rejected a tax levy for its support, the Charlotte Public Library closes its doors.

Less than a year later, another election will be held, and the library tax passes by a five-to-one margin.

1945

Seeking to meet, in the words of his sister, "more normal, run of the mill Americans," New Yorker Allard Lowenstein arrives at the University of North Carolina. Presaging his future as a liberal activist, the 16-year-old Lowenstein immediately becomes embroiled in an all-night dormitory bull session about political philosophy.

He will become a campus leader, then a civil rights leader, and finally a leader against the Vietnam War; it is his long-shot peace campaign that eventually forces Lyndon Johnson to step aside as president in 1968.

1957

A coal-burning narrow-gauge engine that once hauled iron ore from an Avery County mine to a Tennessee smelter returns from retirement as the centerpiece of a Blowing Rock amusement park.

The East Tennessee & Western North Carolina Railroad began doing business in the late 1800s. Locals dubbed the E.T. & W.N.C. the "Eat Taters and Wear No Clothes" railroad, then the "Tweetsie," after the "tweet-tweet" of its whistle.

After competition from trucking shut down the line in 1950, actor Gene Autry purchased engine No. 12 for an attraction that never materialized. Autry then sold it to entrepreneur Grover Robbins, Jr., who laid three miles of track around Roundhouse Mountain and brought Tweetsie back home in a 50-mile motorcade that shut down whole towns along the way.

Tweetsie Railroad will prove to be a popular and financial success for many decades, helping to finance such real-estate developments as Hound Ears and Beech Mountain.

1960

Desperate to survive in a market dominated by Wachovia Bank of Winston-Salem, Charlotte's American Commercial Bank merges with Greensboro's Security National Bank to form North Carolina National Bank.

Because Wachovia has locked up blue-chip corporate borrowers and Charlotte rival First Union National Bank is emphasizing consumer loans, NCNB chooses to target medium-sized businesses.

That strategy—and a rapid series of acquisitions in the 1980s and 1990s—will lead to the creation of NationsBank in 1991.

1990

Despite pro wrestling's longstanding regional popularity, a *Charlotte Observer* poll finds that only 1 percent of North Carolinians say they believe what goes on in the ring is "very real." Another 21 percent, however, consider it "somewhat real." The majority, 72 percent, say it is "not at all real."

The North Carolina Highway Patrol [July 2]
is commissioned in a ceremony at the Capitol.

July

Carry Nation sees Salisbury as a "hell hole"
Headline writer invents "Dixiecrats"
Morehead City swimmer killed by shark

1823

Alfred Mordecai of Warrenton, one of the army's first Jewish career officers, graduates first in his class at West Point.

Mordecai will become an internationally known expert on gunpowder, but when the Civil War breaks out, he resigns his commission and retires to private life rather than contribute to the war against his Southern kin.

1898

Lieutenant William Shipp, born in Asheville and reared in Lincolnton and Charlotte, dies while leading his troops up San Juan Hill during the Spanish-American War.

"It was Shipp who brought me word to advance with my regiment," Colonel Theodore Roosevelt will recall. "He had been riding to and fro with absolute coolness and fearlessness, paying no more heed of bullets than if they were hail stones."

Charlotte later erects a monument to honor Shipp—who in 1883 became the first Southerner to graduate from West Point since the Civil War—and to commemorate the military reinstatement of the Southern states after the war.

JULY 1, 1913

William Jennings Bryan delivers the opening address at the Grove Park Inn in Asheville. In future years, the inn's guests will include half a dozen presidents. F. Scott Fitzgerald writes there, as does Béla Bartók, who characterizes his Concerto No. 3 for Piano and Orchestra as "a monument to the birds of North Carolina."

1914

As Woodrow Wilson's secretary of the navy, former Raleigh newspaper editor Josephus Daniels bans alcohol at officers' mess aboard United States ships.

The ban will go unbroken until 1980, when crew members of the aircraft carrier *Nimitz* are issued two beers apiece in recognition of their having been at sea for more than 100 days.

Daniels's other innovations meet more resistance.

To facilitate the training of recruits, he orders the terms *port* and *starboard* replaced with *left* and *right*. He has to abandon that effort, as well as one to make sailors wear pajamas.

In 1915, he halts the navy's issuance of condoms, saying, "The use of this packet I believe to be immoral." One result is that the navy suffers the highest incidence of venereal disease among the services. The onset of World War I causes Daniels to reluctantly give in; he leaves on an inspection trip, allowing his assistant— the young Franklin D. Roosevelt—to reverse the order.

The war gives Daniels leverage to clean up red-light districts that have fed off sailors. The most famous of these is Storyville in New Orleans, where the mayor argues strenuously, though futilely, for "the God-given right of men to be men." By making Storyville's brothels off-limits, Daniels removes the economic base of early jazz musicians, scattering them to Chicago, Kansas City, and St. Louis—and earning himself the wry title, "the Johnny Appleseed of Jazz."

Daniels will look back proudly on his cleanup effort: "It gave America the soberest, cleanest and healthiest fighting men the world has known."

1941

Just five months after the publication of his groundbreaking book, *The Mind of the South*, W. J. Cash hangs himself with a necktie in his Mexico City hotel room.

Cash, 41 years old, suffered from alcoholism and depression; in Mexico City, where he had gone to write a novel, he came to believe he was being pursued by Nazi assassins.

The Mind of the South, completed while Cash was an editorial writer for the *Charlotte News*, will remain a classic study of class, religion, and politics.

1992

State senator Joe Johnson of Wake County, pulled over by Raleigh police for not wearing a seat belt while driving to a lobbyists' reception, cites a 1787 law protecting legislators "except in cases of crime, from all arrest and imprisonment during the time of their going to, coming from, or attending the General Assembly."

Johnson will persuade the district attorney to drop the citation, but two weeks later, he gives in to public protest by paying the $25 fine and apologizing for having demanded that two police officers be fired.

The legislature, embarrassed, will rewrite the law to clarify that it does not apply to infractions such as seat-belt violations and expired inspection stickers.

1995

Robert Weston Smith—known to the world as disc jockey Wolfman Jack—dies of a heart attack at his home in Belvidere at age 57. He had moved to the Perquimans County town, his wife's birthplace, six years earlier.

Wolfman Jack had just completed a 20-day book tour promoting *Have Mercy! Confessions of the Original Rock 'N' Roll Animal*. His career stretched back to the 1950s, but it was an appearance as himself in the 1973 movie *American Graffiti* that cemented his status as a pop-culture icon.

1929

Only a day old, the North Carolina Highway Patrol suffers its first fatality: G. I. Thompson, stationed in Marion, dies when his motorcycle collides with a truck.

The highway patrol will begin switching to cars in 1935; the last motorcycle is gone by 1939.

1935

A detachment of 243 Civilian Conservation Corps workers arrives in Stokes County to build Hanging Rock State Park.

In North Carolina, the CCC, a New Deal program, mainly preserves forests and prevents soil erosion, but it also jump-starts the state's slow-developing parks system.

At Hanging Rock, workers live first in tents, then create an army-style community of barracks, mess hall, infirmary, and PX. They build a mile-long access road, two dams to impound a 12-acre lake, a sand beach, 200 miles of hiking trails, and a stone-and-timber bathhouse that can accommodate up to 1,000 swimmers.

1939

Ted McElroy, competing in a tournament in Asheville, sets a world record for receiving Morse code: 75.2 words per minute.

1967

The nation's first year-round Outward Bound school opens in Morganton.

North Carolina Outward Bound was originally envisioned as a sea school, probably to be located on the Outer Banks, but high land and equipment costs drove it inland.

At first, the school accepts only 16- to 25-year-old men. Gradually, however, it becomes all-inclusive. By its 25th anniversary, it will have graduated some 30,000 students.

JULY 3

1929

A monument to North Carolina's Civil War dead, created by sculptor Gutzon Borglum, is dedicated at the Gettysburg battlefield. The project is a brief sideline for Borglum, who is less than two years into his consuming masterwork: Mount Rushmore.

In 1925, Borglum had proposed carving a memorial to Confederate heroes Robert E. Lee, Jefferson Davis, and Stonewall Jackson on the cliffs at Chimney Rock above Lake Lure. Estranged from the sponsors of a similar memorial already begun at Stone Mountain, Georgia, Borglum was scouting for a new site and patron.

The Lake Lure idea didn't pan out, however, and the Stone Mountain project, finally completed in 1969, went on without him.

1966

Iron Station native Tony Cloninger, pitching for the visiting Atlanta Braves against the San Francisco Giants, hits two grand-slam home runs in a single game. No other National League hitter—much less another pitcher—has ever accomplished this.

JULY 4

1783

Except for Salem's Moravian community, North Carolinians ignore Governor Andrew Martin's call for the first statewide observance of the Fourth of July.

The Moravians, committed to a celebration "as impressive as our circumstances allow," listen to a sermon in the morning, sing in early afternoon, march in late afternoon, and ring bells and illuminate their houses at night.

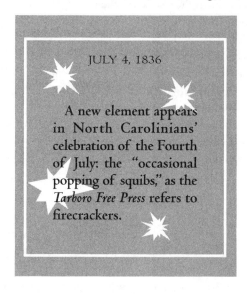

JULY 4, 1836

A new element appears in North Carolinians' celebration of the Fourth of July: the "occasional popping of squibs," as the *Tarboro Free Press* refers to firecrackers.

1863

Union cavalry troops destroy a Kenansville factory that makes bowie knives, bayonets, and other small weapons for the Confederacy.

1868

The Republican-controlled North Carolina General Assembly ratifies the 14th Amendment,

effectively returning the state to the Union. The amendment, passed by Congress in 1866 when no Southern states were represented, grants full citizenship to blacks and denies public office to anyone who participated in secession after taking an oath to uphold the Constitution.

1876

The United States celebrates its centennial with a grand exposition in Philadelphia, but some Southerners have yet to reconcile with the Union. As passengers wait at the Concord depot to board a train to Philadelphia, diehard Confederates assault them with rocks.

1889

Chatham County farm boy Clarence Poe, age 18, becomes editor of the *Progressive Farmer*, a struggling eight-page weekly in Raleigh.

In an era when Southern agriculture still pays more heed to phases of the moon than to science, Poe, who never finished high school, almost single-handedly popularizes "book farming." The *Progressive Farmer* will grow to a circulation of nearly 1.5 million; at one time, it runs more advertising than any other monthly magazine in the nation. Poe battles not only hookworm, cattle ticks, and hog cholera but also child labor, usury, and lynching.

He remains actively involved with the publication until suffering a fatal stroke in 1964 at age 83.

The decline of the small farm will gradually undercut the circulation and influence of the *Progressive Farmer*—in contrast to its extraordinarily prosperous 1966 offshoot, *Southern Living* magazine.

1907

Carry Nation, billed as "an extra added attraction," appears in Salisbury's Fourth of July parade. After inspecting local saloons—at 61, she no longer busts them up—she declares the town a "hell hole."

Nation's month-long tour of the state will conclude in Raleigh. Raleigh Electric Company, whose streetcars clear a nice sum ferrying her supporters to and from Pullen Park, pays her $35, and she makes an additional $25 from the sale of souvenir cardboard and pewter hatchets.

JULY 4, 1937

Paul Green's *The Lost Colony*, the nation's first outdoor drama, debuts at Fort Raleigh on Roanoke Island. Fifty years later, North Carolina alone will support 10 ongoing outdoor dramas, from *Horn in the West* in Boone to *Strike at the Wind* in Pembroke.

1955

The Soupy Sales Show, first aired as *Soupy's On* on a Detroit station, makes its network debut on ABC.

Sales was born Milton Supman in Franklinton, where his parents ran a dry-goods

store. He joined the navy, earned a journalism degree from Marshall College in West Virginia, and worked as a disc jockey before finding fame catching pies in the face and dodging paw swats from White Fang, "the biggest and meanest dog in the United States."

1984

As Ronald Reagan looks on—the first sitting president to watch an auto race—Randolph County's Richard Petty outduels Cale Yarborough to win the Firecracker 400 at Daytona International Speedway. The victory is the 200th of Petty's career, and, though he races eight more years, it turns out to be his last. His winning Pontiac goes to the Smithsonian Institution.

1991

NCNB's Hugh McColl, Jr., and C & S/Sovran's Bennett Brown, negotiating a merger that will create the nation's fourth-largest bank, use clamshells to rough out an organizational chart in the sand at Litchfield Beach, South Carolina.

NationsBank, headquartered in Charlotte, is announced 18 days later.

JULY 5

1836

New York newspaperman Horace Greeley marries Mary Cheney in Warrenton, where she teaches at a girls' academy.

Greeley is the publisher of a weekly literary paper but will later found the *New York Tribune*, play a key role in the antislavery movement, and popularize a piece of advice given to unemployed New Yorkers: "Go west, young man."

1917

General Leonard Wood visits Charlotte to inspect possible sites for a World War I training camp.

The result will be Camp Greene, built on 2,500 acres and named for Revolutionary War hero Nathanael Greene. Though the camp trains soldiers for less than two years, it rouses Charlotte's economy and hastens its rise from small-town obscurity.

1932

In the waning hours of a party at his family's Reynolda House estate in Winston-Salem, tobacco heir Z. Smith Reynolds, age 20, is fatally shot in the head with one of his own handguns.

Police charge his wife of seven months, onetime torch singer Libby Holman, and his best friend, Ab Walker. Holman claims Reynolds shot himself out of "despondency."

The case attracts national attention, but the district attorney drops the charges because of insufficient evidence, and Reynolds's death is ruled a suicide.

Holman, 26, is pregnant at the time of the shooting. She gives birth to a son, Christopher Reynolds, then returns to Broadway. Because of her notoriety, however, she never regains her popularity.

After bitter litigation, Holman is awarded

$750,000 from Smith Reynolds's estate; her son receives a trust fund of $6.7 million.

In 1936, Smith Reynolds's two sisters and brother form the Z. Smith Reynolds Foundation, which becomes a major philanthropic force in the state.

Over the years, the Reynolds-Holman case will inspire several books and movies, including the 1935 comedy *Reckless*, starring Jean Harlow.

In 1971, at age 65, Holman commits suicide at her home in Stamford, Connecticut.

1957

Althea Gibson becomes the first black player to win the most prestigious event in women's tennis—the singles at Wimbledon.

Born in Silver, South Carolina, but reared in Harlem, Gibson moved to Wilmington in 1946 to live with Dr. Hubert Eaton, a black physician and amateur tennis player who had spotted her potential and didn't want to see it wasted. Gibson, a 19-year-old high-school dropout, enrolled at Williston High School, played saxophone in the band, and refined her tennis game on Eaton's backyard court.

"Living in Dr. Eaton's house," she will recall in her 1958 autobiography, "I gradually learned how to obey rules and get along with people. It was the first real family life I had ever known."

JULY 6

1977

Bojangles', a 600-square-foot fast-food restaurant that will grow into a regional chain, opens in Charlotte. The menu features fried chicken, dirty rice, and pinto beans, but a year will pass before its renowned biscuits replace dinner rolls.

JULY 7

1863

Private D. L. Day, Company B, 25th Massachusetts Volunteer Infantry, writes in his diary at Hill's Point, overlooking the Pamlico River, "Today a sergeant, corporal and eight privates from each company have been detailed to manipulate the big guns. I had the honor of being selected from my company, and was assigned the left gun, a most dangerous and hazardous position. I feel proud of my promotion and am sure I shall sustain the honor of the artillery service."

JULY 8

1933

Two semipro teams square off at Wearn Field in what is billed as Charlotte's first official interracial baseball game.

The *Charlotte News* will report that Highland Park, a white mill team, beat the North Charlotte Black Yankees 11–10; the *Charlotte Observer* has the Black Yankees winning 10–7.

1972

"The Happiest Girl in the Whole U.S.A." by Donna Fargo debuts on *Billboard*'s top-40 chart.

The upbeat country tune will peak at number 11; six months later, Fargo's song "Funny Face" reaches number five, but her recording career soon stalls.

Fargo was born Yvonne Vaughan in Mount Airy in 1949.

1951

Twenty-three Charlotte debutantes, "looking as gracious as any ante-bellum belles," appear on the cover of *Life* magazine.

Inside, *Life* devotes a four-page spread to Charlotte's recent challenge to "the social supremacy" of Raleigh:

> For many a decade an old social tradition has plagued North Carolina's country belles: the only affair that would surely stamp them debutantes was Raleigh's big Terpsichorean Ball. Once every year young ladies all over the state would keep a wistful eye on the mails for Raleigh's cherished invitation. Then, hearts aflutter, a few of them would set out for the capital and twirl around for a while in white-gloved elegance at the one dance that really counted.
>
> But others thought it unfair that Raleigh should set itself up to be the social arbiter of the state. So last year the ladies of Charlotte decided to throw off the yoke. Charlotte, they reasoned, was bigger, richer and nicer than Raleigh, and should have a say of its own. They seceded from Raleigh society and announced their plans for the Charlotte Debutante Ball.
>
> This June the ball's second staging proved Charlotte was ready to give the Terpsichorean a real race for prestige. Charlotte's debutantes . . . were every bit as dainty and decollete [as

Raleigh's], Charlotte's young men were just as gracious.

1863

Private D. L. Day, Company B, 25th Massachusetts Volunteer Infantry, writes in his diary at Hill's Point, overlooking the Pamlico River,

> This being an isolated post and several miles from any commissary or sutler, the officers feared it would be terribly infected with malaria; having regard for the health and welfare of the men, they prevailed on our assistant surgeon, Doctor Flagg, to order whiskey rations. Up went the order and down came the whiskey, and now the order is to drink no more river water, but take a little whiskey as a preventive. . . .
>
> When I wish to reward any of my braves for gallant and meritorious conduct, I manage to slop a little extra into their cups. That keeps them vigilant and interested and gallant. Meritorious conduct consists of bringing in watermelons, peaches and other subsistence, of which they somehow become possessed.

1942

Alice Broughton, wife of the governor, orders a rubber mat ripped off the servants' staircase in the Executive Mansion. It is to be donated to the war effort.

Accompanied by a reporter and a photographer from the *Raleigh Times*, she then delivers the 58-pound mat to a nearby service station to be recycled. "Either the attendants never heard of the drive," the *Times* reports, "or they didn't care whether the nation got the rubber as a means of whipping the Axis. . . .

"So the rubber was placed back in the box and carted across the street. There the fellows seemed to know what it was all about, and gladly accepted the rubber.

"Perhaps it is because of stations like the first that more rubber has not been turned in."

JULY 11

1813

During the War of 1812, a British fleet lands at Ocracoke and Plymouth. North Carolina holds little strategic importance, however, and the invaders stay only a few weeks before sailing away.

1966

Kemp's record shop, a Chapel Hill landmark in the 1950s and 1960s, is destroyed by fire.

Kemp Battle Nye sold classical, folk, jazz, and blues music with an endless procession of stunts—record albums by the inch; balance five on your head for five minutes and get one free; closed all day, open all night.

An older generation of students knew the 1825-vintage clapboard, tin-roofed building on East Franklin Street as Ab's—ancestor of the Intimate Bookshops.

1967

A sellout crowd of teens and preteens, primed for the Monkees, boos the little-known opening act off the stage at the Charlotte Coliseum.

A year later, Jimi Hendrix, by now a rock-icon-in-the-making, will return as a headline act.

1970

Connie Lerner of Asheville, the daughter of World War II concentration camp survivors, becomes the first Jewish Miss North Carolina.

In the talent competition, she plays Chopin's "Revolutionary" étude on the piano—a tribute to her parents, who remembered its being played in defiance of the German invasion of Poland in 1939.

1979

On Howard Knob above Boone, the world's largest windmill is dedicated.

Funded by NASA and the Department of Energy, the experimental power project will prove less efficient at generating electricity than at creating TV static for its neighbors. It is dismantled in 1983.

JULY 12

1833

Frankie Silver becomes the first North Carolina woman executed by hanging.

A Burke County jury decided she had used the family ax to chop her husband, Charles, into little bits, which she then burned in a fireplace.

1886

The rambling Battery Park Hotel, set on 25 acres overlooking downtown Asheville, opens its doors. It soon becomes the symbol of Victorian Asheville, hosting such events as the annual Rhododendron Ball.

In 1922, however, developer E. W. Grove, the former St. Louis pharmacist who built the Grove Park Inn, will ignore citizen protests and

ture modifies the name to Kingstown in the bill of incorporation.

level both the old hotel and the hill it sits on to make way for a new Battery Park Hotel.

1966

Hamlet native Tom Wicker, 40, replaces Arthur Krock, 78, as Washington columnist on the editorial page of the *New York Times*.

Wicker, educated at the University of North Carolina, apprenticed at such papers as the *Sandhill Citizen* in Aberdeen, *The Robesonian* in Lumberton, and the *Winston-Salem Journal* before joining the *Times* in 1960.

He will be thrust onto an even wider stage in 1971, when rebelling inmates at New York's Attica state prison ask him to mediate and publicize their fight for better conditions. *A Time to Die*, his narrative about the experience, moves novelist Kurt Vonnegut to call Wicker "clearly a friend of the downtrodden, a modest, gifted Southern country boy, who has become perhaps our most trusted newspaperman."

1989

The North Carolina House ratifies a bill incorporating the Cleveland County community of Kingstown. The town is the county's fifth-largest (population 956, according to the 1990 census) and the nation's first to be named after the Reverend Martin Luther King, Jr.

In 1973, the Eskridge–Weathers Grove area had informally renamed itself Kingston in honor of the slain civil rights leader.

To reduce the likelihood of confusion with Kinston in eastern North Carolina, the legisla-

JULY 13

1584

Two ships dispatched by Walter Raleigh to find a site for a New World colony land near Cape Hatteras. Captains Philip Amadas and Arthur Barlowe claim the land in the name of Queen Elizabeth.

1857

The *New York Tribune*, edited by abolitionist Horace Greeley, devotes a full page to a review of *The Impending Crisis of the South: How to Meet It* by Hinton Rowan Helper. Helper, born near Mocksville, blames slave owners—whom he calls "robbers, thieves, ruffians and murderers"—for the South's economic backwardness and for the plight of its yeoman class. He urges slaves to gain freedom by violence if necessary.

The book causes a sensation in the North, where it sells phenomenally, and in the South, where it is banned. The Republican Party distributes an abbreviated version for Abraham Lincoln's 1860 presidential campaign; at one point, Greeley's *Tribune* is sending out 500 copies a day.

The Impending Crisis of the South ranks with *Uncle Tom's Cabin* in its impact on public opinion, but Helper is no Harriet Beecher Stowe. His argument against slavery is entirely economic. After the Civil War, he will advocate rounding up blacks and placing them on reservations prior to their expulsion from the country.

1986

Bo Jackson's first professional home run, a broken-bat line drive over the left-field fence, comes at Charlotte's Crockett Park. Even more impressive, he leaps a five-foot chain-link fence from a standstill while going after a foul ball.

Jackson, a former Heisman Trophy winner, is serving a brief baseball apprenticeship in the Southern League with the Memphis Chicks. By 1990, he will become the first athlete chosen to play in both football's Pro Bowl and baseball's All-Star Game.

1989

Lawyer Thomas Root blacks out while flying his Cessna 210 on a business trip from Washington National Airport to Rocky Mount. Tailed by 19 military planes for four hours, Root winds up ditching in the Atlantic Ocean near the Bahamas. He is rescued but is found to be suffering from a mysterious gunshot wound in the abdomen. He speculates that the .32-caliber handgun in the plane's glove compartment may have gone off on impact, although Smith and Wesson says this is impossible.

In 1991, Root will be sentenced to 33 months in prison after pleading guilty to counterfeiting, forgery, and fraud charges involving license applications for FM radio stations before the Federal Communications Commission.

JULY 14

1920

The first S & W Cafeteria opens in Charlotte.

At the chain's peak, 19 S & W's stretch from Atlanta to Washington, but by the 1980s, the operation will have shrunk to half a dozen restaurants, none in North Carolina.

JULY 15

1916

Altapass in Mitchell County is hit with 22.22 inches of rain in 24 hours. The downpour remains a state record.

JULY 15, 1949

Edging out Greensboro's WFMY, which has been delayed by a fallen tower, WBTV signs on as the first television station in the Carolinas. An announcer reads a brief statement that concludes, "Now we present test pattern and tone for set adjustment."

1957

Rupert Wade of Morehead City, swimming several hundred yards off Atlantic Beach, is fatally bitten by a shark.

The death will be the last of four attributed to sharks in 20th-century North Carolina as of this writing; only nine attacks are confirmed during the century. Worldwide, shark attacks rarely occur until water temperatures reach 85 degrees, several degrees above North Carolina's maximum.

JULY 16

1857

The future Stonewall Jackson—Thomas Jonathan Jackson, an instructor at Virginia Military Institute—marries Anna Morrison at her father's plantation home in Lincoln County.

Both the marriage license, which the groom has forgotten, and the bride's trousseau, which was delayed in shipment from New York, arrive by courier at the last moment.

JULY 17

1967

Jazz saxophonist John Coltrane, born in Hamlet and reared in High Point, dies of complications of liver cancer.

Coltrane had complained of severe headaches but refused to see a doctor, instead treating himself with enormous doses of aspirin. He dies the day after finally entering a New York hospital.

His funeral will conclude with an original work by saxophonist Ornette Coleman, "Holiday for a Graveyard."

JULY 18

1986

Actor Patrick Reynolds, whose grandfather

founded R. J. Reynolds Tobacco Company, tells a United States House of Representatives subcommittee, "If the hand that once fed me is the tobacco industry, then that same hand has killed many millions of people and will continue to kill millions unless people wake up to the hazards of cigarettes."

JULY 19

1844

Mary Baker Eddy, future founder of the Christian Science Church, leaves Wilmington to return to her family farm in New Hampshire following the death of her husband from yellow fever.

She and businessman George Washington Glover, married barely six months, lived in Wilmington while he was planning a construction project in Haiti.

1967

A Cessna aircraft flying 12 miles south of its assigned course crashes into a Piedmont Airlines 727 over Hendersonville. All 82 aboard the two planes die in North Carolina's worst air disaster.

JULY 20

1920

High Point leads the state into the age of the dial telephone.

1991

Leslie and John Rountree of Greensboro and

Scout, their six-year-old German shepherd, appear on *Late Night with David Letterman*.

The Rountrees tell Letterman how Scout, fearful of an oncoming storm, let himself into their 1990 Mazda, couldn't free himself for 12 hours, and did $4,400 worth of damage to the interior.

JULY 21

1820

The Star of Raleigh reports that serial husband Anthony Metcalf has been jailed in Roxboro:

> It is hoped some of the friends of the numerous women he has married (to say nothing of his other offences) will come forward and prosecute him. . . . As far as the history of his life is known, he was raised in Portsmouth, Virg.—when quite young was sentenced to 3 years imprisonment in the Penitentiary for stealing a Pocket Book—married a woman in Hertford county, another in Wilmington, another in Lincoln, another in Pitt, all in this state, and how many others are not known; but if his own confession (made when confined in our jail) is to be believed, he had married 14 wives in 1818, and we have heard of one since—his age does not exceed 30 or 35.

JULY 22

1967

Carl Sandburg, 89, dies of an apparent heart attack at Connemara, his Flat Rock home since 1945.

The organ prelude for his funeral is "John Brown's Body," one of his favorite songs. His body is cremated and his ashes removed to his birthplace in Galesburg, Illinois.

1975

Visiting Asheville for the first time since 1955, when he was a warmup act for Hank Snow, Elvis Presley performs three times in three days at the civic center—and shoots out the television in his motel room.

The episode occurs during a month-long binge of bizarre behavior in which Presley also gives away nearly $50,000 worth of jewelry during concerts and buys 14 Cadillacs in midnight shopping sprees for friends, associates, and total strangers.

JULY 23

1959

University of North Carolina coach Jim Tatum dies, causing quarterback Jesse Jackson of Greenville, South Carolina, to decide against becoming the first black Tar Heel football player.

Instead, Jackson accepts a scholarship to Illinois and later winds up at North Carolina A & T before discovering that politics is his calling.

JULY 24

1948

Southerners who have bolted the Democratic Party over its civil rights platform meet in Atlanta and christen themselves "States' Rights Democrats."

The unwieldy name proves a problem for *Charlotte News* headline writer Bill Weisner. His solution: "Dixiecrats."

Presidential candidate Strom Thurmond of South Carolina dislikes the label and considers it "a five-yard penalty" in winning over non-Southerners.

Regardless, the party will lose both the election (capturing only four Deep South states) and the battle against being known as "Dixiecrats."

JULY 25

1729

Most of the Lords Proprietors sell their New World rights to the English Crown, and North Carolina becomes a royal colony.

JULY 25, 1941

Photo caption in the *Smithfield Herald*: "Miss Ava Gardner is Hollywood-bound. This 18-year-old Johnston County girl goes to the movie capital this week to begin a career in acting. Metro-Goldwyn-Mayer has signed her up for a 7-year contract—and it's easy to understand why."

1975

Brian Dowling, the former Yale star who inspired the "B. D." character in Garry Trudeau's "Doonesbury," starts at quarterback in the Charlotte Hornets' World Football League opener.

JULY 27

1585

Walter Raleigh's first colonization expedition, led by Richard Grenville, reaches Roanoke Island and begins the first English settlement in the New World. When the ships return to England, 108 men are left behind to build an earthen fort—which they call Fort Raleigh—and construct crude living quarters of poles and bark.

1925

At a session in New York City, Charlie Poole and his North Carolina Ramblers record their most popular number. In an era when Columbia's typical country record sells 5,000 copies, "Don't Let Your Deal Go Down Blues" will sell more than 100,000.

Poole, a native of Randolph County, is a pioneer in the three-finger style of banjo picking; his technique probably resulted from a childhood baseball accident that deformed the fingers on his right hand.

The Ramblers will cut more than 70 sides

for Columbia, but alcoholism burdens Poole's career, and he dies of a heart attack at age 39.

1934

Primo Carnera, the only Italian ever to hold the world heavyweight boxing title, stops for supper at the Charlotte Tourist Camp. Carnera, who weighs 260 pounds, finishes off six ham sandwiches, six fried eggs, six raw eggs, and four bottles of beer.

He tells fans he is "touring the country" and blames a bad ankle for his knockout by challenger Max Baer six weeks earlier.

JULY 28

1877

The telegraph line reaches Asheville.

1943

In a war-benefit exhibition game at Yankee Stadium, Babe Ruth and Ted Williams meet in uniform for the second and last time during their careers.

Ruth, 48 and long retired, manages and pinch-hits for a team of New York Yankees and Cleveland Indians. Williams, 24, plays for the North Carolina Pre-Flight Cloudbusters, made up of major leaguers undergoing training at marine preflight school in Chapel Hill.

JULY 29

1859

High Point's town commissioners vote to require "each or every person or Company of Stage Players, Slight of hand performers, Rope dancers, Tumblers and Wire dancers, or Company of Circus riders or Equestrian performers" to pay a $10 fee. For exhibitions of "Natural or Artificial Curiosities," the fee is $5.

JULY 29, 1918

Tobacco magnate R. J. Reynolds, probably the state's wealthiest man, dies of pancreatic cancer at his estate in Winston-Salem. He is 68 years old.

Fearing that sons Dick and Smith will lack his work ethic, Reynolds has stipulated in his will that they be awarded $2 for every dollar they earn themselves. The incentive plan proves ineffectual, however, and the sons will achieve most of their renown as playboys.

1940

Jack Dempsey, 45, who lost his heavyweight championship in 1926, floors former wrestler Ellis Bashara in the second round of a bout at Charlotte Memorial Stadium.

It is the third and last fight of a comeback tour that the cash-strapped Dempsey had hoped would lead to a title shot at Joe Louis. It won't.

A skimpy crowd of 6,500 pays $1.15 to

$3.40 to see him make short work of Bashara, who boxed at the University of Oklahoma before embarking on a wrestling career as the masked "Purple Flash."

Although his share of the purse comes to more than $2,500, the fight must be embarrassing for Dempsey. His autobiography not only omits mention of Charlotte but also claims that his last bout was 28 days earlier.

JULY 30

1861

L. P. Walker, Confederate secretary of war, approves the purchase of an abandoned cotton mill at Salisbury for use as a prison for captured Union soldiers. The owners, to their eventual regret, agree to take Confederate bonds in payment.

1935

Just days after Senator Josiah Bailey of North Carolina helped filibuster to death a federal antilynching bill, a black man is lynched in Franklin County.

The lynch mob—unmasked and in full daylight—takes Govan "Sweat" Ward from the custody of Sheriff John Moore and two deputies and hangs him from a scrub oak with a cotton plow line. Ward, 25 years old, was accused of decapitating a white farmer with an ax.

The sheriff will later claim that he recognized none of the two dozen lynchers and failed to note the license number of the car that carried away his prisoner. ("I wish we had," he says.)

In spite of Governor J. C. B. Ehringhaus's calls for action, Ward's murderers will remain anonymous.

About 100 lynching deaths have occurred in North Carolina since 1882; Ward's is the last in which the killers go unpunished.

1973

Franklinton native Jim Bibby, a rookie with the Texas Rangers, throws a no-hitter against the Oakland A's.

Bibby's decade in the major leagues will be highlighted by a World Series championship with the Pittsburgh Pirates in 1979.

His older brother, Henry, wins his own championship ring the year of Jim's no-hitter—in the NBA as a guard on the New York Knicks. Henry also started on three consecutive UCLA college basketball champions.

JULY 31

1966

The same day that the Reverend Martin Luther King, Jr., addresses without incident a crowd of 4,500 at Raleigh's Reynolds Coliseum, Ku Klux Klansmen in boots and helmets jeeringly remove blacks from a Klan rally at Nash Square.

The incident will force Governor Dan K. Moore, who has tried to treat the Klan and civil rights advocates with equal wariness, to condemn "an attempt by swaggering demagogues to terrorize, intimidate or assume synthetic authority and [threaten] the dignity of the law." Previously, Moore had ventured no further than to say the Klan "has nothing of value to offer North Carolina."

Earle Hyman, born in Rocky Mount and reared in Warrenton, is nominated for an Emmy for best guest performer in a comedy series. Hyman plays Russell Huxtable, father to Bill Cosby's Cliff Huxtable, on *The Cosby Show*.

That role on television's top-rated show runs eight years, giving Hyman his greatest prominence in the United States. But his lifelong interest—sparked when he was 11 years old and Warrenton's public library opened its doors to blacks—remains Shakespeare. His performances on the classical stage, especially in *Othello*, have made him a household name in Scandinavia.

Not all North Carolina suffragists [August 19] were women.

August

French botanist scales Grandfather Mountain
Homemaker patents hexagonal house
Nixon campaign hits bump in Greensboro

AUGUST 1

1887

After volunteer firefighters disband their companies and turn in their equipment to protest the appointment of a full-time fire marshal, Charlotte's city council creates a professional fire department with four full-time firefighters earning $25 a month.

1968

Governor Dan K. Moore dedicates the state's first welcome center, on I-85 north of Henderson.

AUGUST 2

1776

Joseph Hewes of Edenton, William Hooper

of Hillsborough, and John Penn of Stovall in Granville County sign the Declaration of Independence in Philadelphia.

AUGUST 3

1863

President Jefferson Davis issues a virtual act of amnesty by requesting that all Confederate absentees return to their regiments.

Since Gettysburg, desertion in Robert E. Lee's army has reached dramatic proportions. More than 1,000 soldiers, mostly North Carolinians, are reported crossing the James River east of Richmond and heading home.

AUGUST 4

1937

The nation's first soil conservation district, covering the badly eroded 120,000-acre Brown Creek watershed, is established in Anson County.

AUGUST 5

1909

After two previous failed attempts, Gaston County voters agree to move the county seat from Dallas to prosperous Gastonia, where businessmen have pledged $43,000 toward a new courthouse and jail.

1944

As Allied troops advance toward Paris, Private First Class James McRacken of Red Springs in Robeson County single-handedly disarms the explosives that retreating Germans had planted to blow up the last remaining bridge in Mayenne, a city of 18,600.

Had the bridge been demolished, the Allies would have had to use heavy aerial bombardment on the 1,000-year-old city.

From their windows, scores of townspeople watch as McRacken races 500 yards to the bridge. Heavy German fire cuts his legs from under him, but before dying, he crawls onto the bridge, reaches over the side, and snips the wires to the explosives.

The citizens of Mayenne will rename the bridge after McRacken, build a monument to him, and hold annual memorial services. Among those to lay a wreath at the site: General Charles de Gaulle.

McRacken is buried in Mayenne, but his body is later brought home to Red Springs. In 1994, a bronze bust of him is unveiled atop the war memorial at the town hall.

1993

A red 1992 Lexus belonging to James Jordan, the father of basketball star Michael Jordan, is found abandoned in a wooded area near Fayetteville. The elder Jordan has not been seen since attending a friend's funeral in Wilmington three weeks earlier.

His body is later found floating in a creek near McColl, South Carolina. Two Robeson County teenagers are charged with robbing and shooting him after he pulled off U.S. 74 outside Lumberton to nap on his way to Charlotte.

1906

A mob breaks down the door of the Salisbury jail and kills three of the six black prisoners awaiting trial for murdering a white family.

Witnesses will make themselves scarce, but Judge Benjamin Franklin Long commands a grand jury that "God Almighty reigns, and the law is still supreme." George Hall, the first white man in North Carolina ever convicted in a lynching, is sentenced to 15 years.

1918

The Diamond Shoals Lightship, moored off Cape Hatteras, is shelled and sunk by a German submarine.

When the sub opens fire on a nearby merchant ship, the lightship wirelesses a warning to other vessels in the vicinity. The sub then locates and sinks the unarmed lightship. Its crew of 12 rows safely to shore.

1945

The *Enola Gay*'s bomb-bay doors swing open above Hiroshima, and Major Thomas Ferebee, a 26-year-old from Mocksville, pulls a cable he has looped around his left hand. A bulbous 9,000-pound bomb nicknamed "Little Boy" tumbles out. "Bomb away!" he shouts.

Estimates of the death toll from the first of World War II's atomic bombs range from 80,000 to 130,000. After the second, Japan surrenders.

In 1991, Ferebee's role will be commemorated with the unveiling of a historical marker outside his boyhood home in Mocksville.

AUGUST 6, 1973

Musician Stevie Wonder, on tour, nearly dies when the car in which he is riding collides with a logging truck on I-85 near Salisbury.

He suffers a brain contusion and will spend two weeks in North Carolina Baptist Hospital in Winston-Salem, but his only long-term impairment is the loss of his sense of smell.

1945

The day after Hiroshima, country musician Fred Kirby composes "Atomic Power," the first song about "The Bomb." *Billboard* magazine calls it the "greatest folk song in 20 years." The chorus: "Atomic power, atomic power . . . It was given by the mighty hand of God."

Other versions will outsell the original by Kirby, who goes on to become a longtime kiddie-show cowboy at Charlotte's WBTV.

1965

"Papa's Got a Brand New Bag," recorded by James Brown at Arthur Smith Studios in Charlotte, debuts on the *Billboard* pop chart. It will peak at number eight—Brown's first top-10 hit.

1926

Firearms inventor David Marshall "Carbine" Williams, imprisoned at Caledonia Farm in Halifax County, writes his mother, "I am not in a writing mood. I am at present under stress of an unusual type of blues caused by a collision of inventive thoughts on a certain subject in my mind that is hard pressed to solve with other thoughts that come in, in the form of a most lonesome mood. Inventive thoughts in themselves to me are serious, and when other thoughts far more serious and of a most lonesome nature bombard each other at the same time in one small head [it] generally gives me the blues."

In prison for the second-degree murder of a revenue agent in a raid on a moonshine still in Cumberland County, Williams develops—with the warden's permission—the M-I carbine, later used by 8 million soldiers during World War II.

His invention wins him a pardon from Governor Angus McLean in 1929. In 1952, Jimmy Stewart will portray him in the movie *Carbine Williams*.

1955

Over statewide radio and television, Governor Luther Hodges gives North Carolina's response to the landmark *Brown v. Board of Education* decision.

Hodges points out that the Supreme Court has outlawed only forced segregation of schools and asks that blacks now send their children to black schools voluntarily. If they don't, he warns, the state might abandon public education altogether.

1986

In the first successful insanity defense in a North Carolina murder case since 1906, George Levander Burke is found not guilty in a shooting outside a Chapel Hill bar.

A defense psychiatrist testified that Burke, 35, suffered from atypical psychosis and was not able to determine right from wrong when he shot 60-year-old Thomas Burnette.

AUGUST 9

1861

Off Cape Hatteras, the U.S.S. *Union* chases the Confederate privateer *York* aground. The *York*'s crew throws its lone gun overboard, sets the vessel on fire, and flees ashore. The Union then reclaims the schooner *George G. Baker*, which the *York* had captured before meeting its end.

AUGUST 10

1954

Charles "Ches" McCartney, a bearded eccentric known as the "Goat Man," arrives in Fayetteville.

Since the late 1930s, McCartney, who winters near Jeffersonville, Georgia, has traveled the South preaching and selling postcards of himself with his wagon and team of goats.

AUGUST 11

1909

The *Arapahoe*, a freight and passenger steamer bound from New York to Charleston, is disabled with engine trouble 21 miles south of Diamond Shoals. The first SOS ever sent is received by a wireless operator on Cape Hatteras.

A year earlier, an international agreement had established three dots, three dashes, and three dots as a world radio distress call. The signal happened to translate in international Morse code as SOS, but it was chosen only because it could be easily transmitted and understood.

1945

Meeting at Guilford College during the last week of World War II, North Carolina Quakers declare, "We bow in penitence for helping to cause this war through selfishness, isolation and lack of vision, for now having loosed history's most barbaric instrument of destruction."

1974

Lee Trevino squeezes out a one-stroke victory over Jack Nicklaus to win the PGA championship at Tanglewood Park in Clemmons, near Winston-Salem.

North Carolina hosted its only other PGA tournament in 1936 at Pinehurst Country Club.

AUGUST 12

1988

Improper wiring in a control panel sends the $1.2-million, 20-ton scoreboard at the brand-new Charlotte Coliseum plummeting to the floor.

Nobody is hurt, the scoreboard manufacturer brings in a replacement, and a photo of the wreckage rates prominent play in *Sports Illustrated*.

AUGUST 13

1961

Pavement at the Asheville-Weaverville Speedway breaks up during a NASCAR race, causing Junior Johnson to be declared the winner after only 258 of the scheduled 500 laps.

Irate fans, seeking half their money back because they've seen only half a race, block the only infield exit for more than three hours until being dispersed by drivers and crewmen armed with tools and two-by-fours.

1989

Fast-driving, fast-living Tim Richmond dies of AIDS in a West Palm Beach, Florida, hospital.

Richmond, who lived on Lake Norman in Mecklenburg County, was 34. In 1986, he was NASCAR's hottest driver, winning seven races. In 1987, he fell out of sight, came back to win two races, then returned to seclusion, all the while denying rumors he had AIDS.

AUGUST 14

1756

Rebecca Bryan, a descendant of the last king of Ireland, marries Indian fighter Daniel Boone in the future Davie County.

The newlyweds, whose families have been close since both moved from Pennsylvania to the banks of the Yadkin River, will build a house near the present-day town of Farmington. Daniel spends his time farming, weaving, and blacksmithing. Eight children are born to the

Boones before the family leaves North Carolina for Kentucky.

1916

With a roar heard for miles, the earthen dam on Transylvania County's Lake Toxaway gives way during a storm. Water from the 540-acre man-made lake rushes south. Fortunately, residents have already fled to safety, and the 20 miles of near-wilderness en route to Walhalla, South Carolina, allows the flow to dissipate itself into a vast expanse of mud.

The dam will be rebuilt in 1961, creating a 900-acre lake—the state's largest under private ownership.

1945

North Carolinians take to the streets to celebrate the imminent victory over Japan and the end of World War II. In Raleigh, the crowd on Fayetteville Street is joined by a hook and ladder bearing a "Victory is complete" sign on its side.

Within an hour, Governor Gregg Cherry orders a statewide suspension of alcohol sales.

1983

North Carolina's first Wal-Mart opens in Murphy.

Within a decade, the Arkansas-based discount chain will grow to 67 stores in the state (and more than 1,700 in the nation) and become the dominant retailer in towns such as Lumberton, Rocky Mount, and Monroe.

AUGUST 15, 1945

Brigadier General Frank Armstrong, a native of Hamilton in Martin County and a graduate of Wake Forest, commands the longest and last nonstop combat flight of World War II, flying round-trip from Guam to Honshu, Japan. His B-29 is still in the air as the Japanese announce their surrender.

In 1942, Armstrong led the first American daylight bombing raid over enemy territory in France; in 1943, he led the first heavy bombing raid over Germany.

Armstrong's European diaries will form the basis for the book, movie, and TV series *Twelve O'Clock High*.

1950

Searchers find the body of Christopher Reynolds, 17-year-old son of Z. Smith Reynolds and Libby Holman. He fell to his death while climbing Mount Whitney in California.

Holman was pregnant with Christopher at the time she was charged with fatally shooting her husband at Reynolda House in Winston-Salem. The death was ultimately ruled a suicide.

Holman uses her son's trust fund to establish the Christopher Reynolds Foundation in New York, which will underwrite peace, disarmament, and civil rights causes. Perhaps its most influential project: financing the Reverend Martin Luther King, Jr.'s, 1959 pilgrimage to India to learn the passive resistance strategies of Mahatma Gandhi.

1975

In a case that has become a national cause célèbre, an evenly biracial Raleigh jury acquits black defndant Joan Little in the ice-pick slaying of white jailer Clarence Alligood.

Defense attorneys—including civil rights stalwarts William Kunstler and Morris Dees—argued that Alligood, 62, had attempted to sexually assault the 21-year-old Little, who was serving time in the Beaufort County Jail for breaking and entering. The prosecution contended that Alligood had been killed in an escape plot.

AUGUST 16

1918

Through burning oil and raging waves, surfmen from the Chicamacomico Coast Guard Station go to the rescue of the British tanker *Mirlo*, torpedoed by a German submarine.

Forty-two crewmen are safely brought ashore in one of the most revered acts in Coast Guard history. The rescue is led by Chief Boatswain John Allen Midgett, Jr., one of the "Mighty Midgetts" who have provided the Outer Banks with lifesaving service since the mid-1800s.

1934

Harcourt Brace publishes *Appointment in Samarra*, John O'Hara's soon-to-be-famous first novel.

In the introduction to a later edition, O'Hara reflects on the difficulty of coming up with pure fiction: "There is a minor incident [in *Appointment in Samarra*] of a girl climbing a flagpole at a country club. At the time I wrote that, it was my invention, but after the book was published, I learned that a girl had climbed a flagpole at a country club in North Carolina, and another girl had climbed a flagpole at a country club in Ohio. So Dayton people and Charlotte people thought I was writing under a phony name and was a former resident of Dayton and Charlotte."

AUGUST 17

1957

Dorothy Brown, a 16-year-old "backwoods beauty" recently discovered in Iredell County, is introduced to a national television audience on *The Ed Sullivan Show*. *Life* magazine devotes two pages to "A Living Doll of the Wilds: Long Sam's Carolina Prototype Turns into a Winsome Celebrity."

"Long Sam," as *Charlotte Observer* columnist Kays Gary has dubbed Brown after the Al Capp cartoon character, loves New York but turns down a bid from *The $64,000 Question*, a part in the Broadway musical *Li'l Abner*, and offers from baseball teams, pizza and sweater makers, and modeling agencies. She wants only to return to North Carolina and get an education—at 14, she'd left school to help her destitute parents and six siblings, all of whom slept in two small bedrooms.

With support from the Mooresville newspaper editor who stumbled upon her and from a Charlotte philanthropist, Brown is able to finish high school, graduate from Woman's College in Greensboro, and become an elementary-school teacher in Charlotte.

1960

Vice President Richard Nixon, in Greensboro for a stunningly successful campaign rally, bangs his left kneecap on a car door.

He at first tries to ignore the pain, but doctors find a staph infection and put him in Walter Reed Hospital in Washington. His leg in traction, he misses two weeks of campaigning.

Nixon's impatience, suggests campaign chronicler Theodore H. White, leads him to overschedule himself in an attempt to hit all 50 states. He drinks three chocolate shakes a day to regain the eight pounds he lost in the hospital but is still haggard and off-form when he arrives for his crucial first TV debate with Senator John F. Kennedy.

As he gets out of his car at the studio, Nixon again strikes his knee on the door.

1969

Camille, one of only two category-five hurricanes (the most powerful designation) known to have hit the United States, makes landfall in Mississippi but causes severe flooding in the North Carolina mountains.

AUGUST 18, 1587

Virginia Dare, the granddaughter of Governor John White, is born on Roanoke Island. She is the first child of English parents born in America.

1590

On Virginia Dare's third birthday, Governor John White returns from a supply trip to England to find the Roanoke Island colony deserted. The word *CROATOAN* is carved into a tree. White tries to sail south to Croatan (Hatteras Island), but storms force him back to England.

No one from the Lost Colony is ever heard from again.

1879

Winds of 135 miles per hour and tides four feet above normal hit the North Carolina coast. "Beaufort and Morehead City are classed as ruined . . . completely wrecked," reports the *Raleigh Daily News.*

Only two lives are lost, both in rescue attempts, but the storm destroys Beaufort's landmark three-story Atlantic Hotel. Among the guests whose belongings are swept away: Governor Thomas Jarvis, who returns to Raleigh two days later wearing a sailor suit.

1920

Under intense pressure from both sides, the North Carolina House rejects the 19th Amendment, which would allow women to vote.

The amendment needs only one more state to become law, however, and gets it the next day in Tennessee.

Half a century later, in 1971, the North Carolina legislature will symbolically ratify the amendment.

1929

Amos 'n' Andy, the brainchild of two small-time producers who met in Durham in 1920, debuts on network radio.

A Chicago production company had sent Charles Correll to Durham to direct a local Elks follies, and Freeman Gosden was brought in to assist. Correll, from Peoria, Illinois, and Gosden, from Richmond, Virginia, hit it off immediately and became lifelong partners. After several years of experimentation, they came up with *Amos 'n' Andy*.

With Correll and Gosden, both white, performing all the black parts, the NBC production becomes perhaps the most popular radio show of all time, lasting until 1954. A television version using black actors runs from 1951 until 1966, when CBS succumbs to pressure from civil rights groups.

"There are three things I'll never forget," British writer George Bernard Shaw says after a visit to America. "The Rocky Mountains, Niagara Falls and *Amos 'n' Andy*."

1956

Friends invited by Agnes MacRae Morton take part in the first Highland Games at the foot of Grandfather Mountain.

In the coming years, the games will become the largest outside Scotland, where tradition says they date to 1100 A.D. Crowds of 15,000 gather on MacRae Meadow, wearing clan tartans and competing in games such as tossing the polelike "caber."

According to the 1990 census, about 7 percent of North Carolinians claim Scottish or Scots-Irish heritage. Typically, Highland Scots sailed straight for the Cape Fear River Valley, while the Scots-Irish arrived by way of Pennsylvania.

1985

Alec Wilkinson of *The New Yorker* profiles Garland Bunting, for 35 years a revenue agent in Halifax County.

The article will grow into a book, *Moonshine: A Life in Pursuit of White Liquor*, and propel the canny and colorful Bunting onto the talk-show circuit.

AUGUST 19, 1991

Testimony begins in Farmville in the sexual-abuse case of Robert F. Kelly, Jr., owner of the Little Rascals Day Care Center in Edenton.

Eight months later, the Pitt County jury will end the longest trial in North Carolina history by finding Kelly guilty on 99 charges. The guilty verdict is overturned.

AUGUST 20, 1862

Private D. L. Day, Company B, 25th Massachusetts Volunteer Infantry, writes in his diary at New Bern,

Until recently I have been quite a popular commander of Sunday church parties. The boys would get up their parties and get me a pass to take them into town to church. I would take them in and halting on some convenient corner, would deliver myself of a little speech. I would say, "Boys, I have always believed in the largest tolerance in matters of religion and politics, and as much as I would like to have you attend church with me, if you have any preferences you are at liberty to enjoy them; far be it from me to impose my authority on your feelings or conscience. I shall expect you on the corner at the appointed time that we may report back in camp in season for dress parade."

. . . One Sunday afternoon when we gathered on the corner, one of the party failed to put in an appearance. After waiting beyond a reasonable time, he was defaulted and we returned to camp. About night he came in, showing unmistakable signs of having been on the hardest kind of fatigue duty. Instead of going to his quarters as he was told to, he thought it was his duty to interview the captain. That interview resulted in a court martial. . . . After that interview I was in command of no more Sunday parties.

1889

Greenville, for decades thwarted in its desire for a branch of the Wilmington & Weldon Railroad, eagerly welcomes its first train.

The *Eastern Reflector* notes how "four of our beautiful young ladies" presented the engineer with "a handsome bronzed pair of antlers," which he proudly mounted on the front of his engine.

1943

Betty Smith's *A Tree Grows in Brooklyn*, destined to become one of the best-selling novels of all time, hits bookstore shelves across the state.

The author is a former Brooklyn telephone operator who arrived in Chapel Hill on a bus with her two young daughters in 1938. She came only to study playwriting at the university but later decided to make Chapel Hill her home.

A Tree Grows in Brooklyn, a warm coming-of-age story set in a city slum, was rejected by 12 publishing houses before being accepted by Harper and Brothers. It will also be made into a movie and a Broadway play.

Although she dies in a Connecticut convalescent home in 1972, Betty Smith returns to be buried in Chapel Hill.

AUGUST 21, 1983
The highest temperature ever recorded in North Carolina: 110 degrees at Fayetteville.

AUGUST 22

1831

Nat Turner leads a slave revolt in Southampton County, Virginia, near the North Carolina border.

In the white panic that ensues, many North Carolina blacks are executed, and the state's slave code is tightened. Under the new law, a slave cannot defend himself even if his owner tries to kill him.

1934

The American Legion baseball team from Springfield, Massachusetts, withdraws from a sectional tournament in Gastonia because of local resistance to its lone black player.

Ernest "Bunny" Taliaferria is barred from the team's hotel, and the *Charlotte Observer* reports that "those in charge of the tournament would not guarantee the safety of the Springfield nine when it went on the field in the face of heckling and manifestations of hostility by the onlookers."

AUGUST 23

1784

North Carolina counties west of the Appalachians, protesting neglect by state government, form the state of Franklin and choose John Sevier as their governor.

Neither North Carolina nor the federal government will recognize the would-be state, however, and within four years, it collapses.

1793

In response to President George Washington's Militia Act, the Fayetteville Independent Light Infantry is formed to protect the city during the uncertain times following the Revolutionary War.

"The Grand Olde Company," as it comes to be known, will continue to hold monthly drills and an annual muster into the 1990s.

AUGUST 24

1566

Spaniards searching for Chesapeake Bay land briefly off the coast of what is now Currituck County. They look around for a few days, encounter no natives, give up, and return to the West Indies.

1814

As British troops invade Washington during the War of 1812, Dolley Madison, wife of President James Madison, coolly oversees the evacuation of the executive mansion.

After returning to the fire-gutted structure (its restorative coat of white paint will inspire the name *White House*), the first lady resumes setting a new standard for Washington social life.

A native of Guilford County, which her Quaker parents left when she was only 11 months old, Dolley Madison knew personally the first 11 presidents of the United States.

1864

Writing from an encampment near Petersburg,

Virginia, Major Joseph Engelhard quotes General Robert E. Lee as saying that North Carolina troops "stand as if they have tar on their heels."

His letter, which will not become public until 1991, gives support to a Civil War origin of the nickname "Tar Heels."

One rival theory traces the nickname to Lord Cornwallis's troops, who emerged from a river with tar stuck on their heels. Another theory has it beginning as a derogatory description of workers in the state's early tar industry.

In light of the Engelhard letter, however, Lee at least gets credit for elevating "Tar Heel" to a term of praise.

1869

Harriet Morrison Irwin, a frail and bookish Charlotte homemaker, becomes the first woman granted a patent for an architectural design—a hexagonal house.

One advertisement touts Ms. Irwin's hexagon as applying "the principle of bee-building . . . to human architecture," but the design wins few converts. Her model home in Charlotte's Fourth Ward—two stories with a central tower, a mansard roof, and an arched porch—will be torn down without fanfare in the 1960s.

1887

Concord merchant James Cannon founds Cannon Mills.

Over the next century, he and son Charles A.

"Mr. Charlie" Cannon will build one of the state's dominant industries and create the world's best-known textile trademark. In 1906, they establish a privately owned town—Kannapolis, a Greek rendering of "Cannon City"—to serve as the capital of their towel-making empire.

In the 1980s, Cannon Mills is sold—first to David Murdock, then to Fieldcrest—and voters at last make Kannapolis an independent municipality.

1911

Baltimore is bedazzled by the illumination of Chapel Hill native Isaac Emerson's latest creation: a 357-foot tower, the city's tallest building. It is modeled after the Palazzo Vecchio in Florence—with one exception. At the top revolves a crown-capped, 17-ton copy of a bottle of Bromo-Seltzer, the flagship product of the Emerson Drug Company.

Reports the *Baltimore Sun*, "People in two counties craned their necks in wonder at the great flashing letters, each one 10 feet high and 6 feet wide. The two names seemed to enfold each other in a loving embrace and twine themselves closely around the blue body of the bottle."

The early history of Bromo-Seltzer is murky—one account has young "Ike" Emerson concocting it in a drugstore on the corner of Chapel Hill's Franklin and Columbia Streets.

After graduating from the University of North Carolina in 1879, Emerson married a divorced woman. Adverse public opinion influenced the newlyweds to move to Baltimore, where he opened several drugstores and in 1889 began manufacturing Bromo-Seltzer. Although its key headache cure—potassium bromide—had previously appeared in many other patent medicines, Bromo-Seltzer won the battle for name recognition by out-advertising the competition. (In the movie *The Front Page*, reporter Hildy Johnson storms out of his editor's office and shouts, "Fix him another Bromo!")

By 1936, five years after Emerson's death, the bottle has deteriorated and is removed for safety reasons. The Bromo-Seltzer Tower escapes destruction, however, and is converted into a city arts center.

1928

Long Lance, the autobiography of a purported Blackfoot Indian, is published to popular and critical acclaim. Writing in the *New York Herald Tribune*, Dr. Paul Radin, perhaps the world's foremost scholar on the American Indian, praises *Long Lance* as an "unusually faithful account of [the author's] childhood and early manhood" and a "corrective of the ridiculous notions still prevailing about the Indians."

In reality, Buffalo Child Long Lance is Sylvester Clark Long, a black native of Winston. Although Long's racial heritage does include some Indian blood, he was classified as "colored" and enrolled at Depot Street Graded School for Negroes.

At age 13, fantasizing about being an Indian, he joined a Wild West show, where the high cheekbones and straight black hair he inherited from his distant ancestors enabled him to "pass." He began learning Cherokee and was accepted to the famed Carlisle Indian School in Pennsylvania. His transformation into an Indian was then complete, although he later changed his tribe to Blackfoot and his name to Buffalo Child Long Lance.

The publication of his "autobiography" propels Long Lance to national fame. Paramount recruits him to star in *The Silent Enemy*, a drama about Indians of northern Canada before the arrival of white people; B. F. Goodrich Rubber Company asks him to design a running shoe based on his moccasins.

Long Lance's success, however, will be undermined by alcoholism and his constant fear of being found out. In 1932, he is found dead, a suicide, at a friend's mansion near Los Angeles. He is 41.

AUGUST 25

1919

In Charlotte's worst labor disturbance, five men are killed and more than a dozen wounded by police guarding streetcar barns against striking conductors and motormen.

Workers had gone on strike two weeks earlier for higher wages and union recognition. When Southern Public Utilities Company brought in strikebreakers, violence broke out.

1962

Little Eva's "The Loco-Motion" hits number one on the charts, and "doing the Loco-Motion" becomes the latest dance fad.

Eva Narcissus Boyd was born in 1945 in Belhaven in Beaufort County. She moved to

New York to get into music but was working as a babysitter for songwriters Carole King and Gerry Goffin when she got her big break—a chance to do a demo tape of her employers' latest composition.

The record's fast rise catches all by surprise, and Little Eva has to improvise a dance to go with the record.

Her stardom will prove short-lived. In 1971, broke, she returns to Belhaven, suffers depression, goes on welfare, waits on tables. In 1987, she tells *People* magazine, "I don't loco-mote no more," but her rediscovery results in her going full-time on the oldies concert circuit.

1977

Elvis Presley's scheduled concert in Fayetteville is canceled by his death, but many fans keep their tickets rather than give them up for refunds.

1980

The North Carolina Transportation Museum opens in the old Southern Railway shops at Spencer.

The shops were built in 1896 at a point judged midway between Atlanta and Washington on the Southern's main line. Routine repairs took place in a 37-stall, C-shaped roundhouse; engines were overhauled in a three-story shop with two football fields of floor space.

During the first half of the 20th century, the shops employed as many as 2,500. Workers and their families lived in the towns of Spencer and East Spencer, named after the railroad's first president, Samuel Spencer. The shops fell into rapid decline, however, when the railroad switched from steam locomotives to low-maintenance diesels in 1953. They were closed in 1960.

AUGUST 26

1747

Spanish forces briefly occupy Beaufort. The War of Jenkins' Ear—fought between British and Spanish naval vessels over the control of New World trade—also leads to attacks on Ocracoke, Core Sound, and Brunswick, but no casualties are reported.

AUGUST 27

1891

Twenty-two lives are lost when a passenger train plunges off the Bostian Bridge into Third Creek west of Statesville.

A grand jury will spread the blame among rotten crossties, excessive speed, and "a loose rail, the bolts and spikes of the same having been taken out by some person or persons unknown." Though none come to trial, a number of vagrants are hauled in as suspects. According to a newspaper report, "The tramps . . . are smiling. They are getting themselves . . . put in jail, getting square meals at the county expense and getting fat."

Also benefiting is a Statesville man who undertakes to manufacture walking canes from timber salvaged from the train cars; it is reported that he is unable to keep up with demand.

1918

Concluding a rustic road trip that began nine days earlier in Pittsburgh, inventor Thomas Edison, automaker Henry Ford, tire manufacturer Harvey Firestone, and naturalist John Burroughs check into Asheville's Grove Park Inn.

Along the way, the celebrity nature seekers camped in tents by the mountain roads and were delayed by crowds of admirers. In Weaverville, Edison declined calls for a speech but answered the *Asheville Citizen*'s request for a comment on the world war: "Man's foolishness. That's all you can make out of it. Man is a fool."

1933

Dock Rogers, a black man accused of shooting and wounding two white people, is lynched in Pender County.

The incident began when Rogers supposedly insisted on eating breakfast with a white farm family.

A sheriff's posse surrounds Rogers's house, shoots inside it for several hours, then sets it afire. When Rogers comes out, he is struck down in a fusillade. Still alive, he is captured and driven toward the jail in Burgaw. The truck stops en route, however, and Rogers is dragged into the road and shot 150 times. In Burgaw, the posse drags his lifeless body around the courthouse square before delivering it to an undertaker.

A coroner's jury will rule that Rogers died "at the hand of a person or persons unknown," a common verdict in Southern lynchings. The inquest is conducted by A. C. Blake, justice of the peace, acting coroner, and one of the leaders of the posse.

1961

During a night of racial unrest in Monroe, local NAACP president Robert Williams takes a white couple into his home. He says his intent is to protect them; police call it kidnapping.

Before his trial, Williams will flee to Canada, then to Cuba and China, where he becomes an international spokesman for black separatism. In 1967, he delivers a speech in Tiananmen Square with Mao Tse-tung at his side.

Williams returns to the United States in 1969. He settles in Michigan and fights extradition to North Carolina until charges are dismissed in 1976.

AUGUST 28

AUGUST 28, 1871

Raleigh shuts down while the remains of 103 Confederates killed eight years earlier at Gettysburg are reburied at Oakwood Cemetery.

1929

Maxwell Perkins finishes editing Thomas Wolfe's *Look Homeward, Angel*. Number of words trimmed: 90,000.

1974

In a landmark union election, J. P. Stevens

employees in seven Roanoke Rapids mills vote to be represented by the Textile Workers Union. The tally: 1,685 for the union, 1,448 against. North Carolina's AFL-CIO president Wilbur Hobby proclaims "a new day in Dixie. . . . J. P. first, the textile industry second and then the whole South."

It will take the union six discouraging years to negotiate a contract with J. P. Stevens, however, and union membership both nationally and in North Carolina drops over the next two decades.

AUGUST 29

1650

Explorers from Fort Henry (later Petersburg), Virginia, enter North Carolina by land. Hoping to arrange fur trading, they initiate contact with the Tuscarora Indians along the Roanoke River.

1948

Former vice president Henry Wallace, presidential candidate of the left-leaning Progressive Party, attends its state convention in Durham. The convention nearly turns into a riot as anti-Wallace demonstrators march with signs, explode firecrackers, and pelt Wallace with eggs.

Running against Harry Truman, Thomas Dewey, and "Dixiecrat" Strom Thurmond, Wallace will fare poorly in North Carolina and everywhere else in the general election; he receives no electoral votes.

1794

After a four-day climb, French botanist and explorer André Michaux reaches the top of Grandfather Mountain.

"Reached the summit of the highest mountain in all of North America," he writes in his journal. "With my companion and guide, sang the 'Marseillaise' and shouted 'Long live America and the Republic of France. Long live liberty, equality and fraternity.'" In reality, Grandfather Mountain stands 5,964 feet high but is no competition for Mount Mitchell, at 6,684 feet the highest peak in eastern North America.

Although Michaux's visit to the Blue Ridge will be remembered largely because of the dozens of plants he discovers and names—within 10 miles of Grandfather Mountain exist twice as many varieties of plant life as in all of Europe—his mission stems from French economic and military needs. France's forests are depleted, and he is looking for trees that might thrive there and provide lumber for, among other things, warships.

1983

William Thornton of Faison in Duplin County, a physician assigned to study space sickness aboard the shuttle *Challenger*, becomes the first North Carolinian in space.

AUGUST 31

1886

The Charleston earthquake, the most destructive ever recorded in the eastern United States, leaves its mark on North Carolina.

Buildings throughout the Piedmont shake and sway. At Swannanoa, a railroad tunnel caves in. Gold mines in Cabarrus County collapse, but miners escape injury because the quake hits between the day and night shifts.

"The old expression 'solid as the Earth' has been brought into disrepute of late," observes the *Concord Times*.

1949

Textile heiress Etta Cone, age 79, dies while visiting the family estate in Blowing Rock, leaving to the Baltimore Museum of Art the extraordinary Picassos, Matisses, Cezannes, Modiglianis, and Van Goghs she and her late sister had collected.

Etta and Claribel were sisters of Ceasar and Moses Cone, who in the 1890s moved from New York to Greensboro and built the South's largest cotton mill and the world's largest denim and flannel mills.

Claribel Cone became a doctor, graduating first in her class at Women's Medical College in Baltimore. But when fellow student Gertrude Stein moved to Paris in 1903, Claribel—and later Etta—followed.

Etta Cone typed the manuscript for Stein's first book, *Three Lives*, published in 1909, and Stein introduced the sisters to modern art. On one visit to Pablo Picasso's studio, the Cones paid about $35 for a lot of 11 drawings and seven etchings; they always took Picasso his favorite feature from their American newspapers—the comic strips.

The sisters, neither of whom ever married, later made their home in Baltimore, where they and their brothers had grown up.

1950

Architect Matthew Nowicki, whose designs include Raleigh's boldly parabolic Dorton Arena, dies in a plane crash in Egypt while returning from a trip to plan India's new capital.

Nowicki, a Polish immigrant who at age 40 already enjoyed a worldwide reputation, was acting head of North Carolina State's Department of Architecture.

1960

Denied admission to all-white Dunn High School, seven Lumbee Indian students, along with several parents, stage a sit-in and are arrested for trespassing.

A few North Carolina counties operate separate school systems for whites, blacks, and Indians. But Harnett County has no high school for Indians and instead buses them to East Carolina Indian Institute in Sampson County, a daily round trip of 70 miles.

When it becomes clear that the Lumbees' protest has failed, the American Friends Service Committee arranges for 11 of them to live with families and attend high schools in Raleigh, Greensboro, and High Point. Among the contributors to their expense fund: Eleanor Roosevelt.

The next fall, the Harnett County School Board will give in and admit Lumbees to Dunn High.

Using a mirror and a news photographer's camera,
Ava Gardner [September 3] snaps a self-portrait
on a 1947 trip back to the state.

The *News and Observer* of Raleigh

September

Tuscaroras execute John Lawson
Hurricane punches through Outer Banks
Walker Percy flunks English placement test

SEPTEMBER 1

1898

The nation's first forestry school, directed by German immigrant Carl Schenck, opens at George W. Vanderbilt's Biltmore Forest.

1919

Residents of the suburb of Myers Park, disgruntled about the roads, schools, and police and fire protection provided by the city of Charlotte, successfully petition to make their community a separate municipality.

Barely five years later, however, residents will decide they have had enough independence and return to the city.

1962

Lucy Morgan retires as director of Penland School in Mitchell County, a community handicraft program she founded in 1924 and built into the nation's best-known center for sophisticated work in glass, metal, wood, and fiber.

1976

Wayne Hays, a once-powerful Ohio Democrat, resigns from Congress rather than undergo an Ethics Committee investigation of charges that he put Elizabeth Ray, a native of Marshall in Madison County, on his payroll as his mistress.

SEPTEMBER 2

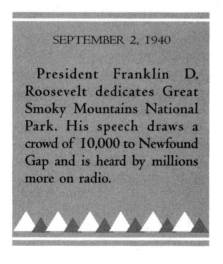

SEPTEMBER 2, 1940

President Franklin D. Roosevelt dedicates Great Smoky Mountains National Park. His speech draws a crowd of 10,000 to Newfound Gap and is heard by millions more on radio.

1952

Hugh Morton, the owner of Grandfather Mountain, opens the 228-foot-long Mile High Swinging Bridge.

The bridge costs $15,000, but over the next four decades, it will allow nearly 6 million visitors to admire the view from the higher of Grandfather's two peaks.

SEPTEMBER 3

1709

North Carolina's Lords Proprietors agree to sell a Swiss company 13,500 acres between the Neuse and Cape Fear Rivers. A year later, Swiss and German immigrants will establish Carolina's second town—Neuse-Berne, named for the river and the Swiss city.

The colonization effort takes hold, and by mid-century, 100,000 more settlers, driven by political and religious unhappiness, will leave Switzerland and Germany for America.

The English continue to dominate North Carolina, however, and common usage anglicizes Neuse-Berne into New Bern.

1922

The morning after their wedding in Atlanta, Margaret Mitchell and Red Upshaw leave by car for their honeymoon at the Grove Park Inn in Asheville. They continue to Raleigh, where they visit Upshaw's parents.

The honeymoon and two-year marriage prove less than idyllic, but Mitchell will make use of Upshaw as a model for the charming bounder Rhett Butler in *Gone With the Wind*.

1934

Scores of textile mills close as North Carolina workers join a national walkout for better wages and working conditions. In Gastonia alone, 92 mills shut down.

1951

Time magazine's cover: Ava Gardner, Smithfield-born actress. "She is far from being the most beautiful babe in the Hollywoods (her mouth is a little too large)," says *Time*. "Her figure is not the best (she is a trifle skinny and by Hollywood standards her legs are only average). Certainly few people least of all herself claim that she is a good actress (though she likes to think of herself as a singer). Yet she seems to exude the kind of allure that sets the mysterious Geiger counters which measure glamor clicking like subway turnstiles."

1991

A hydraulic line ruptures near a deep-fat fryer at the Imperial Food Products chicken-processing plant in Hamlet, creating an instant fireball. Workers are trapped behind doors that owner Emmett Roe has ordered locked to curb the theft of chicken nuggets. The death toll in the state's worst-ever factory accident: 25.

Roe will go to prison after pleading guilty to involuntary manslaughter.

SEPTEMBER 4

1957

On the same morning the nation watches National Guardsmen bar black students from Little Rock's Central High School, four black students break the color barrier in Charlotte.

Dorothy Counts, the 15-year-old daughter of a Johnson C. Smith University professor, receives the most attention. She makes her way through an angry, heckling crowd into Harding High, but four days of harassment will persuade her to transfer to a Pennsylvania school.

The same year, three years after the Supreme Court's historic desegregation decision, black students are also admitted to formerly all-white schools in Greensboro and Winston-Salem.

SEPTEMBER 5

1802

In New Bern, John Stanly kills Richard Dobbs Spaight, signer of the Constitution and the state's first native-born governor. In a duel provoked by Stanly, who has succeeded Spaight in Congress, Spaight is mortally wounded on the fourth shot.

Criminal charges will be brought, but Stanly is pardoned by the governor. The legislature later outlaws dueling, making participants ineligible for public office and prescribing the death penalty for survivors and their seconds.

1917

Pamlico County inaugurates North Carolina's first motorized school-bus service. Previously, the few state schools that transported children used horse-drawn vehicles.

Local school officials concluded that it would be cheaper to pay $1,379 for a bus to haul 26 pupils from seven miles away than to operate a second school in the Oriental district.

Children are seated on long plank benches along each side of the bus, inspiring the nickname "rabbit box."

1923

Billy Mitchell, controversial brigadier general of the United States Army Air Corps, makes the case for air power by sending planes from a Dare County landing field to bomb obsolete battleships anchored 20 miles off Cape Hatteras.

Two years later, Mitchell's advocacy of air warfare will result in his court-martial for defiance of superior officers.

World War II proves his theories correct, however, and Congress awards him the Medal of Honor.

1987

Some 2,000 fans storm the field at Raleigh's Carter-Finley Stadium to celebrate East Carolina University's 32–14 victory over North Carolina State. The crowd tears down a restraining fence, both goalposts, and a row of shrubbery and fights with security guards and Wolfpack fans.

Leery of a repeat, North Carolina State decides to suspend the 18-year-old football series, but in 1995, legislative pressure will force both North Carolina State and the University of North Carolina to schedule games with ECU.

SEPTEMBER 6

1875

The University of North Carolina reopens to enroll students after the Civil War.

SEPTEMBER 7, 1846

A hurricane punches through the Outer Banks into Pamlico Sound, creating Oregon Inlet—named for the first ship to pass through, the side-wheeler *Oregon*—and Hatteras Inlet. Before the storm, Hatteras Island was joined to Ocracoke Island.

1881

Sidney Lanier, the South's best-known poet, dies at his retreat in Lynn in Polk County. He had moved to the mountains at the end of his life in a futile search for a climate that would ameliorate his tuberculosis.

Lanier had been in bad health since 1864, when he was captured aboard a Confederate blockade runner off the North Carolina coast and held for four gruesome months at a Federal prison at Point Lookout, Maryland.

SEPTEMBER 8

1862

At the age of 32, Colonel Zebulon Vance, destined to become the most popular political leader in North Carolina history, takes office as governor while still commanding Confederate troops.

1886

The *New York Tribune* responds to North Carolina's efforts to attract Northerners and their investment capital:

> Every such movement is deserving of and receives the heartiest encouragement. . . . But [Northerners must know] that if they cast in their lot with the people of North Carolina they will be perfectly secure in all their political rights and privileges. Everybody knows that in portions of the South unless one swears by the Democratic party the community in which he resides will make it unpleasant for him. He may not be positively maltreated, but he will be let alone in an emphatic manner.
>
> We rejoice at the assurance that comes to us that North Carolina has set her face against this un-American, suicidal policy; that she welcomes alike Republicans and Democrats and proposes that they shall have equal rights. Inviting immigration in this spirit and offering superior inducements, there is no reason why she should not increase and multiply.

SEPTEMBER 9

1961

Maria Beale Fletcher of Asheville, a former Radio City Rockette, becomes the only Miss North Carolina to be chosen Miss America.

1965

Emmylou Harris, valedictorian at her high school in suburban Washington, D.C., enrolls at the University of North Carolina at Greensboro to study drama.

In her three semesters there, she will act in several campus productions, including Shakespeare's *The Tempest*, but it is her folk singing for $10 a night at the Red Door bar that presages her career as one of country music's most respected performers.

SEPTEMBER 10

1811

In Carteret County, Edward Tinker, the first captain known to have sunk an American cargo ship for the insurance money, is convicted of a murder growing out of his plot.

After taking out a policy on a nonexistent shipment of gold, Tinker had two crew members—Durand and Potts—drill and plug holes in the ship's bottom. A convenient storm came up, Tinker pulled the plugs, and the schooner was scuttled off Roanoke Island. When a third crewman, a cabin boy named Edwards, balked at going along with the scheme, Tinker took him on a duck hunt and murdered him. He weighted the body with stones and threw it in the sea, but the tide brought it in. Tinker, the last man seen with Edwards, was apprehended in Philadelphia.

The captain wasn't finished, however. From jail, he wrote crewman Durand, suggesting the two pin the murder on Potts, the third conspirator. The worst that could happen to Durand, the captain assured him, was losing a slice of ear—the penalty for perjury at the time.

But Durand, frightened of Tinker's incessant plotting, turned the letter over to the authorities.

After being convicted, Tinker is hanged.

1936

Charlotte's weather is dark and rainy, but just as President Franklin D. Roosevelt arrives from Asheville for his "Green Pastures" campaign rally, the clouds part. He gets out of his open car and exclaims to the soaked audience filling brand-new Memorial Stadium, "I see a rainbow in the sky!"

SEPTEMBER 11

1974

Eastern Airlines Flight 212 crashes and burns three miles short of the Charlotte airport, killing 72 of the 82 people aboard.

1976

President Gerald Ford signs a bill adding 26.5 miles of the New River in Ashe and Alleghany Counties to the National Wild and Scenic River system. Geologists estimate the New River's age at 100 million years—second only to the Nile.

The designation nullifies the Federal Power Commission's approval of two hydroelectric dams on the river in Virginia, but environmentalists will be disappointed in coming years by the inability of North Carolina officials to prevent development along the New.

1987

Fifty-two years to the day after ground was broken in Alleghany County, the Blue Ridge Parkway is formally dedicated in Buncombe County.

The Linn Cove Viaduct, an architectural marvel that curves around Grandfather Mountain, is part of an eight-mile "missing link" that went unfinished for more than 20 years.

The 470-mile highway was scheduled for completion in 1950, but it was delayed by land disputes, money problems, and nearly impenetrable rock formations.

SEPTEMBER 12

1962

Carl Sandburg, age 84, makes his final public performance, reading poetry, singing, and playing the guitar at Flat Rock Playhouse. To cap off the evening, he waltzes in the wings with Maria Beale Fletcher of Asheville, who has just finished her year as Miss America.

1977

Jeff MacNelly's "Shoe," a comic strip whose protagonist was inspired by University of North Carolina journalism professor Jim Shumaker, debuts in newspapers across the country.

MacNelly was a student for a time at UNC but found that classes disagreed with him.

SEPTEMBER 13

1925

Reacting to a brutal drought across the South, Governor Angus McLean proclaims "a day of humility and prayer to God who sendeth rain on the just and the unjust."

Among those responding is the Reverend

A. A. McGeachy of Charlotte's Second Presbyterian Church, who prays for rain for 30 minutes before his Sunday service.

Relief will be minimal. Seventy years later, the summer of 1925 remains the driest on record in many areas of the state.

1971

H. R. "Bob" Haldeman, chief of staff for President Nixon (referred to as "the P"), writes in his diary about evangelist Billy Graham, "This afternoon [Nixon] got into a little harangue on IRS investigations, saying that he had been told by Billy Graham that the IRS is currently investigating him. . . . The P wants now to be sure that we get the names of the big Democratic contributors and get them investigated. Also the Democratic celebrities and so forth."

The entry is one of many that portray Graham, longtime counselor of presidents, in a more political than spiritual light.

Haldeman also reports Graham's being used as an emissary to potential rival George Wallace and former president Lyndon Johnson and his discussing with Nixon "the terrible problem arising from the total Jewish domination of the media."

SEPTEMBER 14

1929

Ella Mae Wiggins is killed by a stray bullet as she rides with a truckload of fellow strikers to a Textile Workers Union meeting.

Nine strikebreakers at Gastonia's Loray Mill are charged with her death, but none will be convicted.

Wiggins's death marks the end of a bloody six-month union drive, which has drawn national attention and fostered generations of antiunion sentiment across the Carolinas.

Almost 60 years later, community leaders and the North Carolina Division of Archives and History will not be able to agree on wording for a historical marker.

1981

Time magazine's cover: Jesse Helms, United States senator from North Carolina. The headline: "To the Right, March!"

1987

Two red wolves set loose on the 118,000-acre Alligator River National Wildlife Refuge near Manteo are the first in more than a century to run free in the area.

In 1991, the United States Fish and Wildlife Service will expand the reintroduction effort to Great Smoky Mountains National Park, west of Asheville.

Red wolves once roamed swampy river bottoms from North Carolina to Texas but were near extinction by the 1970s.

SEPTEMBER 15

1938

After being operated on for tubercular infection of the brain, Thomas Wolfe dies at Johns Hopkins Hospital in Baltimore. He is 37 years old.

A coffin must be brought in from New York to accommodate his six-foot-seven body.

1942

A torpedo from a Japanese submarine blows an 18-by-32-foot hole in the USS *North Carolina*, killing five sailors.

The battleship lists but manages to return to Pearl Harbor for repairs.

1958

New York stockbroker George "Snuffy" Stirnweiss, a former football and baseball star at the University of North Carolina, dies when a commuter train plunges through an open drawbridge into New Jersey's Newark Bay. He is 39 years old.

Stirnweiss played second base on three New York Yankees world-championship teams but is most remembered for winning the 1945 league batting championship by the smallest margin in history—.30854 to the .30846 of Chicago's Tony Cuccinello.

1991

Actress Elizabeth Taylor, visiting Charlotte with fiancé Larry Fortensky to promote her new perfume, is apparently unrecognized when she stops her limousine and enters Bojangles' to order a takeout bucket of chicken.

SEPTEMBER 16

1711

John Lawson, explorer, surveyor, and author of *A New Voyage to Carolina*, is executed by Tuscarora Indians in what will later become Greene County. He is 36 years old.

Lawson's writings, eagerly read in Europe at the time, were among the most informative and ambitious of early American literature. He listed words in various Indian dialects, described plants and wildlife in detail, and laid out geography.

His death results from white settlers' deteriorating relations with the Indians, who increasingly resent losing their hunting grounds, seeing their women and children kidnapped and enslaved, and being cheated by traders.

The Tuscaroras, Lawson wrote two years earlier, were "really better to us than we to them."

1968

The Andy Griffith Show airs for the last time in prime time on CBS.

Since debuting in 1960, the show has never missed Nielsen's top seven; it exits at number one. Even a quarter-century later, its reruns will attract large audiences on cable and local stations.

1979

A Bob Timberlake exhibit at the North Carolina Museum of Art in Raleigh brings protests that he is an illustrator and a promoter rather than an artist. One reviewer calls his work "a contrived world of plastic nostalgia." Critics also contend that Timberlake's limited-edition prints fail to satisfy professional criteria.

The show draws huge crowds, however, and Timberlake's standing as the state's most popular artist is unshaken.

SEPTEMBER 17, 1870

The Cape Hatteras Lighthouse, destined to become perhaps the state's most recognizable landmark, is lighted for the first time.

The 208-foot brick lighthouse, painted a distinctive black-and-white candy stripe, replaces a 90-foot sandstone lighthouse built in 1803 and extensively damaged in the Civil War—the Confederacy wanted to extinguish the light, the Union to protect it.

The Cape Hatteras beacon relies first on whale oil, then kerosene, before being converted to electricity in 1934. It will save countless ships from the treacherous Diamond Shoals, but in later years the lighthouse is itself imperiled by beach erosion.

1906

Charles McIver, founder and first president of the State Normal and Industrial School for Girls (now the University of North Carolina at Greensboro), suffers a fatal stroke while riding the campaign train of William Jennings Bryan between Raleigh and Hillsborough.

Children across the state will later donate pennies to erect a statue of McIver on the State Capitol grounds.

1960

Democratic presidential candidate John F. Kennedy's motorcade winds from the airport to the Charlotte Coliseum, where Arthur Smith and the Crackerjacks have been entertaining the capacity crowd. When the convertible bearing Kennedy and gubernatorial candidate Terry Sanford enters the building, it meets a frenzied rush of supporters.

Kennedy's speech makes no mention of his Catholicism, considered his greatest electoral handicap.

But local Democratic stalwart Gladys Tillett shows no such reluctance in her introduction: "He was not denied the right to fight for his country because of his religion."

SEPTEMBER 18

1933

University of North Carolina freshman Walker Percy flunks the English placement test.

"I had just finished reading Faulkner's *The Sound and the Fury*," Percy will recall half a century later, "and I wrote my placement theme in a Faulknerian style—no capitalization, no punctuation. They put me in the retarded English class, and the professor really thought I was hot stuff. Compared to the rest of the dummies, I guess I was."

Percy will graduate from UNC and from Columbia University's medical school, but he becomes best known for writing such novels as *The Moviegoer*, *The Last Gentleman*, and *Love in the Ruins*.

1935

Shelby Foote of Greenville, Mississippi, arrives at the University of North Carolina hoping to join high-school pal Walker Percy.

"We rejected you," a registration official tells him. "I know," Foote replies, "but I also know you have classes you can't fill. Besides, I came up here all the way from Mississippi. Give me a chance."

Foote's cheekiness pays off.

He proves an indifferent student, however, except for contributing several Faulkner-flavored short stories to *The Carolina Magazine*. He ultimately drops out.

In later life, Foote will become known for his trilogy, *The Civil War: A Narrative*, and for his appearances on the PBS series *The Civil War*.

1940

Two years after his death, Harper and Brothers publishes Thomas Wolfe's *You Can't Go Home Again*.

Although the title comes to be popularly associated with him, the novel as printed falls far short of Wolfe's best work.

In fact, future literary researchers will find that editor Edward Aswell, perhaps too eager to recoup a $10,000 advance, took unacceptable liberties in assembling both *You Can't Go Home Again* and the previous year's *The Web and the Rock*. Laments Chapel Hill critic Louis D. Rubin, Jr., "He combined, spliced, selected, deleted, and rearranged; he changed names, scenes, descriptions; he used material from letters; he even wrote some transitional sequences himself."

1958

In New York, Harry Golden's publisher receives an anonymous letter asking, "Do you know that your author . . . is a swindler, a cheat, and an ex-con and jail bird who has victimized widows and orphans?"

In fact, almost no one knows that Golden, whose *Only in America* ranks number one on the nonfiction bestseller list, is the Harry Goldhurst who served four years in a New York prison for mail fraud and stock manipulation. Golden was released in 1933 and in 1940 moved to Charlotte, where he became nationally known as the publisher of the *Carolina Israelite*, an iconoclastic monthly, and as the author of warm and witty memoirs.

The revelation about his prison record will not only prove harmless to Golden's writing career but will also expand his fame to television, where Jack Paar makes him a regular guest on *The Tonight Show*.

SEPTEMBER 19

1936

F. Scott Fitzgerald writes editor Maxwell Perkins from the Grove Park Inn in Asheville, "I wrote Ernest [Hemingway] about that story of his, asking him in the most measured terms not to use my name in future pieces of fiction. He wrote me back a crazy letter, telling me about what a great Writer he was and how much he loved his children, but yielding the point 'If I should outlive him' which he doubted."

Hemingway's offending story is "The Snows of Kilimanjaro." As published in *Esquire* magazine, it has the hero remembering "poor old Scott Fitzgerald and his romantic awe of [the rich] and how he had started a story once that began, 'The very rich are different from you and me.' And how someone had said to Scott, yes they have more money. But that was not humorous to Scott."

When his story is later published in a book, Hemingway changes the writer's name to Julian, but the exchange becomes one of the most-quoted anecdotes in American literary history.

1970

Future star Chris Evert, who is 15 years old and weighs 98 pounds, stuns the Carolinas Invitational Tennis Tournament in Charlotte by knocking off Margaret Court, the world's top-ranked woman.

SEPTEMBER 20

SEPTEMBER 20, 1879

In Raleigh, the state's first telephone system cranks up. B. W. Starke, Western Union manager, activates a line between his home and his office at Fayetteville and Martin Streets.

Three years later, Southern Bell will begin 24-hour service in the city; the 29 initial subscribers pay 80 cents a year.

1958

Capping an 18-year legal struggle, the Ackland Art Museum is dedicated at the University of North Carolina. As specified in his bequest, the museum's benefactor, William Hayes Ackland, is interred within the building, with a recumbent statue on his marble sarcophagus.

When he died in 1940, Ackland, a Washington lawyer, left $1,395,000 to Duke University for an art museum. The school's trustees declined, reportedly out of the belief that the sarcophagi and recumbent statues of three members of the Duke family in Duke Memorial Chapel were ample. The University of North Carolina and Rollins College, Ackland's second and third choices in an earlier will, were left to wage a long court struggle over the bequest. UNC, whose lawyers were not above arguing that Duke and UNC were "alike as two peas in a pod," finally won out.

SEPTEMBER 21

1940

With footsteps, police sirens, and aircraft engines in the background, Edward R. Murrow opens his *London after Dark* broadcast on CBS, "I'm standing on a rooftop looking out over London. . . . For reasons of national as well as personal security, I'm unable to tell you the exact location from which I'm speaking."

Murrow's nightly broadcasts will give American audiences an unprecedented intimacy with war and make him a national hero.

1987

Salvage workers remove the first of two terra-cotta and concrete globes from atop the columns of Charlotte's ornate Masonic Temple. Despite protests, First Union National Bank is razing the 73-year-old temple to make way for a plaza and snack bar.

One of only six remaining Egyptian Revival buildings in the South, the temple has been praised by such architectural critics as Robert A. M. Stern—who noted, "If you've got it, flaunt it"—as downtown Charlotte's most distinguished building.

The temple was designed by the city's first resident architect, C. C. Hook, whose Charlotte-born grandson, Charles Gwathmey, will go on to become even better known in the profession. Gwathmey's most prominent credit: the 1992 addition to Frank Lloyd Wright's Guggenheim Museum.

In 1990, the Masonic Temple's globes and columns will be used in creating a "gateway" to Rock Hill, South Carolina.

SEPTEMBER 22

1711

The Tuscarora War, the bloodiest Indian war fought on North Carolina soil, begins with attacks on colonial settlements near New Bern and Bath. More than 130 whites are killed by war parties.

The fighting will become so intense over the coming months that many colonists flee and public life nearly ceases.

1926

Thomas Wolfe and James Joyce share a tour bus visiting the battlefield at Waterloo but do not meet.

1947

Alfred A. Knopf publishes John Hope Franklin's *From Slavery to Freedom: A History of Negro Americans*, the first scholarly work to present the integral role of blacks in American life.

Franklin, a professor at what will become North Carolina Central University, was born in Oklahoma and studied at Fisk University and Harvard University. *From Slavery to Freedom* establishes him as one of the preeminent historians of the 20th century; by the 1990s, it is in its seventh printing and Franklin is James B. Duke Professor Emeritus at Duke University.

1963

John Baker, a Pittsburgh Steelers defensive end, sacks New York Giants quarterback Y. A. Tittle, leaving him dazed. A shot of Tittle kneeling on the field with blood trickling from his forehead is one of the most famous sports photos ever taken.

In 1978, Baker, a Raleigh native and North Carolina Central University graduate, will be elected sheriff of Wake County—the state's first black sheriff since Reconstruction.

1989

Hurricane Hugo stuns the Piedmont, ripping 250 miles inland from Charleston and causing North Carolina a record $1 billion in damages.

The day before, the National Weather Service had predicted that Hugo would come no closer than 100 miles east of Charlotte, bringing winds of up to 40 miles per hour. In fact, Hugo hits 27 miles west of Charlotte with 87-mile-per-hour winds.

1991

William Moffett, director of the Huntington Library in San Marino, California, opens the library's photos of the Dead Sea Scrolls to all qualified researchers.

The unexpected and controversial decision by Moffett, a Charlotte native and Davidson College graduate, ends a 40-year monopoly by a handful of editors over one of the great finds of biblical archaeology.

SEPTEMBER 23

1867

The *Wilmington Morning Star* begins publication. It will become the state's oldest continuously published daily newspaper.

1916

Kiffin Rockwell of Asheville is killed in a dogfight over France.

A member of the volunteer Lafayette Escadrille, Rockwell was the first American to shoot down an enemy plane in World War I.

1926

Heavyweight champion Jack Dempsey loses a 10-round decision to Gene Tunney in Philadelphia.

Dempsey trained for the fight outside Hendersonville. The developers of Laurel Park Estates paid him $35,000 and "other considerations" to set up camp there. The minister of Hendersonville's First Methodist Church opposed Dempsey's month-long visit because of the undesirables he would attract—and 200 sportswriters did show up.

Dempsey liked the mountain air but found the water, according to local accounts, "too pure."

1930

Representative Charles Manly Stedman of Greensboro, the last Confederate veteran serving in Congress, dies at age 90.

1940

Raleigh's Eden, the first of Inglis Fletcher's 12 historical novels set in North Carolina, is published by Bobbs-Merrill.

It causes a sensation in a state that has lacked a homegrown novel from a living writer since Thomas Wolfe's *Look Homeward, Angel* 11 years earlier. Many readers praise *Raleigh's Eden* for playing up North Carolina's role in the Revolution. So many others challenge its accuracy, however, that Fletcher participates in a public meeting in which she counters each accusation with documentation.

A widely traveled native of Alton, Illinois, Fletcher became caught up in North Carolina history in the early 1930s while doing genealogical research in Tyrrell County.

She and her husband will eventually make their home in an antebellum mansion on the Chowan River near Edenton.

SEPTEMBER 24

1660

Fur trader Nathaniel Batts buys a tract of land on the Pasquotank River from the Yeopim Indians. The deed is the oldest in existence for North Carolina property.

1770

A mob of 150 Regulators, settlers in the western Piedmont who want tighter regulation of the eastern-controlled government, temporarily seizes Hillsborough after the assembly failed to pass laws to remedy grievances.

1956

A two-page spread in *Life* magazine depicts Governor Luther Hodges promoting the state with a "lively display of home-manufactured and home-grown products." Hodges is shown feeding his cat with food "manufactured from fish scraps in Beaufort," preparing for bed with "headache powders from Durham and chest rub from Greensboro," and, most memorably, taking a shower fully clothed "in quick-drying synthetic fabrics made in North Carolina."

SEPTEMBER 25

1988

In an auditorium at Wake Forest University, presidential candidates George Bush and Michael Dukakis collide in the first of two nationally televised debates. Their exchanges over such issues as deficits, drugs, and the Pledge of Allegiance are intense but inconclusive. Democrat Dukakis accuses Republican Bush of questioning his patriotism; he likens Bush to Joe Isuzu, the unctuous and unscrupulous TV-commercial car salesman.

SEPTEMBER 26

1780

Lord Charles Cornwallis, still enjoying his brilliant victory over American forces at Camden, South Carolina, six weeks earlier, arrives in Charlotte intending to fortify the town and enlist Tory volunteers. Instead, he encounters a "hornets' nest" of resistance—a nickname the city will later make official.

The Battle of Charlotte is more of a skirmish, and the British chase the retreating colonials up what is now North Tryon Street. But Cornwallis's push toward Virginia has been crucially stalled.

During his 16-day encampment, he finds Charlotte "an agreeable village but in a damned rebellious country. . . . The people were more hostile to England than any in America."

After departing, Cornwallis's fortunes will sink ever lower until he surrenders at Yorktown barely a year later, effectively ending the Revolutionary War.

SEPTEMBER 27

1792

Sarah Decrow is commissioned postmaster at Hertford, becoming the third female postmaster in the United States and the first since the adoption of the Constitution.

She will complain to the postmaster general about being underpaid, but she keeps the post until her death in 1795.

1865

The *Raleigh Daily Standard* reports on what may be the state's first road gang, organized under the military government immediately following the Civil War:

> The military on yesterday picked up a large number of gentlemen of color, who were loitering about the street corners, apparently much depressed by ennui and general lassitude of the nervous system, and, having armed them with spades and shovels, set them to play at street cleaning for the benefit of their own health and the health of the town generally.
>
> This is certainly a "move in the right direction;" for the indolent, lazy, Sambo, who lies about in the sunshine and neglects to seek employment by which to make a living, is undoubtedly "the right man in the right place" when enrolled in the spade and shovel brigade.

1931

Addressing the Durham Rotary Club, Duke University law professor John Bradway emphasizes that his new legal-aid clinic—the first in the South—will give students useful experience in dealing with clients.

The local bar at first resists the clinic as unwelcome competition, but Bradway's "poor man's law office" will handle more than 2,500 legal matters in its first decade.

1947

The University of North Carolina avenges the previous season's Sugar Bowl loss to the University of Georgia by defeating the Bulldogs 14–7, but coach Carl Snavely is less than pleased with the play of Charlie "Choo Choo" Justice.

Afterward, he sends Justice a note: "It seems that no matter how thoroughly you practice, Charlie, you have difficulty in remembering in a game the things which are stressed on the practice field. . . . When you get in a game you are too interested in what the other boys are doing; you are governed too much by your impulses and not enough by good sound thinking. . . .

"Charlie . . . these lapses of yours are serious."

SEPTEMBER 28

1880

Shortly after being unloaded in Charlotte, The Chief, a circus elephant, turns on John King, his keeper, and crushes him to death against a rail car.

"The man sank down without a groan," reports the *Charlotte Observer*,

> and the elephant turned and started up the railroad track, the excited crowd fleeing in every direction. The loose elephant got into the main streets of the city, and a crowd was being formed to hunt him down and shoot him when it was learned that the circus people were after the truant beast.
>
> They took the other two elephants, Mary and The Boy, and, driving them rapidly through the streets, overtook The Chief, chained him

to the others and finally got him back to the circus grounds.

The Chief continues with the circus.

John King will be buried in Charlotte's Elmwood Cemetery beneath a five-foot monument donated by his fellow circus workers. On it is carved the image of an elephant and a palm tree.

SEPTEMBER 29

SEPTEMBER 29, 1913

Old Joe, a dromedary in the Barnum & Bailey Circus passing through Winston-Salem, poses for the Camel cigarette package.

Because the camel image on the current pack does not suit R. J. Reynolds, Roy Haberkern, his secretary, goes to the circus in search of a replacement. Haberkern finds the trainer unwilling to allow photographs until he threatens to end the company's tradition of closing its factories when the circus comes to town.

Even then, Old Joe balks until the trainer slaps him on the nose, motivating him into his soon-to-be world-famous stance.

1918

The 60th Infantry Brigade, composed of North Carolina troops, is the first American unit to break through Germany's supposedly impenetrable Hindenburg Line.

SEPTEMBER 30

1786

A judge in Pasquotank County certifies that "John Rose, an inhabitant of this county and State aforesaid, being with part of his left ear left off, had the misfortune to be deprived of that by a bite of a Malicious Mare."

As late as the early 1800s, North Carolina courts commonly punish offenders by the loss of one or both ears. A perjurer in Ashe County, for example, is fined 10 pounds and sentenced to "stand in the pillory for one hour, at the expiration of which time both his ears be cut off and entirely severed from his head, and . . . be nailed to the pillory and there remain till the setting of the sun."

To avoid being taken for a convicted criminal, citizens such as John Rose petition the courts to certify that their missing or maimed ears resulted from other causes.

1864

Rose O'Neal Greenhow, Washington socialite turned Confederate agent, drowns off Fort Fisher.

After serving eight months in a Union prison, Greenhow is attempting to reenter the Confederacy from England, but the blockade runner *Condor* runs aground while trying to evade capture. Greenhow is sent ashore in a small boat, which capsizes in the surf.

Recovered when her body washes ashore: a sheet of coded symbols for "Lincoln," "infantry," "horses," etc.

1911

James B. Duke's Southern Power Company, the forerunner of Duke Power Company, brings electricity to Durham.

Among the impressed is a reporter for the *Durham Recorder*: "From the water driven generators on the Rocky Creek below Great Falls, S.C., the mysterious energy flashed over the lines or tower to tower, over hill and valley, through the fields of ripening corn and the forest in which the leaves are turning red and gold into the sub-station located on the hill just beyond the Pearl Cotton Mill."

The 175-mile run from Rocky Creek to Durham is touted as the longest distance over which electric power has ever been transmitted.

1927

Tom Zachary, a Washington Senators pitcher from Graham in Alamance County, lands in the record books twice. In the eighth inning of a game against the New York Yankees, Zachary gives up Babe Ruth's record 60th home run. In the ninth, he is pinch-hit for by pitching great Walter "Big Train" Johnson, who is making his final appearance in the majors.

1933

Black Mountain College, destined to become one of the most important breeding grounds of American art, literature, music, and dance in the 20th century, holds its first faculty meeting.

The college is a Depression-era confluence of the progressive education movement in America and the Bauhaus design school in Germany, carried over by Jewish emigrants exiled by the Nazis.

It is at Black Mountain that composer John Cage will oversee the first "happening," a spontaneous reaction by a group to stimuli. It is also here that R. Buckminster Fuller will build his first geodesic dome and choreographer Merce Cunningham will found his dance company. Among the school's advisers: Albert Einstein and Carl Jung.

Its heyday past, Black Mountain College will succumb to financial problems in 1956. Its campus is sold and becomes a boys' camp.

1959

McDonald's opens its first restaurant in North Carolina, on Summit Avenue in Greensboro. Hamburgers are 15 cents, French fries 10 cents.

Greensboro greets visitors to its centennial in 1908 [October 11].

October

"Patriotic ladies" hold
Edenton Tea Party

N.C. State students
send message to Hitler

Magic Johnson makes final Laker appearance

OCTOBER 1

1963

Harold Hayes, born in Elkin, reared in Winston-Salem, and educated at Wake Forest, takes over as editor of *Esquire*.

Hayes will make the magazine a trailblazer in the iconoclastic "New Journalism," publishing Tom Wolfe's jetstream-of-consciousness notes on a custom-car show as "The Kandy-Kolored Tangerine-Flake Streamline Baby," dispatching black humorists Terry Southern, Jean Genet, and William S. Burroughs to cover the 1968 Democratic Convention, and printing a cover photo of a glowering Sonny Liston in a Santa hat.

1972

Continuing a feud from the previous season, Richard Petty and Bobby Allison smash into each other repeatedly during a NASCAR race at North Wilkesboro.

The violence continues in Victory Lane, where winner Petty is attacked by a drunken fan. His brother, Maurice Petty, beats the fan away with a driver's helmet.

1976

Newspaper executive Derick Daniels, whose grandfather Josephus Daniels was the founder of the *News and Observer* of Raleigh and one of the state's most prominent moralists, is named president of Hugh Hefner's Playboy Enterprises.

OCTOBER 2

OCTOBER 2, 1880

The first train across the Blue Ridge arrives at Asheville, ending the city's isolation and igniting a tourist explosion.

In the coming decade, Asheville's population will jump from 2,610 to 10,237.

1961

Despite brushing against a floating restaurant in the Cape Fear River, the USS *North Carolina* is safely guided by tugboats into its new berth at Wilmington.

The first of the navy's modern battleships, the *North Carolina* received so much attention during its sea trials that it was nicknamed "Showboat."

The ship completed its shakedown cruise just prior to Pearl Harbor and spent most of the war protecting aircraft carriers and supporting island-hopping invasions in the Pacific.

Mothballed in 1947, the *North Carolina* was destined for scrap before a statewide campaign raised $330,000 to convert it to a museum and a memorial to North Carolinians who died in World War II.

OCTOBER 3

1938

With war on the horizon, the most extensive military exercise ever held in the United States takes place in eastern North Carolina between Fort Bragg and the coast. The joint antiaircraft–Air Corps exercise involves civilian volunteers at some 300 lookout stations. "Their purpose," says a newspaper account, is "to observe the approach of enemy airplanes and to report promptly to the Defense Commander at Fort Bragg the strength, types of planes, altitude, speed and direction of movement of the attacking air force."

1949

University of North Carolina halfback Charlie "Choo Choo" Justice, described as looking "a little like Rudolph Valentino made up as Superman," makes the cover of *Life* magazine.

"All of the residents of Chapel Hill and many citizens of other communities think Choo Choo is the best collegiate football player in the world," says *Life*.

"Part of this adulation . . . results from Choo Choo's undoubted technical talents on the gridiron, but part of it also can be attributed to the sense of drama he brings to the game. When

Justice goes back to receive a punt he somehow looks like a man who is going to run 60 or 70 yards for a touchdown. He often does."

Justice finishes second in the Heisman Trophy balloting in both 1948 and 1949.

1951

Russ Hodges, who got his start broadcasting Charlotte Hornets minor-league games, earns a place in baseball history with his radio call of Bobby Thomson's home run off Ralph Branca of the Dodgers, "the Shot Heard Round the World": "There's a long fly. . . . It's gonna be . . . I believe . . . The Giants win the pennant! The Giants win the pennant! The Giants win the pennant!"

OCTOBER 3, 1960

The Andy Griffith Show, set in Mayberry, North Carolina, premieres on CBS.

The first episode, entitled "The New Housekeeper," introduces Aunt Bee (Frances Bavier), who comes to live with widowed sheriff Andy Taylor and his son, Opie (Ron Howard). Don Knotts plays novice deputy Barney Fife.

The series' original concept casts the Mount Airy–born Griffith as a yarn-spinning, guitar-picking good old boy on whom each episode is centered. Griffith quickly sees, however, that the show will work better if he steps back and allows his supporting cast to shine.

1962

An "open letter" advertisement in the *New York Times* urges President John F. Kennedy to delay implementation of recent Supreme Court school desegregation decisions until *Biology of the Race Problem,* a new book by W. C. George, can be introduced as evidence.

Governor John Patterson of Alabama had earlier commissioned George, retired head of the Department of Anatomy at the University of North Carolina School of Medicine, to write a scientific defense of white supremacy.

OCTOBER 4

1856

Benjamin Hedrick, a chemistry professor at the University of North Carolina, publishes a defense of his abolitionist views in the *North Carolina Standard* of Raleigh.

In response, the faculty denounces him, the board of trustees dismisses him, and an unsuccessful attempt is made to tar and feather him at an educational conference in Salisbury.

Hedrick, a native of Davidson County, will flee to New York and spend the rest of his life in the North.

1887

The North Carolina Farmers' Alliance is organized in Rockingham. In addition to seeking political reforms, the alliance tries such cooperative ventures as processing tobacco and manufacturing shoes, but within several years, it will fold.

1902

The *Tar Heel* newspaper reports that the well and the moss-covered oak buckets that previously supplied University of North Carolina students with drinking water have given way to "the new-fangled idea, the pump" at the request of state health authorities.

Five years earlier, university president Edwin Alderman had created an elegant campus landmark—since known by generations of students as "the Old Well"—by ordering the "squalid and ramshackled" well shelter rebuilt to resemble "the Temple of Love in the Garden at Versailles."

1970

Curtis Turner, dubbed by *Sports Illustrated* as "the Babe Ruth of stock car racing," dies when his small plane crashes into a Pennsylvania hillside.

In addition to his on-track exploits, Turner led a short-lived effort to unionize drivers and was a founder of Charlotte Motor Speedway.

OCTOBER 5

1929

Duke University dedicates its new 35,000-seat football stadium, the largest in the South. The game is less grand: the University of Pittsburgh wins 52–7.

1993

The Charlotte Hornets of the NBA announce the signing of all-star forward Larry Johnson to the largest contract in professional team sports in the United States: 12 years, $84 million.

"Pray for me," says team owner George Shinn.

OCTOBER 6

1988

On the fall premiere of *The Cosby Show*, Temple University alumnus Bill Cosby pays off a basketball bet by wearing a Duke University cap and shirt.

1991

Using only a seven-iron and a putter, Chick Evans shoots 126—54 over par—in the last round of the Vantage Championship at Tanglewood Park in Clemmons.

A shoulder injury prevents Evans from raising a club above his waist, but he has to finish 18 holes in order to claim his $1,000 minimum paycheck.

His score is the highest ever recorded on the Senior PGA Tour.

1993

Still in his prime at age 30, former University of North Carolina star Michael Jordan retires from the NBA. He is the world's most famous athlete and perhaps the best ever to play basketball.

In search of a new challenge, Jordan will switch to baseball, but after a season struggling in the minor leagues, he returns to the Chicago Bulls.

1930

President Herbert Hoover visits the textile town of Kings Mountain for the 150th anniversary of the Battle of Kings Mountain, a turning point in the Revolutionary War.

Thousands watch from the curb, store windows, and rooftops as the president and First Lady Lou Henry Hoover, accompanied by no visible security personnel, ride slowly past in an open convertible.

At the battleground, eight miles away in York County, South Carolina, Hoover gives a 22-minute talk before a crowd estimated at 75,000.

The *Charlotte Observer* reports that Hoover, showing the "cares of his office," indirectly responds to charges that he hasn't done anything to ease the Depression precipitated by the previous year's stock-market crash. According to the *Observer*, he compares "the material well-being of the United States with that of other nations of the world," pointing out that twice as many Americans own homes as Europeans and that seven times as many own cars.

A lone heckler yells, "Well, Hoover, all us jackasses are here to get our hay." Nobody laughs, and Hoover doesn't respond.

1942

Students at North Carolina State gather enough scrap metal in two hours and 45 minutes to fill three freight cars. Afterward, they pose with their accumulation and a banner reading, "To Hitler & Co. from N.C. State College."

1964

The Lady Bird Special, the first lady's campaign train through the South, winds up a series of whistle-stop speeches for Lyndon Johnson in Ahoskie, Rocky Mount, Wilson, Selma, Raleigh, and Charlotte.

1864

Captain James Iredell Waddell of Pittsboro in Chatham County, assigned by the Confederacy to cripple the Northern economy by sea, sails from England.

He will take the clipper ship *Shenandoah* as far as Australia, then head north, burning and scuttling ships as he goes. In the Bering Strait, he burns eight American whalers.

More than two months after Appomattox, the *Shenandoah* will fire the last shot of the Civil War—at an American whaling ship off the coast of Alaska.

Waddell's next plan is to sail into San Francisco and hold the city for ransom, but en route he encounters a British ship bearing newspaper accounts of the war's end. Realizing he faces possible piracy charges, Waddell disguises the *Shenandoah* as a merchant vessel and sets sail for England, where he turns it over to British authorities.

1912

Millie McCoy, age 61, dies of tuberculosis at home in her native Columbus County. Her sister Christine, with whom she is joined at the pelvis, will succumb a day later.

Born slaves, the Siamese twins were sold to a series of promoters who exhibited them as curiosities. Freed after the Civil War, the McCoys prospered under their own management. They toured with P. T. Barnum's circus and performed as the "Carolina Nightingale"—Christine singing soprano, Millie alto. On one occasion, Queen Victoria presented them matching brooches.

OCTOBER 9

1837

The steamship *Home*, seeking to break its own record for the fastest passage from New York to Charleston, fails to survive a storm off Cape Hatteras; of its 135 passengers and crew members, 90 perish.

The storm is not especially violent by Outer Banks standards, but the sleek, 220-foot sidewheeler, converted from inland to sea use, can't handle the high waves.

When the boiler fires go out, the captain turns the *Home* toward land and grounds it off Ocracoke Island. As the ship begins breaking up, chaos rules; only three lifeboats and two life preservers are aboard.

At the time, the *Home* disaster stands as the deadliest ever on United States shores. In response, Congress will pass the Steamboat Act, requiring all passenger ships to carry a life preserver for each person on board.

1888

The long-delayed Washington Monument opens to the public. Among the 193 carved memorial stones lining its inner walls is a block of leopardite—a rare, black-spotted granite—representing North Carolina.

The stone is the second submitted from the Charlotte quarry; the first was turned down by the monument committee.

The rejected stone is brought back to Charlotte and used as an "upping block" to help passengers into their carriages. It remains on the Square in downtown until street improvements in the 1940s require its removal to the grounds of the Mint Museum.

1918

The University of North Carolina purchases the collection of North Caroliniana accumulated over 34 years by historian Stephen Beauregard Weeks.

The 10,000 books, perioicals, and maps will become the cornerstone of the university's North Carolina Collection—the most comprehensive single source of printed material about any state in the country.

1983

Richard Petty's win in the Miller 500 at Charlotte Motor Speedway is marred by the revelation that his Pontiac was powered by an illegal engine. NASCAR officials strip Petty of the prize money and Winston Cup points but allow him to keep the victory.

Petty denies knowing his engine exceeded the cubic-inch displacement allowed.

His engine-building brother, Maurice Petty, will later confess to placing wax in the cylinders to trick NASCAR inspectors.

OCTOBER 10

OCTOBER 10, 1934

President Franklin D. Roosevelt appoints University of North Carolina historian R. D. W. Connor, a Wilson native, as the nation's first archivist.

In his new post, Connor, who has made North Carolina's archives a model for other states, faces an unfinished building, an unhired staff, and an unsorted backlog of 150 years of documents. He will spend the next seven years in Washington successfully organizing the National Archives along the lines of North Carolina's, then return to the classroom.

1953

Greensboro planner Romeo Guest, having conceived a research center linked to the University of North Carolina, Duke University, and North Carolina State, comes up with the name Research Triangle Park and writes it in his diary.

The next year, Guest will present the idea to Governor Luther Hodges, who becomes the park's most prominent advocate.

By the mid-1960s, the park will land such tenants as the National Institute of Environmental Health Sciences, IBM, and Burroughs Wellcome.

1960

At the urging of the crowd, whistle-stopping vice presidential candidate Lyndon Johnson becomes the latest celebrity to climb into the seat of Thomasville's famed Big Chair.

The concrete-and-steel chair, 18 feet high on a 12-foot base, is modeled after a Duncan Phyfe in the Smithsonian Institution. Erected in 1951, it is the second to mark Thomasville's standing as the "Chair City of the South." The original, built around 1922, stood 13 feet tall and was made of pine with a steer-hide seat; it succumbed to the elements and had to be dismantled, but not before a photo of visiting evangelist Billy Sunday posing in it made the cover of the *New York Times Magazine*.

OCTOBER 11

1908

Greensboro opens a week of centennial festivities, including a reenactment of the Battle of Guilford Courthouse, a parade of Confederate veterans, and the dedication of the 20,000-seat Hippodrome Auditorium. (The corrugated-iron building, purchased from the Jamestown Exposition of 1907, is billed as second only to Madison Square Garden in seating capacity.)

The *Charlotte Observer* reports favorably on "the generosity shown by the Greensboro white people to the negroes in their midst. At the fair the darky has been given a show and in the auditorium a section. This broad-minded way of dealing with the negro caused favorable comment by visitors."

1975

Sophomore Joe Montana, who opened the season as Notre Dame's fourth-string quarterback, makes his college debut at Chapel Hill with the University of North Carolina leading the nationally ranked Irish 14–6 in the fourth quarter.

Montana, who will go on to become one of the NFL's greatest quarterbacks, takes only 62 seconds to pass for two touchdowns. The final score: Notre Dame 21, UNC 14.

OCTOBER 12

1793

The fledgling University of North Carolina lays the cornerstone for Old East, the nation's first public-university building.

Students pay $5 a year for their rooms in Old East—and are responsible for bringing their own bed, coal, wood, and candles.

1961

Before a crowd of 30,000 in Kenan Stadium, President John F. Kennedy accepts an honorary doctorate from the University of North Carolina.

Showing his characteristic aversion to hats—he thinks they make him look silly—he shuns the traditional mortarboard.

1980

"Romare Bearden: 1970–1980," a retrospective exhibit in honor of a native son, opens at Charlotte's Mint Museum.

Bearden has been called America's foremost master of collage and the most gifted African-Amercan artist of the century.

Born in his great-grandfather's house in 1911, he left Charlotte for New York with his parents when he was about five years old, returned for occasional visits, then stayed away for 50 years. But Bearden came back again and again in his imagination, using colored paper scraps and magazine snippets to depict black life in such works as *Carolina Shout*.

OCTOBER 13

1913

In North Wilkesboro, promoter *extraordinaire* J. Hampton Rich organizes the Boone Trail Highway and Memorial Association to advocate building "an arterial highway to reclaim the counties of the northwestern part of the state."

This goal soon proves too limiting for Rich, a former editor and Baptist preacher and a self-styled "major." Over the next two decades, he will travel first to eastern Tennessee and western North Carolina, then as far as San Francisco and Boston. Rich informs local officials that his research shows that Daniel Boone once passed their way and asks if they are interested in his building a commemorative monument and delivering historical lectures to their schoolchildren. "If a town could raise the money," a federal archivist later observes, "Rich could raise the evidence."

About the marker he placed at the Golden Gate, Rich writes, "The spot was never reached by Boone perhaps except in his dreams but we know that he longed to reach the Pacific and asked many questions about the far famed country of California."

One typical Rich creation resembles an eight-foot-high arrowhead, made of stone and mortar and marked with a metal plaque depicting Boone with rifle, powder horn, and dog.

OCTOBER 13, 1927

The schooner *Maurice R. Thurlow* runs aground during a storm off the Outer Banks. It signals for help, and its crew of nine is taken ashore in a Coast Guard surfboat.

Few ships stranded on Diamond Shoals are ever refloated, but after the storm, the Coast Guard can find no trace of the *Maurice R. Thurlow*. Thirteen days later, a Dutch tanker will sight it in the North Atlantic. Every few days, the wayward schooner is reported in a different location, but it is never overtaken. Its fate remains unknown.

1982

In Lausanne, Switzerland, the International Olympic Committee restores two gold medals won by the late Jim Thorpe.

Thorpe, an American Indian voted the greatest athlete of the first half of the century, won his medals in the pentathlon and decathlon in the 1912 games at Stockholm. A few months later, however, a newspaper revealed that Thorpe had been paid $2 a game to play semipro baseball with the Rocky Mount Railroaders. The practice was common among collegians at the time, but the IOC declared Thorpe a professional, wiped out his records, and reclaimed his medals.

Almost three decades after his death, the campaign led by his descendants finally persuades the IOC to reverse its decision.

OCTOBER 14

1927

Six months after his historic transatlantic flight, Charles Lindbergh circles Greensboro's Tri-City Airport several times, eyeing a waiting crowd of thousands, before touching down in the *Spirit of St. Louis*.

Lindbergh, on a coast-to-coast tour promoting aviation, is welcomed by Governor Angus McLean and the mayors of Greensboro and High Point. He makes a brief talk at World War Stadium, then flies to Winston-Salem, where he dedicates Miller Municipal Airport, addresses schoolchildren at Hanes Park, and attends a banquet in his honor. He leaves for Richmond the next morning.

1951

WBTV in Charlotte and WFMY-TV in Greensboro carry the state's first Washington Redskins telecast. The image is grainy black-and-white and the Redskins lose to the Cleveland Browns 45–0, but North Carolinians like what they see.

The Redskins network is the creation of team owner George Preston Marshall and is sponsored by Amoco gasoline—the NFL's lucrative TV packages are still years away.

Marshall plays to white Southern fans, maintaining an all-white roster until 1962. He signs such regional favorites as Charlie "Choo Choo" Justice, plays exhibitions in Winston-Salem, and even includes in the team fight song—"Hail to the Redskins"—the line, "Fight for old Dixie," later chnged to "Fight for old D.C."

OCTOBER 15

1929

As part of Light's Golden Jubilee—the international commemoration of the 50th anniversary of Thomas Edison's invention of the light bulb—the State Capitol is illuminated by floodlights for the first time.

On hand for the ceremony is Governor Franklin D. Roosevelt of New York, who had spoken earlier at the state fair and the state homecoming. The *News and Observer* refers to Roosevelt as "the man most often mentioned as Democracy's next standard-bearer."

1946

In the eighth inning of game seven of the World Series, Enos "Country" Slaughter of Roxboro in Person County dashes home from first base on a single.

The tie-breaking run holds up, giving the St. Louis Cardinals the world championship and ensuring endless controversy over Boston Red Sox shortstop Johnny Pesky's delayed throw home; Slaughter blames Pesky's teammates for failing to alert him to the play at the plate.

1951

A Winston-Salem crowd of 20,000 hears President Harry Truman defend American involvement in the Korean War as necessary for world peace. He is the first president to visit the city since George Washington in 1791.

Truman, a Baptist, has come for the groundbreaking at the new site of Wake Forest, the nation's oldest and largest Baptist college.

Lured by a 600-acre estate donated by the Reynolds family, trustees decided to abandon the school's original campus in the town of Wake Forest.

1954

Thomas Wolfe's birthplace is sold for salvage.

Mostly vacant for the past decade, the house on Woodfin Street in Asheville has fallen into disrepair; its fate brings scant complaint from Wolfe's family or preservationists.

However, a one-room playhouse built by Wolfe's father, W. O., is moved to the backyard of the Thomas Wolfe Memorial—the former Old Kentucky Home, where Wolfe's mother,

Julia, took in boarders after she and the children moved when Tom was six years old.

1954

Hazel, the most lethal hurricane ever to hit North Carolina, leaves 19 dead.

1971

President Richard Nixon comes to the Charlotte Coliseum to honor hometown boy Billy Graham, whom he labels "the top preacher in the world."

But Nixon's speech plays second fiddle to a civil liberties issue: using hair length as their main criterion, the Secret Service and police bar suspected antiwar activists, including members of the radical Red Hornet Mayday Tribe, on the grounds that they might disrupt the ceremonies.

Eighteen protesters will unsuccessfully sue for damages.

OCTOBER 16

1749

Attempting to quell the popular no-holds-barred sport of "gouging," the North Carolina legislature makes it a felony "to cut out the tongue, or pull out the eyes."

The law proves no match, however, for combatants' creativity. Five years later, the proscription must be extended to "the slitting of noses, the biting or cutting off of a nose or lip, and the biting or cutting off of any limb or member."

In colonial North Carolina, the gentry favors horse racing and cockfighting, but the yeoman class prefers "rough and tumble" fighting and "gouging." One contemporary account describes "two men . . . fast clinched by the hair . . . while several of the bystanders were betting upon the first eye to be turned out of its socket. . . . At length the uppermost sprung up with his antagonist's eye in his hand!!! The savage crowd applauded."

As late as 1810, the *Raleigh Star* will acknowledge the widely held belief "that a North Carolinian cannot salute you without putting his finger in your eyes," even though it insists that civilization has driven "gouging" to "Georgia and the wilds of Louisiana."

1928

Concord native Robert Phifer, a retired cotton merchant and investor, dies in a sanatorium in Battle Creek, Michigan.

Phifer, a bachelor, leaves not only his art collection but also a trust fund of more than $1 million to the North Carolina Art Society. His bequest eventually will form the backbone of the North Carolina Museum of Art in Raleigh.

1939

One month after the passage of the Selective Service Act, North Carolina election officials and volunteers register—in a single day—more than 450,000 men between the ages of 21 and 36.

By the end of World War II, 258,000 North Carolinians will serve in the army, 90,000 in the navy, and 13,000 in the marines. Of these, 4,088 die in action.

1865

Sidney Andrews, Southern correspondent for the *Boston Daily Advertiser* and the *Chicago Tribune* during the early days of Reconstruction, sums up his observations of North Carolina:

Spindling of legs, round of shoulders, sunken of chest, lank of body, stooping of posture, narrow of face, retreating of forehead, thin of nose, small of chin, large of mouth—this is the native North Carolinian as one sees him outside the cities and large towns.

There is insipidity in his face, indecision in his step, and inefficiency in his whole bearing. His house has two rooms and a loft, and is meanly furnished—one, and possibly two, beds, three or four chairs, half a dozen stools, a cheap pine table, an old spinning-wheel, a water-bucket and drinking gourd, two tin washbasins, half a dozen tin platters, a few cooking utensils, and a dozen odd pieces of crockery. Paint and whitewash and wall-paper and window-curtains are to him needless luxuries.

His wife is leaner, more round-shouldered, more sunken of chest, and more pinched of face than her husband. He "chaws" and she "dips." The children of these two are large-eyed, tow-headed urchins, alike ignorant of the decencies and the possibilities of life. In this house there is often neither book nor newspaper; and, what is infinitely worse, no longing for either. The day begins at sunrise and ends at dark; its duties are alike devoid of dignity and mental or moral compensation. The man has a small farm, and once owned six or eight negroes. How the family now lives, the propping hands of the negroes being taken away, is a mystery, even if one remembers the simple cheapness of mere animal life.

1908

William Howard Taft becomes the first Republican presidential candidate ever to campaign in North Carolina. His train makes whistle stops in Statesville, Salisbury, Lexington, High Point, and Greensboro before continuing to Virginia.

Because Taft has a sore throat, his Salisbury speech is moved indoors, from a vacant lot on the square to the opera house. "I have come here because I deeply sympathize with the South," Taft says. "I am anxious that it should take its place at the council board of the nation. I am anxious that you should exercise the influence through your able and great men, of whom you have many, in the same way that Ohio and Indiana and New York and Massachusetts do. But, my dear friends, if you are going simply from historic tradition to keep voting the Democratic ticket . . . then you are bound to stay on the outside and look in at others enjoying the power."

Taft will easily defeat Democrat William Jennings Bryan for the presidency, but it is another 20 years before North Carolina goes Republican, choosing Herbert Hoover over Al Smith.

1988

Gertrude Elion, 70, and George Hitchings, 83, longtime research partners at Burroughs Wellcome in Research Triangle Park, win the

Nobel Prize for medicine. Among their accomplishments: paving the way for the anti-AIDS drug AZT.

Elion's career almost didn't get off the ground. After graduating from Hunter College in New York in 1937 with a degree in biochemistry, she had to teach high school for several years because laboratories would hire only men for research jobs. Only in 1944, when World War II forced open new job categories for women, did Burroughs Wellcome hire Elion as Hitchings's assistant.

OCTOBER 18

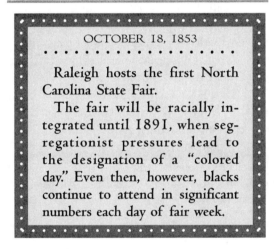

OCTOBER 18, 1853

Raleigh hosts the first North Carolina State Fair.

The fair will be racially integrated until 1891, when segregationist pressures lead to the designation of a "colored day." Even then, however, blacks continue to attend in significant numbers each day of fair week.

1877

"More than once I have been called upon to hear agricultural addresses at our annual fairs," Governor Wade Hampton of South Carolina says at the North Carolina State Fair in Raleigh, "and I have had the misfortune to make them myself. . . . I must say that to the listener and speaker I have always found them great bores."

To the relief of his audience, Hampton instead speaks on the Civil War. The 1877 fair is the first since the end of Reconstruction, and North Carolinians' appetite for martial entertainment is high. Hampton, alongside Governor Zebulon Vance of North Carolina, a fellow Confederate general, reviews 20 marching units.

1888

In the state's first recognized intercollegiate football game, played during the North Carolina State Fair in Raleigh, Wake Forest defeats the University of North Carolina 6–4.

At a first-aid station staffed by young women from St. Mary's School, injured players receive a slap in the face with Fair Special Cologne.

1900

Orville Wright, uncomfortably encamped at Kitty Hawk, writes his sister,

> This is "just before the battle," sister, just before the squall begins. About two or three nights a week we have to crawl up at 10 or 11 o'clock to hold the tent down. When one of these 45-mile nor'easters strikes us, you can depend on it, there is little sleep in our camp for the night. Expect another tonight. We have passed through one which took up two or three wagon-loads of sand from the N.E. end of our tent and piled it up eight inches deep on the flying machine. . . . We certainly can't complain of the place. We came down here for wind and sand, and we have got them.

1929

Thomas Wolfe's first novel is published by Scribner's. It dazzles reviewers; Sinclair Lewis, in Stockholm to receive the Nobel Prize for literature, tells his audience that *Look Homeward, Angel* is "worthy to be compared with the best in our literary production, a Gargantuan creature with great gusto of life."

But Wolfe's hometown of Asheville is shocked and embarrassed. Many of his characters are readily identifiable as local citizens. His old teacher, Margaret Roberts, is among the most affected. "You have crucified your family and devastated mine," she writes him.

In the *News and Observer* of Raleigh, Jonathan Daniels, a friend of Wolfe's from their college days at the University of North Carolina, rages that "North Carolina and the South are spat upon."

It will be eight years before Wolfe goes home again.

1945

Ava Gardner marries bandleader Artie Shaw, the second of her three husbands, in Beverly Hills.

OCTOBER 19

1874

R. J. Reynolds pays the Moravian Church $388.50 for a lot in Winston.

The 24-year-old Reynolds has been selling tobacco products for his father out of Critz, Virginia, but is attracted to Winston's new railroad and warehouses and its proximity to flue-cured tobacco.

His "Little Red Factory" on Chestnut Street will turn out 150,000 pounds of plug tobacco in its first year.

1905

President Theodore Roosevelt, making a Raleigh stop on his Southern rail tour to promote Appalachian conservation and railroad regulation, presents John Charles McNeill with the Patterson Memorial Cup, awarded to the North Carolina writer who has displayed "the highest literary skill and genius" in the past year.

McNeill, born on a farm near Wagram in Scotland County, is perhaps the first North Carolina writer to achieve regional recognition. His poetry and journalism appear widely, from the *Charlotte Observer* to the *Atlantic Monthly*.

Roosevelt ends his day by making brief remarks from a gazebo in a Charlotte park. After accepting a bouquet of roses from five-year-old Miriam Methany, he evokes a roar from the crowd by hoisting her in his arms and proclaiming, "Here is the best product, the finest crop."

1911

The Glidden Tour, a cross-country caravan promoting the automobile, approaches North Carolina from Virginia, where residents have complained about their dogs being run over. The *Charlotte Observer*, however, doesn't hesitate to roll out the welcome mat: "Roaming dogs are not held in high esteem in this community. . . . Speed up and enjoy yourselves."

1913

The first modern-type tobacco blend goes into production in Winston-Salem.

Within a decade, Camels will account for almost half the cigarettes sold in the United States.

R. J. Reynolds considered naming his new brand after Kaiser Wilhelm but was saved by second thoughts: "I don't think we should name a product for a living man. You can never tell what the damn fool will do."

Indeed, soon after Camels hit the market, the kaiser's war breaks out—and free cigarettes for doughboys in France create a generation of loyal Camel smokers.

1923

Efird's Department Store, billed as "the Only Store South of Philadelphia with Escalators," opens on North Tryon Street in Charlotte.

1940

Mountain Folk, a clumsily stereotypical documentary, premieres in Franklin.

Audience reaction is so negative that the University of North Carolina Extension Service, which has partly underwritten the project, will insist that the New York and Texas producers retitle the film *Remnants of Frontier Life in the Southern Highlands* and erase from the soundtrack references to Franklin and Macon County—and the word *typical*.

1948

President Harry Truman, speaking on the State Capitol grounds in Raleigh at the unveiling of the *Three Presidents Statue*—which honors Andrew Jackson, James K. Polk, and Andrew Johnson—takes a discreet poke at Southerners who have broken away from the Democratic Party because of his civil rights proposals. Jackson, says Truman, understood that "the way to correct injustice in democracy is by reason and debate, never by walking out in a huff."

1957

At College Park, Maryland, Queen Elizabeth II and Prince Philip watch their first football game, the University of Maryland's 21–7 upset of the University of North Carolina.

Among those seated with the royal party: Governor Luther Hodges, who leaps to his feet and waves his hat when the Tar Heel band breaks into "Dixie."

OCTOBER 20

1862

Annie Carter Lee, 23-year-old daughter of General Robert E. Lee, dies soon after arriving in Warren County.

General Lee, concerned about the well-being of his wife and four daughters in Virginia, had sent them to the White Sulphur Springs spa near Warrenton in Warren County, but Annie was already fatally stricken with typhoid fever.

In wartime, returning her body to Virginia is impractical, so she is buried in the family plot of the spa's owner.

Lee cannot attend the funeral. In 1870, however, he will arrive in Warrenton on the train, unannounced, to visit the grave. Old and ill, he is only months from death. Willie White, a Confederate veteran, recognizes him instantly and takes him in. Word of Lee's visit spreads, but the community respects his wishes not to be disturbed.

The next morning, as Lee prepares to drive out to the grave, he finds his carriage filled with freshly cut flowers. Townspeople stand silently by the roadside to get a glimpse.

In 1994, against the wishes of the local chapter of the United Daughters of the Confederacy, the Lee family will have Annie's remains unearthed from beneath an 11-foot obelisk erected by Warren Countians. She is reburied in the family crypt at Washington and Lee University in Lexington, Virginia.

1905

The Greater Charlotte Club, forerunner of the modern Charlotte Chamber of Commerce, is organized in the law office of Edmund Randolph Preston. Its slogan: "Watch Charlotte Grow."

Preston will describe Charlotte as "the center of the finest section of the United States, blest as it is with the best all-year-round climate and sturdy, Christian, Anglo-Saxon population in the world, and literally teeming with the possibilities of business and industrial development that stagger the imagination to contemplate. . . . From this time on, all that we ask of those within and without our border is 'Watch Charlotte Grow.'"

1928

Exemplifying the cigarette industry's effort to win over women, a full-page ad in *Progressive Farmer* magazine offers this testimonial from Amelia Earhart: "Lucky Strikes were the cigarettes carried on the *Friendship* when she crossed the Atlantic. They were smoked continuously from Trepassey [Newfoundland] to Wales. I think nothing else helped so much to lessen the strain for all of us."

By keeping the log for the *Friendship*'s two pilots, Earhart had recently become world-famous as the first woman to fly across the Atlantic Ocean.

1942

Fifty-seven black Southerners meet at North Carolina College for Negroes in Durham for the Southern Conference on Race Relations.

Out of the conference comes a statement denouncing segregation and urging that steps be taken to end all discriminatory practices against blacks. In turn, the Durham Statement (or Manifesto) will lead to the creation in 1944 of the influential Southern Regional Council.

1955

No Time for Sergeants, a hayseed-in-the-army comedy that gives Mount Airy native Andy Griffith his first major national exposure, opens on Broadway.

It will run for 796 performances, inspire a movie and a TV sitcom, and introduce Griffith to fellow cast member Don Knotts, the future Barney Fife of Mayberry.

1958

"A Lover's Question," sung by Durham native Clyde McPhatter, reaches the top-40 chart en route to number six. His other big hit, "Lover Please," comes three years later and makes number seven.

McPhatter, also known as the founder and lead singer of the Drifters, will die of a heart attack at age 39 in New York City in 1972.

1969

After Governor Bob Scott complains to the press about problems with the 78-year-old Executive Mansion, WBTV in Charlotte joins his call to raze and replace it:

> Though Victorian architecture leaned toward the frilly, there are many such buildings that have a graceful and airy charm. By contrast, the Executive Mansion is a hodgepodge of turrets, balconies, gables and architectural gingerbread assembled into one tasteless mass. At its best, it's pompous; at its worst, it's ludicrous. . . . The governor's mansion was a mistake when it was built, continues to be a mistake and has little value beyond the furnishings it holds and the price that could be gotten out of the sale of its salvage.

At the instruction of the legislature, plans will be drawn for a "French country" residence for the governor; reaction is overwhelmingly negative, however, and the tide turns in favor of renovation, which is completed in 1975.

1986

A Phoenix newspaper columnist covering an NBA owners' meeting predicts that "the only franchise Charlotte gets will have golden arches."

Although entrepreneur George Shinn's bid for an expansion team starts out as a long shot, within six months the NBA is won over. The Charlotte Hornets open play in 1988.

OCTOBER 21

1882

Presbyterian minister Joseph Wilson, the father of Woodrow Wilson, laments in a letter to his son the demands of his latest flock: "My work here in Wilmington seems to be done, and I think I see evidences amongst the people that some of them think so too. Yet I never preached so well. . . . The fault they find with me is as to visiting. They want a gad-about gossip."

OCTOBER 21, 1993

In Raleigh, *Madonna and Child in a Landscape* is unveiled as the year's traditional Christmas postage stamp.

The oil painting, completed by Giovanni Battista Cima da Congeliano in 1497, had hung in the North Carolina Museum of Art's Italian Renaissance gallery for more than 30 years with little fanfare. But its selection by the United States Postal Service spawns a cottage-industry bonanza, including greeting cards, postcards, key chains, tie tacks, lapel pins, earrings, cuff links, and a miniature Christmas ornament. Americans will buy a billion of the *Madonna* stamps.

1936

The state's first art museum opens in Charlotte.

The structure housing the Mint Museum of Art originated 100 years earlier as the first branch of the United States Mint, striking coins from the output of the Carolina gold rush. It shut down during the Civil War, reopened afterward as an assay office, and closed for good in 1913.

The building was scheduled for demolition until a citizens' group paid to have it dismantled, moved stone by stone from downtown to suburban Eastover, and converted into a museum.

1959

Governor Luther Hodges and the state's civil defense director unveil an atomic fallout shelter in the basement of the Executive Mansion.

The shelter is outfitted with a two-week supply of food and water for the governor and five family members.

1965

Roy Woodle, a bricklayer and itinerant preacher, tells a subcommittee of the House Un-American Activities Committee that the Ku Klux Klan is a "fake" organization that preaches "good things"—segregation and Christianity—but does nothing about them. Its true purpose, he says, is furnishing its leaders with "Cadillacs, rib-eye steaks . . . and first-class motel rooms."

Woodle says he recently quit the Klan after serving as chaplain—"Grand Kludd"—for North Carolina.

The Klan has grown, he says, by promising "victory, that the schools wouldn't integrate. But the Klan don't have no program."

Woodle is one of more than a dozen Klan witnesses from North Carolina called to testify; most refuse. The hearings are held in response to President Lyndon Johnson's call for a congressional investigation of the Klan after the murder of civil rights worker Viola Liuzzo in Alabama.

1994

Comic actress Martha Raye, tireless entertainer of troops during three wars, becomes the first civilian buried in the cemetery at Fort Bragg.

Raye, who died at age 78, was especially beloved by Green Berets for her service during the widely protested Vietnam War.

1896

The United States Post Office tests rural free delivery in China Grove.

The new service must overcome resistance from Rowan County farm families who don't like neighbors being able to snoop in their mailboxes, but by 1898, R.F.D. will spread from China Grove (and Charleston, West Virginia, the other test site) across the nation.

1945

Addressing a conference at Duke University, endowed by James B. Duke's tobacco fortune, New Orleans surgeon Alton Ochsner cites "a distinct parallelism between the incidence of cancer of the lung and the sale of cigarettes. . . . Smoking is a factor because of the chronic irritation it produces."

OCTOBER 23, 1985

Merle Watson, 36-year-old son and partner of Doc Watson, dies in a tractor accident in Caldwell County.

Together, the Watsons performed traditional North Carolina mountain music before worldwide audiences, recorded 23 albums, and shared Grammy awards in 1974 and 1980.

Merle Watson was 15 when his father, the blind guitar virtuoso from Deep Gap, first brought him onstage.

1990

Seven bronze figures by sculptor Julia Belk are erected in front of Davis Library at the University of North Carolina.

In short order, more than 500 students will petition to have *The Student Body* removed, saying it perpetuates "racial and sexual stereotypes already ingrained in society."

Found particularly offensive: a black man balancing a basketball on his finger, a black woman balancing a book on her head, and a white woman holding an apple and apparently leaning on a white man for support.

The administration later responds by moving the sculpture to a less prominent site.

OCTOBER 24

1918

Influenza claims the life of 42-year-old Edward Kidder Graham, president of the University of North Carolina.

More than 13,000 North Carolinians, most of them between 20 and 40 years of age, will die before the flu runs its course.

The worldwide epidemic proves a boon, however, to Vick's Chemical Company of Greensboro. Thanks to heavy advertising and good timing, Vick's VapoRub, a menthol salve invented years before by founder Lunsford Richardson, becomes a staple in American sickrooms.

1992

The opening of the 60-story NationsBank Corporate Center gives Charlotte the South's tallest building (unless you count NationsBank Plaza in Atlanta, which is about 100 feet taller by virtue of the spire atop its 55 stories).

The $150-million tower, designed by acclaimed architect Cesar Pelli, ousts 42-story One First Union Center, erected in 1987 by NationsBank's archrival, as Charlotte's (and the state's) tallest.

OCTOBER 25

1774

In what comes to be known as the Edenton

Tea Party, 51 self-described "patriotic ladies" meet and resolve, in writing, to boycott East Indian tea as long as it is taxed by the British—one of the first political actions by American women.

Although their behavior is treasonous and their names will be reported in a London newspaper, they are not taken seriously.

1864

Captain Conley of the 101st Pennsylvania Volunteers, an escaped prisoner of war for the past three weeks, recalls his arrival with two other escapees at a Union sympathizer's farm "just over the crest of the Blue Ridge" in Polk County: "Mr. Stanton brought out to us his two sons, young men about 18 and 20 years of age, who as we learned were compelled to keep in hiding to escape the conscription which prevailed through the Confederacy and included every man able to do military duty. Mr. Stanton suggested that his sons join us and go with us to Knoxville, saying that he thought it would be best for them to get inside the Union lines and remain there until the close of the war."

1924

More than 50,000 people pack the grandstands and infield for the inaugural race at the first Charlotte Speedway. The 250-mile contest features the same drivers who competed in the Indianapolis 500.

The track, a daringly banked mile oval, is built of two-by-four wooden boards. The cars, one-seat ancestors of modern-day Indianapolis-style racers, reach speeds of 130 miles per hour. The drivers wear pilot-style caps and goggles.

The speedway is part of a national circuit of board tracks that lifts racing from its dirt-track origins. But the Charlotte Speedway closes in 1927, the victim of a dangerously deteriorating surface—boards pop out and stand upright—and shrinking crowds.

In 1960, some 25 miles to the north, the Charlotte Motor Speedway will open, again making Charlotte a racing hub.

1937

Time magazine's cover: Wallace Wade, Duke University football coach. The headline, noting the South's newfound football prowess, is classic *Time*speak: "Southward the Course of History Takes Its Way."

1954

Time magazine's cover: Billy Graham, Charlotte-born evangelist. "Practical jokes are standard operating procedure," reports *Time*. "One [ministry] team member, noting that the usually hatless Graham had bought himself a new hat in Dallas, filled it with shaving cream and rocked with laughter when Billy put it on. Billy gives as good as he gets. On the ship to London, he emptied [aide Grady Wilson's] seasickness capsules and filled them with mustard."

OCTOBER 26

1895

The first forward pass in intercollegiate

football is thrown by the University of North Carolina against the University of Georgia in Atlanta. Perhaps.

According to witness John Heisman, the man for whom the Heisman Trophy is named, the UNC punter panicked under a heavy rush and tossed the ball to George Stephens, who ran 70 yards for the game's only score. Although years later Stephens will be unable to recall a pass, Heisman insists that he witnessed the then-illegal play from the sidelines—and that Georgia coach Pop Warner futilely protested it.

Regardless, Heisman quickly takes up advocacy of the pass. It will be legalized in 1906 but not popularized until Notre Dame uses it to upset Army in 1913.

Stephens goes on to found both Charlotte's landmark Myers Park suburb and American Trust Company, predecessor of NationsBank.

1920

In Durham, Trinity College (the future Duke University) defeats Guilford College 20–7, ending Trinity's 25-year absence from intercollegiate football.

Fearing professionalism, the faculty banned the sport in 1895.

1993

The NFL awards Charlotte an expansion franchise, to be named the Carolina Panthers. Speaking into television cameras in Chicago, team owner Jerry Richardson has a message for fans back home, who have bought more than 40,000 permanent seat licenses to pay for the Panthers' stadium: "Thank you, thank you, thank you, thank you!"

OCTOBER 27

1827

The *Tarboro Free Press* expounds on the benefits of tobacco: "It forms the traveler's companion and the philosopher's aid. It is the old bachelor's antidote, the epicure's last resort and the sailor's and soldier's third daily ration. It keeps open the sentinel's eyes, and besides medical and many other good effects, it cheers the watchman in the silence of the night."

• • • • • • • OCTOBER 27, 1864 • • • • • • •

The Confederate ironclad ram *Albemarle*, which has fled up the Roanoke River to Plymouth to avoid naval bombardment, is sunk during a daring raid by a Union launch. A torpedo extended beneath the ram's hull on a spar ends the *Albemarle's* six-month challenge to Union control of the North Carolina coast.

OCTOBER 28

1864

Captain Conley of the 101st Pennsylvania Volunteers, escaped prisoner of war, describes life at a mountain hideout in Transylvania County:

Mr. Bishop brought us a large Dutch oven which would at least hold a half bushel, and had a cast iron lid. This was our only cooking utensil. In this we baked our corn bread and cooked our pork and potatoes. Three times a day we would put on a large supply of pork and while it was cooking, we would pare enough potatoes to fill it and when cooked, we would set it down and our whole company now eight in number (including the two men who owned the shanty) would surround it. We seasoned with salt and cayenne pepper in pods. Having no plates, knives or forks or spoons, we made forks and spoons of wood and with them we all helped ourselves from the Spider, or Dutch Oven, as we call it in Pennsylvania. The Stanton boys, with Mr. Bishop's permission, would go to the orchard every day and bring us a good supply of apples. So with corn bread, pork and potatoes, and apples we were able to live very well.

1959

Charlottetown Mall, the first enclosed mall in the Carolinas, opens in Charlotte. It is the third shopping center developed by the Rouse Company, whose future projects will include Harborplace in Baltimore, Faneuil Hall in Boston, South Street Seaport in New York, and Underground Atlanta.

1985

Bhagwan Shree Rajneesh is arrested when his Learjet lands at Charlotte/Douglas International Airport. Federal agents say the impish, bearded guru, who preaches a blend of Eastern religion and free love and has acquired more than 90 Rolls-Royces and a 64,000-acre Or-

egon commune, is attempting to evade immigration authorities by fleeing to Bermuda.

Awaiting a bond hearing before being flown back to Oregon, the 53-year-old bhagwan will spend eight days as the Mecklenburg County Jail's most celebrated prisoner. He pleads guilty to violating federal immigration laws and is deported to India, where he dies of heart failure in 1990.

OCTOBER 29

OCTOBER 29, 1618

In England, Sir Walter Raleigh, the colonizer of Carolina, is beheaded to appease the Spanish, against whom he led raids in South America. His historic influence notwithstanding, Raleigh never set foot in North America.

1901

Sharpshooter Annie Oakley, considered by Will Rogers to be "the best-known woman in the world," nearly dies in a train wreck near Linwood in Davidson County.

After playing to a crowd of 12,000 in Charlotte, she and the Buffalo Bill Wild West Show are en route to Danville, Virginia, for their season finale. About 3 A.M., the Wild West train collides head-on with a southbound freight. Although no people are killed, 110 horses die or have to be destroyed.

The show will be out of business for a year. Southern Railway barely survives the damages it has to pay Buffalo Bill Cody.

Oakley, 40, suffers internal injuries and is partly paralyzed; it will be two years before she performs again.

In 1915, she and husband Frank Butler move to the Carolina Hotel in Pinehurst, where they teach shooting for several years.

1937

The Robesonian's announcement of a new Lumberton movie house illustrates the special complexity of segregation in a triracial community.

Whites, it says, will use the white front entrance and sit on the lower floor. Indians will use the Indian front entrance and sit in the Indian section of the balcony. Blacks will use a side entrance and sit in the black section of the balcony.

1956

The Huntley-Brinkley Report debuts on NBC. The format, cutting back and forth between Chet Huntley in New York and David Brinkley in Washington, breaks ground for TV news, and "Good night, Chet," "Good night, David" becomes an instant trademark.

Huntley, whose roots are in Montana, plays straight man to the droll and quirky Brinkley, a Wilmington native who skipped college and once worked for United Press International in Charlotte.

Brinkley hates the famous sign-off, devised by producer Reuven Frank. As he reveals later, "I thought it was stupid—two grown men saying good night to each other—and so did Chet. We should have said good night to the audience. But Reuven insisted."

1993

Tarboro requires six overtimes to defeat Hertford County 70–69. The combined 139 points are the most ever scored in a North Carolina high-school football game.

OCTOBER 30

1992

In an exhibition game at the University of North Carolina's Smith Center, Magic Johnson, who has announced he is HIV-positive, makes his final appearance as a member of the Los Angeles Lakers.

Johnson hits only one of 10 field-goal attempts against the Cleveland Cavaliers, but it is the reaction to a small cut he suffers on the court that spurs him to end his comeback plan.

"You know, you could see the fear upon people's faces," Johnson says later. "Did he bandage it all? Is it all bandaged up? Is it all right? It's not leaking? You know, that whole thing."

OCTOBER 31

1931

William Faulkner, whose lurid novel *Sanctuary* has just rescued him from obscurity, arrives in Chapel Hill as the guest of Milton "Ab" Abernethy—student radical, founder of the fledgling Intimate Bookshop, and publisher of the literary review *Contempo*.

Faulkner spends his three days in town on a drunken binge. He agrees to provide material for an all-Faulkner issue of *Contempo*, but literary historians will find his visit most notable for the fact that he loses—forever—page 12 from his *Light in August* manuscript.

1933

In the midst of the Depression, Governor J. C. B. Ehringhaus's official car, a four-year-old Lincoln with 190,000 miles on the odometer, is sidelined for repairs for the sixth time in his months-old administration.

Scheduled to open the Cumberland County Fair, Ehringhaus borrows a Ford, but it, too, breaks down, 25 miles short of Fayetteville.

Several cars pass the thumbing governor and his chauffeur before a salesman from Missouri stops. "Well, now ain't this something, giving the governor a lift," he says. "I wish I had a picture of this to send my factory."

1934

In an unlikely industrial recruitment session at the Sir Walter Hotel in Raleigh, chamber of commerce officials from across the state discuss what to do if, in the words of the *News and Observer*, "Upton Sinclair, the Big Bad Wolf of California politics, chases the Three Little Pigs and the rest of the movie people out of Hollywood."

Novelist Sinclair's socialistic gubernatorial campaign does indeed have the moguls in a swivet, but his big lead vanishes—in large part because of Hollywood's ahead-of-its-time newsreel propaganda—and North Carolina will have to wait half a century to welcome its moviemaking colony.

1947

Disc jockey and promoter Connie B. Gay, born on a tobacco farm near Lizard Lick in Wake County, produces a breakthrough country-music extravaganza at Washington's Constitution Hall. His headliners include Eddy Arnold, Minnie Pearl, T. Texas Tyler, Cowboy Copas, and Kitty Wells, and his invitation-only audience, at $6 a head, includes senators, cabinet members, and important lobbyists.

The turnout helps disprove the conventional wisdom that only the poor, ignorant, and powerless enjoy the *Grand Ole Opry* and gives "country"—the term Gay prefers to "hillbilly"—a significant push into the metropolitan radio markets that have shunned it.

Gay, who first came to Washington to announce the Department of Agriculture's daily network radio show, will parlay his entertainment acumen—he discovers or manages such performers as Grandpa Jones, Roy Clark, Jimmy Dean, Kitty Wells, and Patsy Cline—into a chain of nine radio stations. "I must have hit it about the right time," he says later. "It was a postwar thing. Adolf Hitler had mixed up everybody, so that the old boy from Maine might have heard his buddy from Arkansas picking a guitar or playing an Acuff record, and he liked it."

One of Gay's lasting achievements, however, will make him no money. In 1958, with rock 'n' roll threatening to steamroll country music into oblivion, he and Nashville music publisher Wesley Rose found the Country Music Association. With the CMA as its dominant promoter, country rebounds to become a phenomenally prosperous mass-appeal medium.

1990
A TV commercial for Senator Jesse Helms shows the hands of a white man holding and then slowly crumpling a job rejection letter.

Democratic challenger and former Charlotte mayor Harvey Gantt, who is black, denies supporting racial quotas, but the "hands" commercial helps Helms take command of the campaign and makes a national issue of race in the workplace.

Recruited to record the theme song for the good-health campaign of 1946 [November 9] were Dinah Shore, Frank Sinatra, and Rocky Mount's Kay Kyser.

North Carolina Collection, University of North Carolina

November

Blackbeard meets end at Ocracoke Island
Art Buchwald hitchhikes to see girlfriend
Jack Nicholson guests on "Andy Griffith Show"

NOVEMBER 1

1935

North Carolina requires that motor-vehicle drivers be licensed.

1980

Esquire magazine profiles Shelby's Rolls-Royce–leasing Earl Owensby as "A Very Minor Movie Mogul." The *Washington Post* will dub him "the red-clay Cecil B. DeMacho."

By whatever title, Owensby churns out low-budget action films—like *Chain Gang; Rottweiler, Dogs from Hell*; and *Rutherford County Line*—that bomb with American audiences but do nicely overseas.

By decade's end, however, Owensby will run into financial problems, and the sound stages at EO Studios fall quiet.

1985

The *Charlotte News*, once the Carolinas' largest afternoon daily, ceases publication at age 97.

NOVEMBER 2

1904

The north wall of Winston's brick reservoir, built in the form of a truncated pyramid, suddenly collapses, sending tons of water rushing down Trade Street toward the railroad tracks.

Within moments, the city has suffered its worst disaster: nine people are dead, the reservoir is rubble, and houses in the water's path are woodpiles.

1919

In Elizabeth City, Margaret Sanger gives the South's first public lecture on birth control.

Sanger, a New Yorker invited by maverick newspaper editor W. O. Saunders, will recall later that she was skeptical of her reception "in a city in which not even a suffragist had delivered a public lecture. To my delight, however, I found that people, both black and white . . . were so eager to know about birth control that every possible moment of my time was given to speaking. . . .

"Never have I met with more sympathy, more serious attention, more complete understanding than in . . . this Southern mill town."

1920

Permitted to vote for the first time in North Carolina history, women turn out in such numbers that ballot counting is delayed.

1962

Dashing state archivist H. G. Jones's hopes of establishing that the song "Carolina Moon"

refers exclusively to North Carolina, lyricist Benny Davis insists that the question leaves him "really at sea."

Jones was inquiring at the behest of Governor Terry Sanford, who had been startled to see Governor Ernest Hollings of South Carolina jump to his feet when "Carolina Moon" was played at a governors' conference. In his letter to Davis, Jones noted that "one has only to read the lyrics to know that you were dreaming of the Tar Heel state as you wrote them. Even the word *pining* gives it away. North Carolina is the state of the long leaf pine. All they grow south of us are palmettos and other nuts."

Jones is similarly unsuccessful in nailing down the state's claim to "Carolina in the Morning."

1984

Velma Barfield, the first woman executed in the United States in 22 years, dies by lethal injection at Central Prison in Raleigh.

Barfield, 52, was convicted of murdering her boyfriend by putting arsenic in his beer. She also confessed to killing her mother and two elderly people she cared for as a live-in housekeeper.

NOVEMBER 3

1864

Captain Conley of the 101st Pennsylvania Volunteers, escaped prisoner of war, describes sentiments in Transylvania County:

> This was . . . just three days before the time
> for starting for Tennessee. We were now in-

formed that it would be necessary to secure five days rations before starting, as we would not be able to get any for that time. So we spent our time among the Union families in that neighborhood, with most of whom we became acquainted soon. We found them to be rugged stalwart mountaineers; most of them had little culture, but answering Union proclivities, most of them seemed to be determined to die rather than serve in the rebel army. All the men who were liable to military duty and consequently to conscription, spent most of their time in the woods, only coming home for supplies. All of them were heavily armed. I met a number of men here who carried, each, two guns and two revolvers. Posses of rebels had frequently been sent in there to hunt up these people, but had almost invariably met with defeat, as these mountaineers would band together and ambush them. We were told that they also tried to capture them with bloodhounds, but that also proved a failure; as not one bloodhound brought in ever got out alive.

I have never anywhere else known such bitterness as existed between neighbors here. The persecution and hardship that the Union men had been subjected to, very naturally, brought a spirit of retaliation. It was not unusual, as we learned, for persons to be waylaid, and assassinated when passing along the public highways.

1979

Five members of the obscure Communist Workers Party are killed by gunfire while preparing for an anti–Ku Klux Klan march at a Greensboro public housing project.

Fourteen Klan members and Nazis are charged in the shootings, but all will be acquitted, first in state court, then in federal court.

NOVEMBER 4, 1862

Hertford County native Richard Gatling patents a revolving six-barrel machine gun.

While practicing medicine in Indiana during the Civil War, Gatling examined the corpses of Union soldiers and found that many more had died from disease than from bullets. He concluded that inefficient weapons prolong war.

Within a year, he has turned out a prototype revolving gun that fires 250 rounds a minute. The Gatling gun won't be refined until after the Civil War, but it soon becomes standard equipment for modern armies.

Do you not sometimes feel remorse, he will be asked, that so many men have been killed by your invention?

No, he replies. "I feel that I have done more to prevent future wars than anyone else of my generation. The man who makes war so terrible that men will be deterred from waging it is doing most to ensure a warless world."

NOVEMBER 5

1827

Former congressman Robert Vance is fatally

wounded in a duel by Samuel Carson, his successor, in Henderson County.

Carson will help establish the republic of Texas and become its first secretary of state. Carson County, Texas, is named for him.

NOVEMBER 5, 1968

Henry Frye, a Guilford County lawyer, wins election to the North Carolina House. He is the first black to serve in the assembly since 1898.

In 1983, Frye will become the first black to sit on the North Carolina Supreme Court.

1974

Myrtle "Lulu Belle" Wiseman, twice voted America's most popular female radio entertainer in the 1930s, is elected to the North Carolina House from Mitchell County.

Before retiring to Spruce Pine in 1958, she and her husband, Scotty, had performed for almost a quarter-century as the Hayloft Sweethearts on the *National Barn Dance* on Chicago's WLS, hosted a daily TV show for eight years, and made seven Hollywood movies.

The Wisemans wrote or cowrote such classics as "Good Old Mountain Dew" (with Bascom Lamar Lunsford), "Remember Me," and "Have I Told You Lately That I Love You?"

In her two terms in the legislature, Lulu Belle Wiseman will make her most dramatic impression when, arguing for the death penalty for rapists, she tells her stunned colleagues about her own rape 10 years earlier.

NOVEMBER 6

1787

Andrew Jackson, age 20, is admitted to the Rowan County bar.

An acquaintance of Jackson's during the several years before he moves to Tennessee will recall him as "the most roaring, rollicking, game cocking, cardplaying, mischievous fellow that ever lived in Salisbury."

Two hundred years later, a gamecock that continues to attack after losing an eye will still be known as a "Jackson."

1864

The number of captives at Salisbury Prison, built to hold 2,500, reaches a peak of 8,740. Some must sleep outdoors, digging trenches to keep warm.

The prison is the Confederacy's second-largest, behind Andersonville in Georgia. More than 4,000 prisoners will die here—twice the population of the town of Salisbury.

1913

As part of his proclaimed "Good Roads Days," Governor Locke Craig, clad in overalls, takes up a shovel on a Buncombe County work crew.

Craig's call for two days of volunteer maintenance on the state's dirt roads elicits diverse responses. In Guilford Conty, more than 1,000 men show up; students at the State Normal and Industrial School for Girls put 400 rakes to use. At Chapel Hill, acting University of North Carolina president Edward Kidder Graham takes the lead in leveling Franklin Street. Lenoir College students, according to the *Charlotte Observer*'s correspondent, "livened up the occasion by giving cheer after cheer for Hickory and Governor Craig." In Raleigh, however, "there was practically no response on the part of citizenship."

1988

Taping a TV special, magician David Copperfield, handcuffed and locked in a safe, escapes from the old Hotel Charlotte moments before its implosion.

The 12-story hotel had been closed since 1973, but in its heyday, it was Charlotte's finest. Among its guests: Presidents Franklin D. Roosevelt, Dwight Eisenhower, Lyndon Johnson, and Richard Nixon; Elvis Presley; Huey Long; Jack Dempsey; and Babe Ruth. Bill Monroe and Roy Acuff recorded in its 10th-floor studios, and Tommy Dorsey, Guy Lombardo, and Kay Kyser performed in its ballroom.

NOVEMBER 7

1942

Art Buchwald, who has run away from his home in New York to join the marines, hitchhikes to Greensboro. His plan is to bid a dramatic farewell to Flossie Starling, a Woman's College student with whom he had a summer romance while the two worked at a New Hampshire hotel. He surprises her by showing up unannounced at her dormitory; she surprises him by telling him she has a date to a big dance with a V.M.I. cadet.

The next morning, the distraught Buchwald bribes a downtown derelict—with a pint of whiskey spitefully stolen from the cadet—to give permission for his 17-year-old "son" to enlist.

Buchwald is then on his way to Parris Island, to the war in the Pacific, and, eventually, to Washington, where he will become a Pulitzer Prize–winning humor columnist.

1951

Ava Gardner marries Frank Sinatra, the last of her three husbands, in Philadelphia.

Later in life, Gardner will say, "I don't know why the hell anybody should talk about my marital record—my three ex-husbands had 20 wives between them."

1972

President Richard Nixon's overwhelming defeat of George McGovern helps North Carolina Republicans elect their first governor, Jim Holshouser, and United States senator, Jesse Helms, since the turn of the century.

1989

Voters in Greensboro, the home of Lorillard Tobacco Company, which makes Newport, Kent, and True cigarettes, approve the state's toughest antismoking ordinance.

The ordinance requires most restaurants to set aside 25 percent of their space for nonsmokers and bans smoking in elevators and many retail areas.

1989

The tabloid TV show *A Current Affair* spotlights Charlotte's mayoral race as "the nastiest campaign in the country . . . a down and dirty dogfight."

Republican Sue Myrick defeats Democratic challenger Craig Madans after a campaign that includes allegations of drug use and adultery and an on-the-air vulgarity by Myrick.

NOVEMBER 8

NOVEMBER 8, 1921

Exum Clement, Asheville's first female lawyer, becomes the first woman elected to the General Assembly.

Her colleagues in the North Carolina House will refer to her as "the legislatrix" and "Brother Exum."

1923

Julian Shakespeare Carr, Durham tobacco manufacturer and former Confederate private, dedicates the Unity Monument near the reconstructed Bennett house, the site of General Joseph E. Johnston's surrender to Sherman: "No people of any age covered themselves with greater glory than did the people of the Confederacy in this, the most heroic conflict ever waged in all the history of man. We fought in the face of adverse public sentiment abroad engendered by the insidious propaganda that we were fighting to perpetuate slavery."

1983

Wilson Goode, one of eight children of a Northampton County sharecropper, is elected the first black mayor of Philadelphia. His family moved from North Carolina to Philadelphia when he was 15.

The low point of Goode's eight years in office will come in 1985, when police trying to evict the radical group MOVE from its row-house headquarters drop a bomb on the roof. The resulting fire kills 11 people, including five children, and destroys more than 60 houses.

NOVEMBER 9

1855

Railroad advocate John Warwick Thomas throws a picnic for 5,000 as the first train pulls into Thomasville, the town he founded three years earlier.

In his 25 years as a legislator, Thomas lobbied for construction of the North Carolina Railroad. He put up at least $18,000 of his own money, bought land on the railroad survey line, and provided the new community with a sawmill, a gristmill, and a store.

1909

The highlights of President William Howard Taft's one-day visit to Wilmington: a cruise to Fort Caswell; a military parade featuring an arch across North Front Street inscribed, "Welcome to the 'Land of the Long Leaf Pine' "; and an automobile tour of the city.

The *Wilmington Morning Star* calls it "a magnificent success in every detail, doing credit even to a city of many times its size."

1914

The first North Carolina Suffrage Convention is held at Charlotte's Selwyn Hotel.

Chapel Hill poet and translator Barbara Henderson, president of the state's Equal Suffrage League, issues this call: "Women of Carolina: The day is here; the time is now! Opportunity knocks at the portal; open your doors to a new tomorrow. . . . Your state needs your service. For the sake of your home and your children lay aside your smaller tasks for the time and flock to the standard of a larger service."

1946

A radio broadcast "direct from Hollywood" kicks off a campaign to arouse North Carolinians' support for better health facilities.

"Did you know," asks entertainer Skinnay Ennis of Salisbury, "that we had the highest percentage of draft rejections of any state in the Union?"

The half-hour evening show, airing on every full-time station in the state, also features Dinah Shore, Red Skelton, Kay Kyser of Rocky Mount, Ava Gardner of Smithfield, John Scott Trotter of Charlotte, and Anne Jeffreys of Goldsboro.

Another weapon of the good-health campaign: "It's All Up to You (to Make North Carolina No. 1 in Good Health)," a song recorded by Shore, Kyser, and Frank Sinatra.

1977

North Carolina voters approve gubernatorial succession.

NOVEMBER 10

1918

In Atlanta, Georgia Tech makes easy work of a North Carolina State football team crippled by influenza and military inductions. Georgia Tech coach John Heisman agrees to halt the game after three quarters. The final score: 128–0.

1931

Aviator Amelia Earhart, on a promotional tour for Beech-Nut Chewing Gum, lands her autogiro in Charlotte.

During her three-day stopover, she will demonstrate the experimental "flying windmill," attend a United Relief Drive luncheon, make a side trip to Fayetteville for Armistice Day ceremonies, and endear herself to city officials by endorsing their plan to buy the airport: "A few years' time will prove it necessary, unless a city wants to suffer the fate some towns brought upon themselves in years gone by when they refused to permit railroads."

1981

Durham, long known as "Bull City" for its Bull Durham heritage, adopts the official title "City of Medicine."

NOVEMBER 11

1861

From the *Carolina Watchman*, a newspaper in Salisbury: "The Government has bought the old Salisbury Factory, and is now preparing to fit it up for a prison to accommodate some thousands or more of Yankees who are encumbering the tobacco factories of Richmond. Our citizens don't much like the idea of such accession to their population; nevertheless, they have assented to their part of the hardships and disagreeables of war, so bring them along. We will do the best we can with them."

NOVEMBER 10, 1926

66 Meeting in Pinehurst, the American Association of Highway Officials approves the final plans for Route 66, which will link Chicago and Los Angeles and open the West to a new wave of migration and development.

By 1984, when the last stretch of the storied Route 66 is decommissioned, it has long since been supplanted by the interstate highway system.

1927

In Murphy, construction is completed on the state's only all-marble courthouse.

After four previous courthouses all burned down, Cherokee County decided to turn to a local quarry at the town of Marble to ensure a fireproof building.

1928

At the request of American Legion officials, Durham police remove a Ku Klux Klan float from line in the annual Armistice Day Parade. The float bears the letters *KKK* and two white-draped figures representing "Purity" and "Honesty."

"Since our post is composed of men of all classes and all religious faiths . . . ," an American Legion official tells the *Durham Morning Herald*, "participation by the Klan in our parade would throw the entire picture out of harmony."

1934

Interior Secretary Harold Ickes, overruling a study committee, chooses to route the southern leg of the Blue Ridge Parkway through North Carolina rather than Tennessee. Ickes notes that Tennessee already has an entrance to Great Smoky Mountains National Park at Gatlinburg.

1990

On the first day of hunting season in Beaufort County, Van Jones and two companions bag the biggest bear ever killed in North Carolina.

It weighs 720 pounds and stands seven feet, six inches. Most North Carolina bears weigh 200 to 400 pounds.

Wildlife officials estimate the age of the male black bear at 8¾ years.

NOVEMBER 13

1836

P. T. Barnum departs Rocky Mount after making the first known stop with his own circus troupe. No show is recorded, but Barnum does preach a sermon.

NOVEMBER 14

1906

Will Harris, a black handyman, arrives in Asheville from Charlotte and goes berserk, eventually killing five people. "Nobody cares who I am," he cries. "I am from Hell and don't care who sends me back."

Two days later, after a pawnbroker hands out 50 guns to a gathering crowd, Harris is killed in the woods of nearby Fletcher.

In Thomas Wolfe's 1937 short story "The Child by Tiger," the character Dick Prosser—called by one critic "the one full-scale Afro-American in his writing"—will be based on Harris.

1910

A fire that starts in a hotel kitchen nearly destroys the thriving mountain town of Webster. Fighting a strong wind, a bucket brigade manages to save only the post office.

In 1913, the Jackson County seat will be moved to Sylva.

1953

A Chapel Hill record company owned by newspaper publisher Orville Campbell releases "What It Was, Was Football," Andy Griffith's comic monologue about football as seen through a country boy's uncomprehending eyes.

The record makes the playlist on NBC radio, is picked up by Capitol Records, sells a million copies, and launches the 27-year-old Griffith onto the national stage.

NOVEMBER 15

1846

Peter Stewart Ney, a Rowan County schoolmaster in his late 70s, dies shortly after insisting to his doctor, "I am Marshal Ney of France."

Thus, he leaves several generations of North Carolinians to debate whether he was in fact the Napoleonic marshal Michel Ney, living in hiding to escape persecution.

No fewer than three books will argue that he was, and his gravestone describes him as "a native of France and soldier of the French Revolution under Napoleon Bonaparte."

According to believers, Marshal Ney, convicted of treason, escaped execution by a Paris firing squad and fled to America. Proficient in Latin, Greek, and Hebrew, he taught school in such places as Lincolnton and Mocksville—and designed the Davidson College seal. His friends said that when he drank too much, he would claim to be Marshal Ney. Sober, he would deny it.

Disbelievers note that a 1887 exhumation of Peter Stewart Ney's body failed to turn up the silver plate supposedly implanted in the head of the real Marshal Ney. Further research in the 1940s and 1950s by William Henry Hoyt suggests that Ney may have been Scottish-born Peter McNee.

1894

North Carolina's first public meeting on women's suffrage is held in Asheville. Speakers include music teacher Helen Morris Lewis and Mayor Thomas Patton.

One week later, a suffrage association is formed with Lewis as president. She will spend much of the next decade traveling the state and speaking to audiences that often number in the hundreds, but the movement fails to take hold and by the early 1900s has entered a long period of dormancy.

1915

Drawn by ads claiming that "No Southern Man Can See It without a Lump in His Throat," a crowd of 5,000 fills the Academy of Music to see the Charlotte premiere of *The Birth of a Nation*. The movie is silent, but a 30-piece orchestra plays a synchronized score—part of which will resurface as the theme for *Amos 'n' Andy*.

"Overwhelming," the *Charlotte Observer* begins its review, "in its stupendousness . . ."

1921

The Lost Colony premieres before Governor Cameron Morrison and other state leaders in the old North Carolina Supreme Court building. The five-reel silent movie, among the nation's first uses of film for educational purposes, is the brainchild of Mabel Evans, superintendent of the Dare County schools.

The state-financed $3,000 budget included hiring Elizabeth Grimball, director of the New York School of the Theatre, to cast and direct the three-week shooting on Roanoke Island.

Four prints of *The Lost Colony* will be shown throughout the state; in areas without electricity, the projector is run by a generator-equipped Model T Ford.

1933

In one of Charlotte's most spectacular crimes, four members of Chicago's Touhy Gang rob a mail truck of $120,000.

The case will vault Police Chief Frank Littlejohn into the national spotlight when his discovery of a Chicago laundry ticket near the crime scene leads to arrests and the recovery of part of the money.

1993

After an absence of almost four decades, Billy Graham returns to the cover of *Time* magazine. This time, he has just turned 75 years old, and the article focuses on his accomplishments rather than his ambitions.

NOVEMBER 16

1765

Citizens of New Hanover County, angered by the British Stamp Act, force the resignation of the new stamp distributor for North Carolina.

NOVEMBER 17

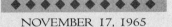

NOVEMBER 17, 1965

Charlotte's Carolina Theater accepts a scroll signed by 20th Century-Fox president Darryl F. Zanuck recognizing it as the first theater in the country to play a movie to more people than live in the city.

Attendance for *The Sound of Music* totals 247,000, versus Charlotte's estimated population of 238,000.

The movie eventually runs 79 weeks before yielding to *Dr. Zhivago.* One woman sees it 60 times.

NOVEMBER 18

1923

R. D. W. Connor, the state's most prominent historian, advises editor Robert B. House on how to put out the new *North Carolina Historical Review:* "Don't let professional North Carolin-

ians and professional southerners ruin the quarterly with 'patriotic' articles. . . . Make it a real scholarly historical publication. Avoid old hackneyed subjects—Mecklenburg Declaration, Regulators, First at Bethel, number of troops in Confed. Army, etc.!"

1944

Former governor O. Max Gardner, a Democrat, enjoys himself in a letter to the president of Massachusetts' Pepperell Manufacturing Company, a Republican, on the occasion of Franklin D. Roosevelt's reelection: "I thought about you around midnight November 7th when the first glimmering results came in from Massachusetts, and I had no difficulty in recognizing that you were again in the minority. . . .

"We are going to start on this glorious Fourth Term on a wider and more complete distribution of the wealth of New England, starting with you and terminating at Shelby, North Carolina, by way of Washington, D.C."

1954

Junius Scales, head of the Communist Party in the Carolinas, is arrested by the FBI and charged under the 1940 Smith Act with membership in an organization advocating violent overthrow of the government. Scales, a longtime resident of Chapel Hill, is a scion of a prominent Greensboro family—both his father and grandfather were state senators.

Scales will be convicted at his trial in Greensboro and sentenced to six years in prison. In 1961, after an unsuccessful appeal to the United States Supreme Court, Scales—who resigned from the Communist Party in 1957, soon after the Soviet invasion of Hungary—begins serving his sentence at the federal penitentiary in Lewisburg, Pennsylvania.

On Christmas Eve 1962, President John F. Kennedy frees Scales—the only American to spend time in prison for being a communist—by commuting his sentence to parole on his own recognizance.

1974

"Minor Heroism" becomes not only Allan Gurganus's first published work but also *The New Yorker*'s first fiction centering on a homosexual character.

Gurganus, a native of Rocky Mount, had so impressed Pulitzer Prize winner John Cheever at the Iowa Writers' Workshop that Cheever submitted the short story to *The New Yorker*.

Gurganus's 1989 first novel, *Oldest Living Confederate Widow Tells All*, will make the bestseller lists.

NOVEMBER 19

1850

The *Raleigh Register*, previously a weekly, becomes the state's first daily newspaper. Daily publication lasts barely two months, however.

1949

Cameron Village, the South's largest shopping center, opens in Raleigh. In addition to 40 street-level stores, its amenities include under-ground wiring, covered sidewalks, and free parking for 1,500 cars.

NOVEMBER 20

1930

Central Bank and Trust in Asheville, the largest financial institution in western North Carolina, goes under, taking with it more than $4 million in city deposits.

The Great Depression has hit once-booming Asheville especially hard; less than 15 percent of its office space is occupied.

Mayor Edward Gallatin Roberts is among six public officials and 11 bankers charged with conspiracy. Roberts commits suicide, leaving a note to the citizens that concludes, "My soul is sensitive, and it has been wounded unto death. I have given my life for my city, and I am innocent. I did what I thought was right."

1932

At Asheville's Riverside Cemetery, F. W. Von Prittwitz, German ambassador to the United States, dedicates a monument to 18 German sailors who died of typhoid while imprisoned nearby during World War I.

"Germany is happy to find herself in the same line with the United States when she advocates disarmament . . . ," Von Prittwitz tells the crowd of several thousand. "May this monument stand as an imperishable symbol of the friendship between our two peoples and a mark of our determination to maintain it for all future to come."

In less than a decade, however, Germans and Americans will again be at war.

1938

University of North Carolina president Frank Porter Graham addresses the opening session of the Southern Conference for Human Welfare in Birmingham, Alabama: "The black man is the primary test of American democracy and Christianity. [We take our] stand here tonight for the simple thing of human freedom. Repression is the way of frightened power; freedom is the enlightened way. We take our stand for the Sermon on the Mount, the American Bill of Rights and American democracy."

The unprecedented convention, foreshadowing the civil rights movement, attracts such figures as Hugo Black, Eleanor Roosevelt, C. Vann Woodward, and Swedish social economist Gunnar Myrdal, who is beginning work on *An American Dilemma*, his landmark work on race relations.

NOVEMBER 21

1672

George Fox, founder of the Quakers, visits the colony's Albemarle (northeast) section, converts a number of settlers, and sows the seeds for what will become a stronghold of Quakerism.

1960

"Stay" by Maurice Williams and the Zodiacs hits number one on the *Billboard* charts.

At one minute, 37 seconds, it is the shortest number-one single of the rock era. (The longest: the Beatles' "Hey, Jude," which will clock in at seven minutes, 11 seconds in 1968.)

Williams is a native of Lancaster, South Carolina, but lives in Charlotte.

1966

Future movie star Jack Nicholson makes the first of his two appearances on *The Andy Griffith Show*, playing a father who abandons a baby on the Taylors' doorstep.

1990

As well-wishers at Maine's Baxter State Park sing "Amazing Grace," Bill Irwin of Burlington becomes the first blind person ever to hike the 2,143-mile Appalachian Trail without a constant human companion.

His only eyes on the 259-day odyssey from Georgia have been those of his German shepherd guide dog, Orient. Along the way, Irwin climbed mountains so steep he had to lift Orient overhead from ledge to ledge, was swept away while crossing a river, and lost his toenails to the constant pounding.

NOVEMBER 22

1718

Carolina's most notorious pirate, Blackbeard, is run down at Ocracoke Inlet. Robert Maynard, the commander of two sloops of British sailors, cuts off Blackbeard's head with a single swipe of his sword and hangs it in the rigging as evidence that he is entitled to the bounty offered by the colony of Virginia.

1855

The first train arrives in High Point, a community created out of farmland at the intersection of a plank road and the new North Carolina Railroad.

Surveyors had marked its locale as the highest point along the rail line between Goldsboro and Charlotte.

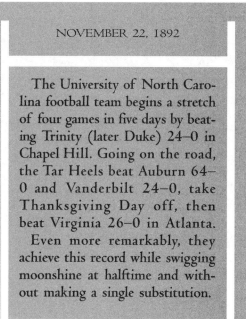

NOVEMBER 22, 1892

The University of North Carolina football team begins a stretch of four games in five days by beating Trinity (later Duke) 24–0 in Chapel Hill. Going on the road, the Tar Heels beat Auburn 64–0 and Vanderbilt 24–0, take Thanksgiving Day off, then beat Virginia 26–0 in Atlanta.

Even more remarkably, they achieve this record while swigging moonshine at halftime and without making a single substitution.

NOVEMBER 23

1789

North Carolina's second constitutional convention, held in Fayetteville, adjourns after ratifying the federal Constitution.

More than a year earlier, a convention in Hillsborough had refused to ratify, thus leaving North Carolina out of the new union. The North Carolinians agreed with the document's division of power and system of checks and balances but balked at the lack of specific protection for states' and individual rights.

By April 30, 1789, some 11 states had ratified the Constitution and the United States of America was born, but only after James Madison agreed to sponsor 10 amendments to be known as the Bill of Rights. Madison justified the addition in part as an "accommodation" to North Carolina.

Satisfied, the Fayetteville convention ratifies by a vote of 195 to 77.

NOVEMBER 24

1877

The USS *Huron*, a navy gunboat on its way to a surveying expedition off the coast of Cuba, runs aground in a storm about 200 yards off Nags Head. Of its 132 crew members, 98 die.

Two months later, another vessel will run aground 20 miles away; 85 die. Responding to public outcry, Congress approves 30 new life-saving stations, 15 of them along the Virginia and North Carolina coasts.

In 1991, the *Huron's* plot in the Graveyard of the Atlantic will become the state's first Historic Shipwreck Preserve.

1892

The magnificently turreted and dormered Zinzendorf, the first of what developers hoped would be a string of resort hotels along a ridge on the western edge of Winston, catches fire on Thanksgiving Day.

Fire companies from Winston and Salem race

each other to put out the blaze, which began in the laundry room, but hydrants put out too little water to be effective.

1919

Clyde Hoey, a member of the "Shelby Dynasty" of Democratic politicians, wins the congressional primary against Johnson D. McCall of Charlotte.

Hoey carries his home county of Cleveland by the vote of 3,369 to 34. Even more remarkably, he receives every one of the 1,242 votes cast in Shelby.

Hoey goes on to win the general election and will later serve as both governor and United States senator.

NOVEMBER 25

1864

Robert Moffat Livingstone, eldest son of the famous missionary Dr. David Livingstone, is fatally injured in a riot at the Confederate prison at Salisbury.

Young Livingstone, born in Africa and reared in Scotland, enlisted with a New Hampshire regiment using a false age (21, instead of 18) and name (Rupert Vincent).

In a letter to his father, he cryptically referred to the alias as a means to avoid "further dishonoring" the family name. He expressed regret at having joined the army. "I have never hurt anyone knowingly in battle," he said, "having always fired high." He was captured at the Battle of New Market Road in Virginia and taken to Salisbury.

A friend will later quote Dr. Livingstone as saying, "I am proud of the boy, and if I had been there, I should have gone to fight for the North myself."

Robert Livingstone is likely buried in a mass grave in what is now Salisbury National Cemetery.

1980

In the eighth round of his welterweight title defense in the New Orleans Superdome, Roberto "Hands of Stone" Duran waves his right fist in resignation and mutters, "No mas"—"No more." The unexpected surrender gives the championship back to Sugar Ray Leonard and fuels years of controversy among boxing fans.

Leonard, 24 years old, was born in Wilmington, but his family moved to Washington, D.C., when he was three.

He will retire in 1991, having held all or part of titles in five weight classes.

NOVEMBER 26

1787

The North Carolina Supreme Court's ruling in *Bayard v. Singleton* is the first American decision to assert the judicial branch's authority to invalidate acts of the other branches of government on the grounds that they violate supreme law—a constitution.

The decision anticipates the United States Supreme Court's landmark decision in *Marbury v. Madison* in 1803.

1927

Governor Angus McLean of North Carolina

and Governor Harry Byrd of Virginia unlock a ceremonial gate across the section of U.S. I linking their states.

The nation's first transcontinental highway will eventually cover 2,467 miles from the Canadian border to Key West, Florida. In North Carolina, it enters in Warren County, runs through Henderson, Raleigh, Sanford, and Rockingham, and exits from Richmond County.

NOVEMBER 27

1948

C. D. "Dick" Spangler, Jr., of Charlotte, a junior at Woodberry Forest School, attends the University of North Carolina–University of Virginia football game at Charlottesville. After UNC's 34–12 victory, he pays a Tar Heel cheerleader $10 for Charlie "Choo Choo" Justice's torn No. 22 jersey.

Four decades later, as president of the University of North Carolina system, Spangler will count the jersey as his most valued souvenir.

1990

The Menhaden Chanteymen of Beaufort, 10 black men in their 60s and 70s wearing ball caps and dark suits, make their debut performance at Carnegie Hall.

From the 1880s to the 1950s, Beaufort processed more menhaden—also known as shad, porgies, or fatback—than anywhere else in America.

Like the men who laid railroad tracks, the fisherman sang to synchronize their efforts. As their muscles gave way to hydraulic net pullers, their distinctive "chanteys" died out until 1988, when they were rediscovered and recorded by folklorists Michael and Debbie Luster.

NOVEMBER 28

1963

Jim Hunter of Hertford in Perquimans County, hunting with his brothers on Thanksgiving Day, comes harrowingly close to ending his Hall of Fame pitching career before it starts. A shotgun goes off accidentally, blowing away his right little toe and embedding 45 pellets in his foot.

1988

An unprecedented late-fall tornado rips through the Raleigh area and parts of eastern North Carolina, killing four and injuring 157. Tornado season is generally April through early June, but the rare combination of low pressure, warm air, and moisture ignores meteorological convention.

NOVEMBER 29

1817

Archibald DeBow Murphey, a state senator from Hillsborough, completes his visionary report advocating a publicly financed education system extending from primary school through university. "I bequeath this Report to the State as the Richest Legacy that I shall ever be able to give it," he writes friend Thomas Ruffin.

It will be many years after his death, however, before the state pays Murphey's proposals serious attention.

In 1851, the county seat of Cherokee County names itself after him, though it misspells his name *Murphy*.

1980

In a game against Middle Tennessee State, Ronnie Carr of Western Carolina University hits college basketball's first three-point goal.

Although the Southern Conference has won NCAA approval to score three points for shots taken outside a 22-foot semicircle, it will be 1986 before the rule goes into effect for all college games.

1981

Actress Natalie Wood, 43, disappears from husband Robert Wagner's yacht and drowns off Santa Catalina Island, California.

Wood's death delays the release of the science-fiction movie *Brainstorm*, which had almost finished shooting in Kitty Hawk, Pinehurst, and the Research Triangle.

NOVEMBER 30

1900

The first carload of automobiles ever shipped to the South is unloaded at the Charlotte rail depot.

Osmond Barringer keeps one steam-driven Locomobile for himself and sells the other to a physician.

1971

Brian's Song, a TV movie dramatizing former Wake Forest running back Brian Piccolo's fight against cancer, airs on ABC.

James Caan plays Piccolo, who died at age 26. Billy Dee Williams plays Gale Sayers, his Chicago Bears teammate.

Brian's Song will win an Emmy for the year's best single program. It is later released to movie theaters.

Durham's illuminated sign [December 15]
was proud but short-lived.

December

Last Cherokees take the "Trail of Tears"
Monitor sinks in gale off Cape Hatteras
First N.C. ski resort opens in Haywood County

DECEMBER 1

1677

Some 100 armed rebels, opposing a tax on tobacco not shipped directly to England, seize control in the Albemarle region and put the acting governor on trial.

Culpeper's Rebellion—named after leader John Culpeper—is short-lived, but it will be 1689 before an acceptable governor is appointed and peace is restored to the unhappy colony.

1875

The Currituck Beach Lighthouse is lighted, filling the remaining "dark spot" on the North Carolina coast between Cape Henry, Virginia, to the north and Bodie Island to the south.

The red-brick structure is left unpainted to clearly distinguish it from the other lighthouses along the Outer Banks.

Automated in 1939, it will continue to flash its warning signal at night every 20 seconds.

1861

Braxton Craven, the president of Trinity College in Randolph County (later to become Duke University), arrives in Salisbury with his "Trinity Guards" to administer the new Confederate prison. The outbreak of war has seriously depleted Dr. Craven's student body, and he acts as both military commander and professor for his young men.

1928

Buncombe County dedicates its new 17-story courthouse on Asheville's Pack Square. "The motley crowd that sauntered back and forth through the ornate $1,750,000 structure were awed by the lavishness," reports the *Asheville Times*.

The courthouse will remain the state's tallest into the 1990s.

1928

Structural work is completed on Winston-Salem's 22-story Reynolds Building, the new headquarters for R. J. Reynolds Tobacco Company and the largest office building south of Baltimore.

New York architects Shreve and Lamb like their design so much that they use it as a model for their next art-deco project—the 102-story Empire State Building, which goes up in New York in 1931.

When the Reynolds Building celebrates its 50th anniversary in 1979, officials of the Empire State Building will send a card inscribed, "Happy Anniversary, Dad."

1966

In *The New Yorker*, a full-page cartoon by Whitney Darrow, Jr., depicts Santa Claus telling his elves, "I have an announcement to make. As of next March, because of conditions too advantageous to be ignored, I'm moving this shop to North Carolina."

DECEMBER 4, 1838

The last party of Cherokees, their land virtually confiscated by Congress, leaves North Carolina for the Indian territory west of the Mississippi River.

Six months earlier, after hundreds of Indians had died on crowded barges in the summer heat, General Winfield Scott agreed to wait and let the rest of the Cherokees walk what will become known as the "Trail of Tears."

1994

Charlotte Smith of the University of North Carolina becomes the first woman in 10 years to dunk a basketball during a game, making a one-handed jam during a 113–58 rout of North Carolina A & T at Chapel Hill.

Only 17 seconds into the game, Smith, a six-foot forward who played at Shelby High, intercepts a pass and drives in uncontested.

Until now, the only woman to dunk during a game was West Virginia University's six-foot-seven Georgeann Wells, who had two in 1984.

DECEMBER 5

1902

The Hall of History, later to be known as the North Carolina Museum of History, opens in Raleigh.

Overseeing the museum is "Colonel" Fred Olds, who has combined his personal collection of memorabilia with that passively accumulated by the North Carolina Museum of Natural History.

Olds, former city editor of the *News and Observer*, has a limited staff (one assistant) but unlimited enthusiasm and imagination. Even though prone to tout every odd-shaped rock as ballast that came over with the Lost Colonists and every old bottle as Blackbeard's rum flask, Olds stirs interest in the state's past, preserves many priceless artifacts, and paves the way for more professional curators.

1938

Accepting an honorary degree at the University of North Carolina three years after the school gave one to his wife, Eleanor, President Franklin D. Roosevelt shrugs off New Deal losses in the recent elections: "The liberal forces have often been killed and buried, with the inevitable result that they have come to life again more vigorous than before."

In a phrase that will come to identify the speech at Woollen Gymnasium, Roosevelt denies that his favorite breakfast dish is "grilled millionaire."

DECEMBER 6

1941

The Liberty ship *Zebulon B. Vance*, the first of 250 ships built at Wilmington during World War II, is launched.

1975

In Washington's power wedding of the year, Federal Trade Commissioner Elizabeth Hanford, a Salisbury native, weds Kansas senator Robert Dole in the National Cathedral chapel.

DECEMBER 7

1941

The Japanese bomb Pearl Harbor.

In protest, Oyama, a community in Durham County named after a city in Japan, will change its name to Few, after William Few, the first president of Duke University.

1946

Benny and Billy McCrary, who will grow up to be the world's heaviest twins, are born in Hendersonville.

By age 32, Billy weighs 743 pounds and Benny 723 pounds. They work as tag-team wrestlers until Billy dies of heart failure after falling from his minibike in 1979.

1987

Gospel singer Shirley Caesar, a five-time Grammy winner, is sworn in as a member of Durham's city council.

1993

Four protesters, including longtime peace activist Philip Berrigan, slip onto Seymour Johnson Air Force Base in Goldsboro and symbolically attack an F-15E Strike Eagle jet with hammers and bottles of blood.

Arrested some 100 times, the 70-year-old Berrigan has spent a total of six years in jail. He and the rest of the "Goldsboro Four" will be found guilty of destruction of government property and serve several months in jail.

DECEMBER 8

DECEMBER 8, 1924

James B. Duke dips into his tobacco and power stocks to create a $40-million endowment to support Durham's Trinity College—to be renamed Duke University—and other educational, medical, and religious purposes.

1965

At North Carolina State, about 1,000 students converge on the student newspaper office to demand that editors apologize for proposing that "Dixie" be stricken from the repertoire of campus musical groups.

About 400 protesters march on to the State Capitol. In the evening's only conflict, a poster reading "Down with Dixie" is ripped from the hands of two black students and destroyed.

DECEMBER 9

1921

A banquet at Monroe's Hotel Joffre welcomes Marshal Ferdinand Foch, the commander of Allied forces during World War I, in the only North Carolina stop on his nationwide victory tour.

Foch was scheduled to dine in Charlotte, but Southern Railway refused to pull his private railroad car from the Monroe yards of rival Seaboard Airline, forcing Governor Cameron Morrison, Josephus Daniels, and other dignitaries to travel to Monroe.

DECEMBER 10

1718

Pirate Stede Bonnet is hanged in Charles Town—now Charleston.

Bonnet, who operated with the seeming tolerance of North Carolina authorities, had been captured two months earlier by South Carolina militia while scraping barnacles from his ship on the Cape Fear River.

1710

The Lords Proprietors, hoping to quell the long conflict between Anglicans and Quakers in the Albemarle region, separate North Carolina from South Carolina and name Edward Hyde, a cousin of Queen Anne, the first governor of North Carolina.

DECEMBER 11, 1988

The *Winston-Salem Journal* refuses to publish a "Doonesbury" installment depicting an R. J. Reynolds Tobacco Company job applicant who is unable to say "Cigarettes do not cause cancer" without laughing.

The *Journal* explains that the strip was pulled because "it singled out for an unfair attack the city's largest company and would be personally offensive to its employees, their families and a large number of the *Journal*'s readers."

When Garry Trudeau returns to the Reynolds theme, the paper first moves "Doonesbury" to the editorial page, then drops it completely in 1991.

1957

On the coldest day in a decade, the first Food Town store opens in Salisbury.

Desperately short of capital, former Winn-Dixie employees Ralph Ketner, Brown Ketner, and Wilson Smith have persuaded friends to put up $10 a share to finance the town's newest and largest supermarket.

By the mid-1990s, Food Town will become Food Lion, that single store will become a chain of more than 1,000 from the East Coast to Texas, and an original $1,000 investment will become as much as $20 million (although the stock will lose almost half its value after a 1992 exposé in which ABC's *PrimeTime Live* uses hidden cameras to show workers repacking old meat and changing expiration dates).

DECEMBER 12, 1986

Lillington's James "Bonecrusher" Smith, filling in because the scheduled challenger backed out, knocks down Tim Witherspoon three times in the first round to win the World Boxing Association's heavyweight championship at Madison Square Garden.

Less than three months later, Smith will be dethroned by Mike Tyson in a unanimous 12-round decision, but the Shaw University alumnus remains the only college graduate to hold the heavyweight title.

DECEMBER 13

1862

In Virginia, Confederates under Robert E. Lee repel Ambrose Burnside's forces in the Battle of Fredericksburg, but the death toll is ghastly on both sides: 12,000 Union, and 5,000 Confederate, more than a third of whom are from North Carolina.

DECEMBER 13, 1969

The first tire comes off the line at Goodyear Tire and Rubber's Kelly-Springfield plant in Fayetteville.

The plant will become Cumber-land County's largest private employer and the world's biggest tire factory.

DECEMBER 14

1801

Joseph Lane, one of Oregon's major historical figures, is born in a double log cabin on Beaverdam Creek near Asheville.

During the same year, his cousin, future North Carolina governor and University of North Carolina president David Swain, is born in the same cabin.

In 1848, Lane will be appointed the first governor of the Oregon Territory; in 1859, after statehood, he becomes its first United States senator; in 1860, the Democrats choose him as John Breckinridge's vice presidential running mate.

Lane County, which includes the city of Eugene and the University of Oregon, is named for him.

1903

Wilbur Wright wins a coin toss with brother Orville for the first chance at piloting their prototype flying machine. It crashes after three seconds. They return to the shop.

DECEMBER 15

1786

James Hogg of Hillsborough petitions the North Carolina General Assembly to change the last name of his sons, Walter and Gavin, to Alves, his wife's maiden name.

Hogg earned distinction as a patriot and educational advocate—he played a key part in selecting Chapel Hill for the site of the university—but he and his family still suffer from their inelegant surname.

The legislature will grant Hogg his request, but ridicule proves not easily shed. Hardly has the ink dried on the name-change bill when a wicked little rhyme spreads across the state:

> Hogg by name, Hogg by nature,
> Changed by act of the legislature.

DECEMBER 15

1792

The assembly names North Carolina's new seat of government in honor of Sir Walter Raleigh, the sponsor of the earliest attempted settlement in America.

1913

Durham boosters unveil a sign designed to catch the attention of train passengers. The 40-by-30-foot sign atop the Wright Building uses 1,230 electric bulbs to alternate the slogan "Durham, Renowned the World Around" with a globe labeled "Progress, Success, Health, Wealth."

The *Durham Sun* describes it as "a beautiful thing to behold [that] inspires patriotic pride," but the sign is soon toppled by heavy winds and will not be rebuilt.

1930

Fay Gardner, the wife of Governor O. Max Gardner, writes in her diary about the worsening Depression: "A run made on Commercial Bank here in Raleigh today, also on the 1st National at Gastonia. Everybody losing confidence and becoming panic-stricken."

The next day's entry notes that "eleven banks closed their doors today."

Before the year is out, 93 banks across the state will go under.

DECEMBER 16

1943

Two Atlantic Coast Line trains collide near Lumberton after one derails onto the other's track, and the oncoming train is unable to see a fireman's warning lantern. Seventy-two die in the Carolinas' worst railroad accident.

1968

Lloyd Bailey, a Rocky Mount ophthalmologist serving as one of the state's Republican presidential electors, casts his vote not for Richard Nixon but for George Wallace.

Nixon has carried the state and the nation, but Bailey, a member of the John Birch Society, decides he can't tolerate such appointees as Henry Kissinger and Daniel Moynihan.

Bailey's rebellion will create a storm of protest in Congress, but the electoral-college system survives unchanged.

DECEMBER 17

DECEMBER 17, 1903

At Kill Devil Hills, brothers Wilbur and Orville Wright, who own a bicycle shop in Dayton, Ohio, achieve the first powered airplane flight. With Orville aboard—Wilbur had his chance three days earlier—the plane stays aloft for more than 100 feet.

"I found the control of the rudder quite difficult . . . ," Orville reports later. "The machine would rise suddenly to about 10 feet, and then as suddenly, on turning the rudder, dart for the ground. A sudden dart . . . ended the flight. Time about 12 seconds."

1867

Union forces depart Charlotte.

The town was spared bloodshed during the Civil War, and relations are cordial between occupying troops and citizens.

"On the occasion of their departure," a 1903 history will note, "Mayor Harris presented the captain with a resolution adopted by the board of aldermen thanking the soldiers for their good behavior and expressing regret at their leaving. The captain acknowledged this courteous act with a pleasant note in which he declared his gratitude for the hospitality of the people of Mecklenburg."

1903

Governor Charles Brantley Aycock addresses the North Carolina Society in Baltimore:

I am proud of my State . . . because there we have solved the negro problem. . . . We have taken him out of politics and have thereby secured good government under any party and laid foundations for the future development of both races. We have secured peace, and rendered prosperity a certainty.

I am inclined to give you our solution of this problem. It is, first, as far as possible under the Fifteenth Amendment to disfranchise him; after that let him alone, quit writing about him; quit talking about him, quit making him "the white man's burden," let him "tote his own skillet"; quit coddling him, let him learn that no man, no race, ever got anything worth the having that he did not himself earn; that character

is the outcome of sacrifice and worth is the result of toil; that whatever his future may be, the present has in it for him nothing that is not the product of industry, thrift, obedience to law, and uprightness; that he cannot, by resolution of council or league, accomplish anything; that he can do much by work; that violence may gratify his passions but it cannot accomplish his ambitions; that he may eat rarely of the cooking of equality, but he will always find when he does that "there is death in the pot." Let the negro learn once for all that there is unending separation of the races . . . that they cannot intermingle; let the white man determine that no man shall by act or thought or speech cross this line, and the race problem will be at an end.

These things are not said in enmity to the negro but in regard for him. He constitutes one third of the population of my State: he has always been my personal friend; as a lawyer I have often defended him, and as Governor I have frequently protected him. But there flows in my veins the blood of the dominant race; that race that has conquered the earth and seeks out the mysteries of the heights and depths. If manifest destiny leads to the seizure of Panama, it is certain that it likewise leads to the dominance of the Caucasian. When the negro recognizes this fact we shall have peace and good will between the races.

1965

Staff Sergeant Barry Sadler, recuperating at Fort Bragg from a punji-stick wound suffered in Vietnam, records "The Ballad of the Green Berets." The tribute to his Special Forces comrades will spend five weeks atop *Billboard*'s top-40 list and become the best-selling single of 1966.

The Special Forces, an elite unit created by President John F. Kennedy in 1961, are head-quartered at Fort Bragg. At the height of the Vietnam War, they number about 15,000 men.

Despite the success of "The Ballad of the Green Berets," the nation is fast losing its appetite for war, reinforcing Sadler's prediction that "in two years I'll be forgotten."

DECEMBER 19

1929

Touting his program to make North Carolina agriculture more diverse and self-sufficient during the coming hard times, Governor O. Max Gardner invites newspaper editors to a "Live at Home" dinner at the Executive Mansion.

Among the menu items: oysters from Hyde County; scuppernong juice from the Coastal Plain Test Farm at Willard in Pender County; ham from the Caledonia Prison Farm in Halifax County; cheese from Kraft in West Jefferson in Ashe County; peach conserves from home demonstration clubs in Moore County; ice cream from North Carolina State; and cigarettes from R. J. Reynolds Tobacco Company, Liggett and Myers, and the American Tobacco Company.

1973

In Mountain City, Tennessee, cross-country hiker Peter Jenkins unfolds his map and plots his course into North Carolina.

Jenkins, whose *A Walk across America* will become a 1979 bestseller, spends five months in Murphy working in a sawmill and living with a poor black family. Robbinsville in Graham County, however, proves less hospitable. "An impregnable, invisible wall stood between me and the local people," he writes. "These paranoid people had me as scared as I'd ever been."

DECEMBER 20

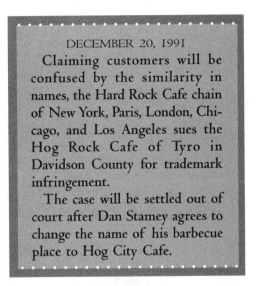

DECEMBER 20, 1991

Claiming customers will be confused by the similarity in names, the Hard Rock Cafe chain of New York, Paris, London, Chicago, and Los Angeles sues the Hog Rock Cafe of Tyro in Davidson County for trademark infringement.

The case will be settled out of court after Dan Stamey agrees to change the name of his barbecue place to Hog City Cafe.

DECEMBER 21

1936

Thad Eure of Gates County takes office as North Carolina's secretary of state.

By the time he retires 52 years later, he will have held one office longer than any other elected official in American history.

Over the years, Eure establishes himself as a man of habits: wearing a red bow tie; ordering a hamburger and a glass of beer at a Raleigh lunch spot; holding onto the mahogany desk, chair, and clock he inherited in his State Capitol office; keynoting the annual ramp-eating festival in Waynesville. (The ramp, a leek that grows on shady, cool mountainsides, resembles a wild onion and has a strong odor and taste.)

1941

To bolster the nation's coastal defenses during World War II, Fort Macon is pressed into service for the first time since its capture from the Confederates in 1862.

Members of the 244th Coast Artillery, turning to the old fireplaces for heat, find what they assume is solid iron shot and roll it into place as andirons.

That's how it happens that shrapnel from a Confederate cannonball wounds two "Union" soldiers 76 years after Appomattox.

1961

Tom and Judy Alexander, looking to occupy their ranch hands during the off-season, open Cataloochee Ski Ranch in Haywood County. Three college students become the first paying customers of North Carolina's infant ski industry.

By the 1990s, as many as 600,000 customers a season will visit the state's 10 ski resorts.

DECEMBER 22

1985

Robeson County district attorney Joe Freeman Britt is profiled on *60 Minutes* as "The Deadliest D.A." According to the *National Law Journal*, no other prosecutor has put more murderers on death row—37 in 12 years.

DECEMBER 23

1838

Noted English actress Frances Anne "Fanny" Kemble, traveling by stagecoach from Philadelphia to Georgia, records her impressions:

> North Carolina is, I believe, the poorest state in the Union. . . . The few detached houses on the road were mean and beggarly in their appearance; and the people whom we saw when the coach stopped had a squalid, and at the same time fierce air. . . .
>
> A custom prevalent in North Carolina [is] the women chewing tobacco, and that, too, in a most disgusting and disagreeable way, if one way can be more disgusting than another. They carry habitually a small stick . . . in their glove, or their garter string, and, whenever occasion offers, plunge it into a snuffbox, and begin chewing it. The practice is so common, that the proffer of the snuffbox, and its passing from hand to hand, is the usual civility of a morning visit among the country people.

1864

Union naval forces pack an old warship with 185 tons of gunpowder and detonate it just 200 yards from Fort Fisher, the L-shaped earthen fort guarding the entrance to the Cape Fear River. The explosion is enormous, but the "Gibraltar of the Confederacy" is unshaken.

On Christmas Eve, 3,000 troops are sent

ashore but are unable to penetrate the fort. It will be more than two weeks before the Union finally succeeds.

DECEMBER 24

DECEMBER 24, 1906

The Bijou, the state's first full-time movie house, opens in Wilmington.

1906

A decade after Guglielmo Marconi of Italy sent the first radio signal, Reginald Fessenden makes the first radio broadcast. From a station in Brant Rock, Massachusetts, he transmits to ships at sea a program of two musical selections (including his own violin rendition of "O, Holy Night"), a Scripture reading, and a short talk.

Fessenden, a native of Canada who was once Thomas Edison's chief chemist, laid the groundwork for his breakthrough during two years' research on the Outer Banks; barely a dozen miles away, the Wright brothers were preparing to fly at Kill Devil Hills.

A storm almost sank the Fessenden expedition on the way to Roanoke Island. Conditions continued harsh—radio workers often had to wear mosquito netting—but 50-foot transmission towers were erected on Roanoke and Hatteras Islands and at Cape Henry, Virginia.

Fessenden was considered by at least one contemporary scientist to be "the greatest wireless inventor of the age—greater than Marconi." But the question of who would profit from radio was complex and treacherous, and Fessenden lost out in extended, bitter litigation over patent rights.

1990

The original Hardee's in Rocky Mount, which dispensed the fast-food industry's first apple turnover, closes after 29 years.

DECEMBER 25

1834

Just down the street from the State Capitol, Representative Robert Potter of Granville County loses $2,800 in a card game. Pulling a pistol and a knife, he pockets the pot and exits.

A week later, Potter will be expelled for reflecting discredit on the legislature.

Previously, however, his colleagues had been more tolerant of Potter's misdeeds. He had once been jailed for castrating two men—an aging minister and a 16-year-old—for carrying on with his wife while he was in Raleigh. Governor David Swain issued a pardon so Potter could take office. Petitions were circulated to prevent Potter from taking his seat, but the House contended it had no right to set standards of conduct—until he cheated at cards.

1852

Peter Evans, 71, dies of throat cancer. Evans's will directs that his 2,700-acre Egypt plantation, on the Deep River in what is now Lee County, be explored for coal.

Although Egypt's coal proves soft and inferior—its yellow smoke makes easy targets of Confederate blockade runners—it remains the state's only significant source and will be mined off and on for several decades.

DECEMBER 26

1986

Junior Johnson, who served 11 months and three days in the federal penitentiary in Chillicothe, Ohio, for a 1956 moonshining conviction, receives a pardon from President Ronald Reagan.

DECEMBER 27

1833

The *Star and North Carolina Gazette* quotes the *New York Evening Star's* praise of Governor David Swain's recent address to the legislature: "The spirit of frankness with which Gov. Swain impugns the torpid inaction of the legislative deliberations of the State for the last half century induces us to imagine he is disposed to countenance the pleasant sarcasm with which North Carolina has been alluded to as the Rip Van Winkle State, that has not yet awoke."

This is perhaps the earliest in-state reference to the "Rip Van Winkle" label. "During the first half of the nineteenth century," historian William S. Powell will write, "North Carolina

seemed unaware of much that was going on anywhere, even within its own boundaries."

1892

The nation's first black intercollegiate football game is played on a snow-covered field in Salisbury. Livingstone College loses 4–0 to visiting Biddle University of Charlotte, now Johnson C. Smith University.

1927

The musical version of Edna Ferber's novel *Show Boat* debuts at the Ziegfeld Theatre in New York.

Ferber researched *Show Boat* not on the Mississippi River but on the North Carolina coast—she had never even laid eyes on the Mississippi.

She heard about the James Adams Floating Theatre, a family-operated showboat working the mid-Atlantic coast, and in 1925 met the boat in Bath, on the Pamlico River, for its first stop of the season.

Ferber spent several days aboard the 700-seat boat. Her hosts, Charles and Beulah Hunter (known as "the Mary Pickford of the Chesapeake") provided her a private bedroom, and the troupe regaled her with tales, which she took down on a yellow pad.

Show Boat scored enormous success not only as a musical (revived in 1994) but also in three movie versions.

1984

Andy Griffith puts the brakes on efforts to find a North Carolina town willing to rename itself Mayberry. He calls the campaign by John Meroney III, 14-year-old founder of *The Andy Griffith Show* Appreciation Society, "enormously embarrassing."

DECEMBER 28

1700

John Lawson, an Englishman who will later become surveyor general of North Carolina, leaves Charles Town on an exploratory trip up the Santee-Wateree-Catawba River, then east across North Carolina to the Pamlico River. Among his discoveries: Carolina barbecue.

In his journal, Lawson records that the Santee Indians served him "fat barbacu'd Venison, which the Woman of the Cabin took and tore in Pieces with her Teeth, so put it into a Mortar, beating it into Rags, afterwards stews it with Water, and other Ingredients, which makes a very savory Dish."

The Waxhaw Indians also provided "Barbakues" for Lawson and his men, and near the Pamlico, an Indian "got a parcel of Shad Fish ready barbacu'd." The party bought 24 of these for the price of "a dress'd Doe-Skin."

DECEMBER 29

1836

The Cherokee Indians, already driven into the southwest corner of the state, surrender their last tribal lands to the federal government under the Treaty of New Echota.

Most Cherokees will soon be forced to resettle on reservations in Oklahoma. But an "Eastern Band" evolves from about 1,400 Cherokees who either hide in the North Carolina mountains or are allowed to stay because they became United States citizens under the provisions of an 1819 treaty.

1891

Asheville welcomes humorist Bill Nye to town with a gala banquet, at which he shares the lectern with former governor Zebulon Vance. Newspapers report that the audience "wept with laughter."

Nye, whose books, syndicated columns, and lectures—teamed, curiously, with poet James Whitcomb Riley—have made him nearly as well known as Mark Twain, will spend the last five years of his life at his "shatto," as he calls it, in Arden on the French Broad River. "George Vanderbilt's extensive grounds command a fine view of my place," he writes.

DECEMBER 30

1812

A ship bearing Theodosia Burr Alston, 28-year-old daughter of former vice president Aaron Burr, is lost at sea, most likely to a storm off Cape Hatteras.

She and her husband, Governor Joseph Alston of South Carolina, had just lost their 10-year-old son to malaria, and she was eager to leave their rice plantation and spend time with her father in New York.

1862

The Union ironclad *Monitor* sinks in a gale

off Cape Hatteras while being towed to Charleston. Sixteen men die; 49 are rescued by the tow ship *Rhode Island*, a side-wheeler.

Less than 10 months earlier at Hampton Roads, Virginia, in the first battle in history between ironclads, the *Monitor* had fought the Confederate ship *Merrimack* to a draw. The battle effectively ended the era of wooden warships.

In 1973, scientists aboard the research vessel *Eastward* will locate the remains of the *Monitor* 15 miles south of Cape Hatteras.

1863

In a letter to Jefferson Davis, Governor Zebulon Vance argues that antiwar sentiment in the state can be appeased "only by making some effort at negotiation with the enemy." Davis's response: Lincoln has refused to negotiate and is demanding unreasonable peace terms.

Confederate defeats at Gettysburg and Vicksburg have spawned some 100 public meetings in 40 North Carolina counties. Although North Carolina will sacrifice more than its share of men in battle, enthusiasm for the war has been far from universal since the beginning, and Vance is continually at odds with Davis over states' rights.

1883

A scow carrying 20 convicts in chains capsizes while crossing the Tuckasegee River. Only one manages to free himself, and he also rescues the guard.

The convicts were part of a crew building a railroad tunnel outside Dillsboro in Jackson County.

1950

Playing for fifth place in the Dixie Classic in Raleigh, Duke rallies from a 54–22 first-half deficit to beat Tulane 74–72—still the biggest comeback in NCAA basketball history.

Leading Duke's comeback: guard Dick Groat, who scores 25 of his 32 points in the second half.

After graduation, Groat will choose baseball over basketball; as shortstop for the Pittsburgh Pirates, he is chosen the National League's Most Valuable Player in 1960.

DECEMBER 30, 1982

Posing for a publicity shot, Food Town president Tom Smith climbs atop store No. 1 in Salisbury to watch the installation of new letters changing the name of his rapidly growing supermarket chain to Food Lion.

The name has been changed to avoid conflicts with Food Town stores in Tennessee and Virginia. Chairman Ralph Ketner—famed for his tight-fistedness—chose the new name because it requires changing only two letters on store marquees.

1957

Pianist Thelonious Monk concludes a landmark engagement at New York's Five Spot Cafe. Following the release of his album *Brilliant Corners*, his Five Spot performances pave the way for his reemergence as a major figure in modern jazz.

Monk's career was stymied during the early 1950s, when drug charges caused him to lose the cabaret card necessary to perform in New York clubs.

Monk was born in Rocky Mount, but when he was four years old, his mother took him and two other children to New York; his father remained in the South.

1990

Three months before winning the Pulitzer Prize for drama, Neil Simon's *Lost in Yonkers* makes its world premiere at the Stevens Center in Winston-Salem.

Lost in Yonkers is the latest in a series of Broadway-bound shows to open at either the North Carolina School of the Arts or Duke University. Among them: Mikhail Baryshnikov in *Metamorphosis* and Rex Harrison in *The Circle*.

North Carolina History:
An Appreciation

In overcoming the obstacle of being neither a historian nor a native North Carolinian, I have relied on the research of academics, authors, and journalists, on the guidance of librarians and archivists.

Tar Heels may take for granted such essential reference books as *The North Carolina Gazetteer* and *Dictionary of North Carolina Biography*, both by William S. Powell (alas, no relation), and *North Carolina Illustrated* by H. G. Jones; such useful periodicals as the *North Carolina Historical Review* and *The State* magazine; such a respected publisher as the University of North Carolina Press; such a stalwart advocate for preservation and education as the North Carolina Division of Archives and History; even such a unique repository as the North Carolina Collection at the University of North Carolina. It is no myopic boast, however, to characterize this lineup as the envy of those who care about the histories of the other 49 states.

North Carolina's historical Golconda did not

appear overnight, or by chance. The North Carolina Collection, for example, is rooted in the Historical Society of the University of North Carolina, formed in 1844 by UNC president David Swain, perhaps the first serious collector of North Caroliniana. Over the years, numerous friends of history, both professional and (in its highest meaning) amateur, have advanced the collection and other state archival resources.

In a larger sense, North Carolina's stewardship of its history has grown out of an unusually strong attachment to place. In part, of course, this phenomenon is simply Southern, a bittersweet residue of the Civil War. But there's more to it than that. To read accounts of early state fairs, centennial celebrations, and local "firsts" is to be touched by an earnest pride in

being a North Carolinian and in putting the state in the best light. When presidential candidate William Howard Taft toured the state in 1908, for instance, the *Charlotte Observer* took pains to note that "the newspaper men, those in charge of the party and Mr. Taft himself took occasion to say nice things about the respectful and kindly treatment given the visitors by the North Carolinians. . . . Not a jeer nor an offensive interruption was heard."

Although today this identity has been muted by the forces of homogenization, from interstate highways to cable TV, and trivialized by our veneration of itinerant athletes wearing our place names on their jerseys, it remains a notable distinction—at least in the eyes of this transplanted Mississippian—to be a Tar Heel.

Selected Reading

Many events I have cited in this book were drawn from such standard sources as *North Carolina through Four Centuries* by William S. Powell. Others, however, had less predictable origins.

For instance, the story of Richard Nixon's campaign-turning knee injury in Greensboro is reported and interpreted in Theodore H. White's groundbreaking *The Making of the President 1960*. Charlotte's decision to punish Charles Lindbergh for his pro-German attitude is glancingly mentioned in *Charles A. Lindbergh and the Battle against American Intervention in World War II* by Wayne S. Cole; in time, newspaper microfilm yielded the details. The Grateful Dead's first North Carolina engagement is found in *DeadBase VIII: The Complete Guide to Grateful Dead Song Lists* by John W. Scott, Mike Dolgushkin, and Stu Nixon. A federal art inspector's disapproving report on the Morganton mural (and on the local citizens whom it suited just fine) comes from *Wall-to-Wall America: A Cultural History of Post-Office Murals in the Great Depression* by Karal Ann Marling. John F. Kennedy's melancholy appearance at his former girlfriend's Charlotte wedding is recounted in *JFK: Reckless Youth* by Nigel Hamilton.

Listed at the end of this section are books about North Carolina that I relied on. Among books not specifically about the state, these were particularly useful: Robert E. Denney's *The Civil War Years: A Day-by-Day Chronicle of the Life of a Nation* and *Civil War Prisons and Escapes: A Day-by-Day Chronicle*, in which military history is given poignant counterpoint by excerpts from the diaries of combatants; *Speak Now against the Day: The Generation before the Civil Rights Movement in the South*, the landmark contribution by John Egerton; and *Contemporary Authors*, the ongoing reference series.

North Carolina incidents turned up in such biographies as *Babe* by Robert W. Creamer, *Never Stop Running: Allard Lowenstein and the Struggle to Save American Liberalism* by William H. Chafe, and *The Sound of Wings: The Life of Amelia Earhart* by Mary S. Lovell.

I relied on numerous periodicals, including but not limited to the *Charlotte Observer*, the *Charlotte News*, the *News and Observer* of Raleigh, the *Raleigh Times*, the *Greensboro Daily News*, the *High Point Enterprise*, the *Durham Morning Herald*, *The Spectator* (especially Noel Yancey's long-running "As I Recall It" column), the *North Carolina Historical Review*, the *North Carolina Folklore Journal*, *The State* (especially Billy Arthur's articles), and *Carolina Comments*.

Finally, the works listed below provided me with both background and detail—and would constitute a respectable basic reading list for those interested in a more in-depth exploration of North Carolina history.

Anderson, Jean Bradley. *Durham County: A History of Durham County, North Carolina*. Durham: Duke University Press, 1990.

Andrews, Sidney. *The South since the War, as Shown by Fourteen Weeks of Travel and Observation in Georgia and the Carolinas*. 1866. Reprint, with a new introduction by David Donald, Boston: Houghton Mifflin, 1971.

Banner, Leslie. *Passionate Preference: The Story of the North Carolina School of the Arts: A History.* Winston-Salem: School of the Arts, 1987.

Barrett, John Gilchrist. *The Civil War in North Carolina.* Chapel Hill: University of North Carolina Press, 1963.

Beard, Ross E., Jr. *Carbine: The Story of David Marshall Williams.* Lexington, S.C,: Sandlapper Store, 1977.

Beverley, Robert. *Western North Carolina Almanac and Book of Lists.* Franklin: Sanctuary Press, 1991.

Blythe, LeGette, and Charles Raven Brockmann. *Hornets' Nest: The Story of Charlotte and Mecklenburg County.* Charlotte: McNally for Public Library of Charlotte and Mecklenburg County, 1961.

Bratton, Mary Jo Jackson. *Greenville, Heart of the East: An Illustrated History.* Chatsworth, Calif.: Windsor Publications, 1991.

Brown, Louis A. *Salisbury Prison: A Case Study of Confederate Military Prisons, 1861–1865.* Wilmington: Broadfoot Publishing Company, 1992.

Brownlee, Fambrough L. *Winston-Salem: A Pictorial History.* Norfolk: Donning Company, 1977.

Bryan, John. *Biltmore Estate: The Most Distinguished Private Place.* New York: Rizzoli International Publications, 1994.

Bushong, William B. *North Carolina's Executive Mansion: The First Hundred Years.* Raleigh: Executive Mansion Fine Arts Committee, 1991.

Butler, Lindley S., and Alan D. Watson, eds. *North Carolina Experience: An Interpretive and Documentary History.* Chapel Hill: University of North Carolina Press, 1984.

Chesnut, Mary Boykin Miller. *Diary from Dixie.* Edited by Ben Ames Williams. Boston: Houghton Mifflin, 1949.

———. *Private Mary Chesnut: The Unpublished Civil War Diaries.* Edited by C. Vann Woodward and Elizabeth Muhlenfeld. New York: Oxford University Press, 1984.

Claiborne, Jack, and William S. Price, Jr., eds. *Discovering North Carolina: A Tar Heel Reader.* Chapel Hill: University of North Carolina Press, 1991.

Clancy, Paul R. *Just a Country Lawyer: A Biography of Senator Sam Ervin.* Bloomington: Indiana University Press, 1974.

Clark, Donna B. *Days on the Hill: A Calendar for Tar Heels.* Charlotte: InfoSupply, 1994.

Clement, Edwin A. *North Carolina Telephone Story: The First Ninety-eight Years, 1879–1977.* Raleigh: North Carolina Independent Telephone Association, 1978.

Coates, Albert. *History of the North Carolina State Highway Patrol As I Have Known It.* Chapel Hill: Professor Emeritus Fund, 1983.

Cope, Robert F., and Manly Wade Wellman. *The County of Gaston: Two Centuries of a North Carolina Region.* Charlotte: Gaston County Historical Society, 1961.

Crow, Jeffrey J., ed. *Public History in North Carolina, 1903–1978: The Proceedings of the Seventy-fifth Anniversary Celebration, March 7, 1978.* Raleigh: Department of Archives and History, 1979.

Crow, Jeffrey J., Paul D. Escott, and Charles L. Flynn, Jr., eds. *Race, Class, and Politics in Southern History: Essays in Honor of Robert F. Durden.* Baton Rouge: Louisiana State University Press, 1989.

Duberman, Martin B. *Black Mountain: An Explo-*

ration in Community. New York: Dutton, 1972.

Encyclopedia of North Carolina. New York: Somerset Publishers, 1992.

Evans, Eli. The Provincials: A Personal History of Jews in the South. New York: Atheneum, 1973.

Fawcett, George D. Quarter Century Studies of UFOs in Florida, North Carolina, and Tennessee. Mount Airy: Pioneer Printing Company, 1975.

Federal Writers' Project. North Carolina: The WPA Guide to the Old North State. 1939. Reprint, with a new introduction by William S. Powell, Columbia: University of South Carolina Press, 1988.

Gardner, Oliver Max. Public Papers and Letters of Oliver Max Gardner, Governor of North Carolina, 1929–1933. Compiled by Edwin Gill and edited by David Leroy Corbitt. Raleigh: Council of State, 1937.

Golden, Harry Lewis. The Right Time: An Autobiography. New York: Pyramid Books, 1971.

Green, Paul. A Southern Life: Letters of Paul Green, 1916–1981. Edited by Laurence G. Avery. Chapel Hill: University of North Carolina Press, 1994.

Greenwood, Janette Thomas. Bittersweet Legacy: The Black and White "Better Classes" in Charlotte, 1850–1910. Chapel Hill: University of North Carolina Press, 1994.

Hamrick, Grace Rutledge. "Miss Fay": A Biography of Fay Webb Gardner. Boiling Springs: Gardner-Webb College, 1978.

Hill, Michael Ray, ed. Guide to North Carolina Highway Historical Markers. Raleigh: Department of Archives and History, 1990.

Historic Minutes. Greensboro: WFMY-TV, 1976.

Hodges, Luther Hartwell. Messages, Addresses, and Public Papers of Luther Hartwell Hodges, Governor of North Carolina, 1954–1961. Edited by James W. Patton. 3 vols. Raleigh: Council of State, 1960–63.

Hoey, Clyde Roark. Addresses, Letters, and Papers of Clyde Roark Hoey, Governor of North Carolina, 1937–1941. Edited by David Leroy Corbitt. Raleigh: Council of State, 1944.

Hunter, Jim "Catfish," and Armen Keteyian. Catfish: My Life in Baseball. New York: McGraw-Hill, 1988.

Jones, H. G. North Carolina Illustrated, 1524–1984. Chapel Hill: University of North Carolina Press, 1983.

Jones, H. G., comp. North Carolina History: An Annotated Bibliography. Westport, Conn.: Greenwood Press, 1995.

Kelly, Richard. The Andy Griffith Show. Rev. ed. Winston-Salem: John F. Blair, Publisher, 1984.

Kratt, Mary Norton. Charlotte: Spirit of the New South. New ed. Winston-Salem: John F. Blair, Publisher, 1992.

Lemmon, Sarah McCulloh. North Carolina's Role in the First World War. Raleigh: Department of Archives and History, 1966.

Marks, Stuart A. Southern Hunting in Black and White: Nature, History, and Ritual in a Carolina Community. Princeton, N.J.: Princeton University Press, 1991.

Maynor, Joe. Duke Power: The First Seventy-five Years. Charlotte: Delmar, 1980.

McLean-Reep, Dinah. The Original Charlotte Area Daily Fact Calendar. Charlotte: InfoSupply, 1994.

Mitchell, Miriam G., and Edward S. Perzel. Echo of the Bugle Call: Charlotte's Role in World War I.

Charlotte: Dowd House Committee, 1979.

Moore, Daniel Killian. *Messages, Addresses, and Public Papers of Daniel Killian Moore, Governor of North Carolina, 1965–1969.* Edited by Memory F. Mitchell. Raleigh: Department of Archives and History, 1971.

Moore, John Robert. *Senator Josiah William Bailey of North Carolina: A Political Biography.* Durham: Duke University Press, 1968.

Morrison, Joseph L. *Governor O. Max Gardner: A Power in North Carolina and New Deal Washington.* Chapel Hill: University of North Carolina Press, 1971.

Morton, Hugh M., and Edward L. Rankin, Jr. *Making a Difference in North Carolina.* Raleigh: Lightworks, 1988.

North Carolina: Reflections of 400 Years. Wilson: JCP Corporation and Branch Banking and Trust Company, 1984.

O'Brien, Robert, with Harold H. Martin, eds. *Encyclopedia of the South.* New York: Smithmark Publishers, 1992.

Orr, Oliver Hamilton, Jr. *Charles Brantley Aycock.* Chapel Hill: University of North Carolina Press, 1961.

Perkins, David, ed. *The* News and Observer's *Raleigh: A Living History of North Carolina's Capital.* Winston-Salem: John F. Blair, Publisher, 1994.

Powell, Dannye Romine. *Parting the Curtains: Interviews with Southern Writers.* Winston-Salem: John F. Blair, Publisher, 1994.

Powell, William S. *The First State University: A Pictorial History of the University of North Carolina.* Chapel Hill: University of North Carolina Press, 1992.

———. *The North Carolina Gazetteer.* Chapel Hill: University of North Carolina Press, 1976.

———. *North Carolina through Four Centuries.* Chapel Hill: University of North Carolina Press, 1989.

Powell, William S., ed. *Dictionary of North Carolina Biography.* 7 vols. projected. Chapel Hill: University of North Carolina Press, 1979–.

Quinn, David Beers. *Set Fair for Roanoke: Voyages and Colonies, 1584–1606.* Chapel Hill: University of North Carolina Press, 1985.

Roller, David C., and Robert W. Twyman, eds. *Encyclopedia of Southern History.* Baton Rouge: Louisiana State University Press, 1979.

Sanford, Terry. *Messages, Addresses, and Public Papers of Terry Sanford, Governor of North Carolina, 1961–1965.* Edited by Memory F. Mitchell. Raleigh: Council of State, 1966.

Schwartz, Frank Joseph. *Sharks, Sawfish, Skates, and Rays of the Carolinas.* Morehead City: Institute of Marine Sciences, 1984.

Sharpe, William P. *A New Geography of North Carolina.* 4 vols. Raleigh: Sharpe Publishing Company, 1954–65.

Snider, William D. *Light on the Hill: A History of the University of North Carolina at Chapel Hill.* Chapel Hill: University of North Carolina Press, 1992.

Spignesi, Stephen J. *Mayberry, My Hometown: The Ultimate Guidebook to America's Favorite TV Small Town.* 1987. Reprint, Ann Arbor, Mich.: Popular Culture, 1991.

Starr, Glenn Ellen, comp. *The Lumbee Indians: An Annotated Bibliography.* Jefferson: McFarland and Company, Publishers, 1994.

Steiner, Jesse Frederick, and Roy M. Brown.

North Carolina Chain Gang: A Study of County Convict Road Work. 1927. Reprint, Montclair, N.J.: Patterson Smith, 1969.

Sturkey, Don. *Slice of Time: A Carolinas Album, 1950–1990*. Asheboro: Down Home Press, 1990.

Sumner, Jim L. *A History of Sports in North Carolina*. Raleigh: Department of Archives and History, 1990.

Tilley, Nannie May. *Bright-Tobacco Industry, 1860–1929*. Chapel Hill: University of North Carolina Press, 1948.

———. *R. J. Reynolds Tobacco Company*. Chapel Hill: University of North Carolina Press, 1985.

Walser, Richard Gaither, and E. T. Malone, Jr. *Literary North Carolina*. Raleigh: Department of Archives and History, 1986.

Waugh, Elizabeth Culbertson. *North Carolina's Capital, Raleigh*. Chapel Hill: University of North Carolina Press, 1968.

Wilborn, Elizabeth W., comp. *North Carolina Historical Almanack: Being a Collection of Notable Events That Have Befallen People and Places in Our Great State*. Raleigh: Department of Archives and History, 1964.

Wineka, Mark, and Jason Lesley. *Lion's Share: How Three Small-Town Grocers Created America's Fastest-Growing Supermarket Chain and Made Millionaires of Scores of Their North Carolina Friends and Neighbors*. Asheboro: Down Home Press, 1991.

Wright, Wilbur, and Orville Wright. *The Papers of Wilbur and Orville Wright, Including the Chanute-Wright Letters and Other Papers of Octave Chanute*. Edited by Marvin W. McFarland. 2 vols. New York: McGraw-Hill, 1953.

North Carolina County Map

Index

House, Robert B., 215
House Un-American Activities Committee, 51
Howard, Ron, 181
Howard Knob, 133
Hudson-Belk, 8
Humphreys, Josephine, 93
Hunt, Jim, 14
Hunter, Beulah, 234
Hunter, Charles, 234
Hunter, Jim "Catfish," 111, 220
Hurricane Camille, 150
Hurricane Hazel, 189
Hurricane Hugo, 172-73
Hussey, James, 19
Hussey, Rufus, 14
Hutchins, Effie, 82
Hutchins, James, 54
Huxley, Aldous, 91
Hyde, Edward, 227
Hyman, Earle, 141

Ickes, Harold, 212
Ingle, Bob, 57
Iredell, James, 26
Irwin, Bill, 217
Irwin, Harriet Morrison, 154

Jackson, Andrew, 6, 44, 53, 208
Jackson, Anna Morrison, 9, 59, 136
Jackson, Bo, 135
Jackson, Jesse, 137
Jackson, Thomas J. "Stonewall," 91-92, 136
Jacobs, Timothy, 22
James, Hinton, 27
Jarrell, Randall, 98
Jarvis, Thomas, 150
Jefferson, Thomas, 13, 69
Jeffreys, Anne, 211

Jenkins, Peter, 231
Jennings, Waylon, 99
John Birch Society, 52
Johns, Sammy, 42
Johnson, Andrew, 24, 35, 52, 112-13, 120
Johnson, Bradley T., 27
Johnson, Jack, 111-12
Johnson, Joe, 127
Johnson, Junior, 106, 147, 234
Johnson, Larry, 182
Johnson, Lyndon, 90, 122, 167, 183, 185, 196
Johnson, Magic, 201
Johnson, Ross, 11
Johnson, William, 120
Johnson C. Smith University, 97
Johnston, Joseph E., 83
Jones, Charley, 111
Jones, H.G., 206
Jones, Van, 212-13
Jordan, James, 144
Jordan, Michael, 48, 62, 118, 144, 182
Justice, Charlie "Choo Choo," 175, 180-81, 188, 220

Keeler, Wee Willie, 72
Keller, Helen, 110-11
Kelly, Robert F., Jr., 151
Kelly, Walt, 29
Kemble, Frances Anne "Fanny," 232
Kemp, Hal, 101
Kenilworth Inn, 76
Kennedy, Jacqueline, 10
Kennedy, John F., 10, 12, 83, 150, 169, 181, 186, 216
Kerouac, Jack, 4
Ketner, Brown, 227
Ketner, Ralph, 227, 236

King, John, 175-76
King, Martin Luther, Jr., 26, 35, 66, 68, 134, 140, 149
King, William Rufus DeVane, 35, 44
King County, 35
Kirby, Fred, 145
Kirk, George, 98
Kirkpatrick, T.L., 97-98
Kitchin, Claude, 68
Klenner, Fritz, 107
Knotts, Don, 4, 18, 181, 194
Koch, Frederick, 53
Krzyzewski, Mike, 50
Ku Klux Klan:
  Birth of a Nation, 31; charitable donations, 57; denied participation in parade, 212; foes, 78, 89, 196, 207; murder, 98; rallies, 11, 140-41
"Kudzu," 115
Kunstler, William, 149
Kuralt, Charles, 34, 89
Kyser, Kay, 211

Labor unrest, 109, 115, 155, 162-63, 167
LaGuardia, Fiorello, 80
Lake, I. Beverly, 85
Lake Toxaway, 148
Land of Oz, The, 115
Lane, Joel, 62
Lane, Joseph, 228
Lanier, Sidney, 164
Latham, Maud Moore, 72
Latta, Edward Dilworth, 28, 34
Lawrence, Emily Blackwell, 83
Lawson, John, 168, 235
Lea, John, 98
Lee, Annice Carter, 193
Lee, Howard, 89
Lee, Robert E., 9, 92, 144, 154,